THE PARENT'S WHEN-NOT-TO-WORRY BOOK

For a healthy life,

THE PARENT'S
WHEN-NOT-TO-WORRY
BOOK

Barry B. Behrstock, M.D.
with Richard Trubo

HARPER & ROW, PUBLISHERS, New York
Cambridge, Hagerstown, Philadelphia, San Francisco
London, Mexico City, São Paulo, Sydney
1817

For Sophia, Victor, Gwen, Jason, and Jennifer,
thinking of you

FIRST EDITION

Designer: Sidney Feinberg

Library of Congress Cataloging in Publication Data

Behrstock, Barry B.
  The parent's when-not-to-worry book.
  Bibliography: p.
  Includes index.
  1. Children—Care and hygiene. 2. Children—Dis-
eases. 3. Medical delusions. I. Trubo, Richard,
joint author. II. Title.
RJ61.B342   649'.4   80–7894
ISBN 0–690–01972–6 (U.S.A. and Canada)
    0–06–337–0174 (except U.S.A. and Canada)

81 82 83 84 85 10 9 8 7 6 5 4 3 2 1

CONTENTS

ACKNOWLEDGMENTS

There were many who contributed to this book—teachers, colleagues, patients, relatives, and friends. I hope they are pleased to see their viewpoints and the lore they shared with me as I have worked them into the pages of this book.

There are a few individuals whom I would like to personally thank. Most of all, I am deeply grateful to Neal Kaufman, M.D., MPH, a valued colleague and warm friend, for his constant encouragement and support from the inception of the idea through the construction of the manuscript. His professional analysis enriches the work that follows.

My colleagues for their constructive comments: Steven Weinstein, M.D., Nan Zaitlen, M.D., Andrew Blumberg, M.D., Francine Kaufman, M.D.

The following specialists who reviewed the material relating to their fields. Ophthalmology, Sheldon Nankin, M.D., and David Barr, M.D.; Otolaryngology, Mervin Goldstein, M.D.; Orthopedics, Eugene Bleck, M.D., and Charles Bellitti, M.D.; Dentistry, David Haag, D.D.S.

For help with reference sources: Librarians Ute Simons and Linda Sleeth of Hoag Presbyterian Hospital Library. For the flawless and punctual typing of the manuscript, Donna Trubo.

For their enthusiasm throughout the process, my parents, Sophia and Victor Behrstock, my wife, Gwen, and children, Jason and Jennifer, and patients and friends, Richard Zaitlen, Sandra Miyawaki, Victoria Mackie, Harriette Hammond.

Finally, a special thanks to my editor, Carol Cohen of Harper & Row, for her encouragement and guidance throughout.

INTRODUCTION

The extraordinary advances of medical science have guaranteed today's child a healthier life than was ever dreamed possible. Medical knowledge doubles every ten years, and as it does, commonly accepted health care principles are constantly being revised. Yet, an enormous amount of misinformation about health care persists. Many myths and folktales, some that originated centuries ago, endure from one generation to the next. With the best of intentions, grandparents often give erroneous advice to their children, while mothers and fathers pass on inaccurate information to other parents. Some physicians disseminate obsolete information, while the advertising industry often engulfs us with questionable data.

So despite the impressive strides in health care, a persistent body of mythology has become stubbornly ingrained in our culture and consciousness. These myths are often accepted as fact. Since most children are essentially healthy and their problems resolve spontaneously, many believe that the treatments suggested by this child-related folklore actually work. But the truth is that many ills of childhood require no unusual attention, frequently disappearing on their own, and many conditions which folklore incorrectly classifies as problems are merely a normal part of childhood growth.

As a pediatrician, I am troubled by how often parents are unduly misled by many of these myths and misconceptions. After all, parents, not doctors, are entrusted with the everyday health care of their children. In their desire to do *something*, parents frequently act on misinformation they have learned over the years, leading to unnecessary anxiety and aggravation, the wasting of time or money. Misconceptions can provoke actions that may actually be detrimental, dangerous, and occasionally even life-threatening. There may be risks each time a parent puts honey on an infant's pacifier, or securely bundles a feverish baby. Conversely, there may also be some unfortunate consequences when misinformation inhibits a parent from carrying out proper child-care procedures. Such is the case when a parent believes that the brushing of baby teeth to prevent cavities is unimportant or that a baby's high fever may be caused by teething.

I believe that every child is entitled to excellent and intelligent health care. This book will assist you in providing your own child with the best care possible, while helping you channel your own parental energies in a constructive, health-facilitating manner. In refuting the often controversial or stubbornly ingrained beliefs presented in the upcoming chapters, I have relied on the most authoritative information available to substantiate my viewpoints. Obviously, each child is an individual with his or her own specific needs, while the information contained in this book is often generalized in nature. Before adopting any particular recommendations, you should consider your child's own needs and consult with your physician.

I am very interested in hearing from you if you have any questions or reactions to the material in the upcoming chapters. Also, you may have learned some myths about caring for children as you grew up and were disappointed to find that they are not included in this book. I'd like to know what they are. You can write to me in care of my publisher, Harper & Row, 10 East 53rd Street, New York, N.Y. 10022.

BARRY B. BEHRSTOCK, M.D.

1

THE NEWBORN

All parents worry.

But as the title of this book indicates, there are times when parental worry is exaggerated and unwarranted. Babies do *not* need to have one bowel movement a day. Crying will *not* cause umbilical hernias. Infants do *not* need to burp after every feeding. All birthmarks are *not* permanent.

By advising a parent when *not* to worry, this book goes beyond other child-care health books. It explores the most common myths and misconceptions which I, as a pediatrician, confront almost daily. You've probably already asked your pediatrician hundreds of questions and consulted several books, all in search of the most accurate advice available. Should your baby have a pacifier? Should your baby be allowed to sleep in your bedroom? Is it all right to let a baby cry? Every pediatrician has opinions on controversial questions like these. When there is no definitive right or wrong answer, I usually advise parents to follow the course they feel most comfortable with. The proper decision in such situations is what feels right to you, based on your own common sense.

In many areas of newborn care, there is much medical information to base decisions on. These are sometimes the areas of the most persistent erroneous beliefs surrounding infants. Let us explore these myths and replace them with factual information.

Crying

MYTH: *Crying helps exercise a baby's lungs.*

Many parents wish their babies didn't cry at all. For both mother and father, an infant's cries can be irritating, frustrating, and even unsettling. But crying is the only reliable means babies have for communicating their needs. In the absence of language and sophisticated body movements, crying is a baby's most important way to signal hunger, discomfort, tiredness, or boredom. Crying, then, is "normal" in healthy, happy babies, and is almost always merely a means of communication.

The thesis, though, that crying fulfills a physiological need—namely, to exercise the baby's lungs—is, at best, questionable. True, at the moment of delivery, it may be comforting to the mother, father, and obstetrician to hear the baby's first cry, indicating that the newborn has expelled the fluid from the lungs, replacing it with air, since the initial few cries open the previously nonfunctioning air sacs and begin the vital oxygenation process. In addition, some research indicates that in the first few days of life, crying can, in fact, increase the volume of air exchanged in the lungs.

But after those initial few days, crying does not appear to have any physiological benefits. The premise that babies must cry to exercise their lungs is unfounded. Infants' lungs get all the exercise necessary simply through breathing.

Interestingly, in the baby's first weeks of life, many parents are already able to discriminate among the various nuances of their child's cries and can determine their child's specific needs at that particular moment. But while the parent may be able to distinguish cries of hunger, pain, anger, and frustration, one study shows that only the cries of pain instantly activate a mother to her child's side. Researchers found that with the infants out of sight, mothers will often not immediately respond to their baby's rhythmical hunger cries. But upon hearing the tape-recorded cry of pain, they universally rush into the child's room.

MYTH: *There is no pattern to the times that babies cry.*

Although it is true that a baby can cry almost anytime, there are particular times of the day when crying is more common. T. Berry Brazelton, writing in *Pediatrics,* says that the baby's fussiest time is usually between 6 and 11 P.M., when the mother is physically tired, the father is at home, and brothers and sisters are making more parental demands. This crying persists even when the baby is fed, burped, changed, and free of any apparent pain. Among two-week-olds, this fussiness lasts on the average about 1¾ hours; at six weeks old, it peaks at 2¾ hours; and then it gradually declines thereafter.

Some pediatricians theorize that this evening fussiness is in response to household tension, and that periods of colic (unexplainable, highly distressed crying) may be caused and/or exacerbated by stress the baby can sense. The baby's crying, for example, may be most difficult for a parent, tired after a long day, to tolerate and the parent's impatience or anxiety may be communicated to the baby, provoking even more crying.

Having been bombarded with TV and magazine images of smiling, cooing babies, many parents anguish over their own parental "inadequacies" during the baby's crying spells. Keep in mind that it's normal for babies to cry a certain amount of time, typically during the same hours each day, despite any attempts at comforting them. The more understanding you have of this crying phenomenon and the reasons for it, the better you and your family will be able to cope with it.

MYTH: *Newborns do not secrete tears.*

It is a common belief that tears are not present at birth. Even many pediatricians and ophthalmologists believe this, simply because it was advanced by their medical school textbooks. However, this widely held belief has been refuted. Using a quantitative test for tear secretion called the Schirmer Test I, in which the level of tear production is measured on a strip of dry tape, investigators at the UCLA School of Medicine demonstrated that by the second day of life, more than 80 percent of the full-term infants tested secreted cleansing tears when they were not crying. When researchers stimulated these babies to cry, more than 96 percent of them exhibited normal tear levels by the age of two days.

So although the level of tears in newborns may not be enough to overflow the eyelids, tears are still present. Tears are absolutely essential from the moment of birth to cleanse the eyes and prevent injurious drying effects. Fortunately, almost all newborns have the capacity to produce them, whether or not they're visible.

Burping and Sneezing

MYTH: *Babies must burp after every feeding.*

While drinking from a breast or a bottle, most babies swallow some air, which collects in the stomach until it is burped up. Babies, however, vary in the amount of air they ingest, and many do not experience any discomfort from the levels of air that they swallow.

Even so, parents often believe that their babies must be burped *every* feeding. Some admit that they have patted their child for thirty minutes before a sound was finally heard. Others say that they have even awakened a sleeping infant to get up one more burp.

But because the purpose of burping is to make the child comfortable, burping is probably unnecessary for a youngster who is already sleeping contentedly and quietly. If your baby seems unagitated, is not colicky after feeding, and does not normally expel food, this heroic burping effort is probably not required.

Unfortunately, some overly ambitious parents, frustrated in being unable to extract a burp, begin thumping their baby with a force equivalent to a tennis racket striking the back of an adult. When your baby does need help in expelling air, a gentle massaging maneuver, beginning in the lower back and pushing gently upward, is all that is needed. As your child becomes older and more active, natural movements will stimulate the burping process.

MYTH: *Sneezing indicates that your newborn has a cold.*

A sneeze is not necessarily the sign of a cold. For babies, sneezing is a protective reflex that helps clear the upper respiratory passages of lint, dust, or dried mucus that could obstruct the breathing process. When this foreign matter causes irritation in the infant's nose, the sneezing process is triggered.

This protective sneezing mechanism is common to almost all infants, at least through the first month of life. Unless it is accompanied by other cold-related symptoms, like a runny nose, it is probably only a reflex action, not a suggestion of illness.

Interestingly, although sneezing is commonly an anxiety-producer for parents, it was once a welcome phenomenon, considered a sacred experience in ancient times. Sneezing was revered in Greece and Rome, as well as in areas of Asia, Africa, and Mexico.

During the sixth-century reign of Pope Gregory the Great, the Phrase "God bless you" was routinely spoken to individuals who had just sneezed. Many people at that time believed that sneezing caused the heart to stop beating for an instant and that "death angels" could be averted with this simple prayer. Another explanation for this custom revolves around the erroneous belief that malaria (meaning "bad air") was caused by noxious vapors from swamps, not by mosquitoes. When someone sneezed, malaria was often blamed, and a simple prayerlike statement ("God bless you") was considered the best way of combating the illness.

MYTH: *Repeated sneezing is harmful to your child's heart.*

There is *no* evidence that sneezing can stop or damage the heart. Whether your child sneezes in response to a cold or to dust particles in the nose, a sneeze is the mechanism that allows the breathing airways to be cleared. As violent as a sneeze may seem, it cannot impair the heart in any way.

Hiccups

MYTH: *Hiccups are abnormal, and attempts should be made to stop them.*

Hiccups in your newborn are caused by the intermittent, sudden contraction of the diaphragm, probably due to the immaturity of the baby's phrenic nerve, which controls the diaphragm. Hiccups may occur frequently in the first month of life, especially following feedings, with one study showing they are 3000 times more common in newborns than in adults. Even so, they are not a cause for concern.

Although a few swallows of water may stop the hiccups in your baby, there's no necessity for such action. They'll usually disappear on their own in a few minutes without intervention. Over the years, I'm certain you've heard dozens of other "cures," including holding one's breath, pinching the upper lip, electric shocks to the skin, breathing into a paper bag, or frightening the individual. In Plato's *Symposium* the physician Eryximachus suggests that hiccups be treated by gargling water, or by tickling "your nose with something and sneez(ing), and if you sneeze once or twice even the most violent hiccough is sure to go." These techniques have little value.

When adults hiccup, they often feel uncomfortable and embarrassed, and thus presume that their babies are having the same experience. But babies are unperturbed by this common physiological process, and are less concerned with hiccups than you are.

I often ask mothers to think back to when their baby was still in the uterus. Most recall a rhythmic bumping pattern, which, in fact, was the fetus hiccuping. This early, normal behavior simply continues into the first weeks after birth. (The rhythmic beating, incidentally, is distinguished from the *irregular* movement—classically called "kicking"—which, in the initial stages of pregnancy, is actually the fetus' back striking the intrauterine wall.)

One of the few hiccup-halting techniques that may have some value (but only for older children and adults) is swallowing a teaspoon of raw, granulated sugar. The coarse granules, scraping against the back of the throat, could stimulate the vagus nerve, which in turn can suppress the hiccuping.

Nutrition and Feeding

MYTH: *Breastfeeding infants may require up to forty minutes to complete their feeding.*

Each mother, it seems, has her own notion of the time necessary for her baby to complete breastfeeding. Many women feel that twenty minutes (ten minutes on each breast) is the magic number. Others insist that as much as forty minutes is necessary.

Recent studies, however, indicate that a baby's hunger needs are fulfilled in the first few minutes of nursing. If you and your baby are spending forty minutes per feeding, or even thirty, your infant is probably spending most of that time fulfilling the need to suck, not for requirements of nutrition. When A. Lucas (*Lancet,* 1979) studied the feeding behavior of 122 six-day-olds, he discovered (through test-weighing) that 50 percent of the mother's milk was consumed during the first two minutes of sucking on each breast, and 80 to 90 percent was consumed by the end of four minutes. Further research indicates that this same pattern probably continues throughout at least the entire first month of lactation—that is, after the first four minutes of active sucking per breast, there is minimal intake of milk by your baby.

Despite this fact, ten minutes per breast is still the suggested nursing time, because of the additional benefits of extended sucking. The positive interaction and bonding between mother and baby are undeniable; also, during the first few days of breastfeeding, extended sucking can stimulate the mother's own milk production. In addition, a baby who sleeps on and off while nursing may need to breastfeed longer than an infant who remains alert. Ten minutes per breast, then, is the most prudent guideline to follow; however, if you and your baby both enjoy the breastfeeding experience, feel free to nurse for longer, keeping in mind that extended nursing is probably filling emotional more than hunger needs.

MYTH: *There is a best time to stop breastfeeding.*

The most appropriate age to quit breastfeeding can vary dramatically from one child to another. While one child may lose interest in breastfeeding at six months of age, another could continue well beyond the first year of life. Each child is different.

The benefits of nursing, of course, have been well documented. Breast milk, besides providing all the essential nutrients during the first months of life, enhances the natural immunity of the infant against many diseases through the antibodies and cells it contains. Breastfeeding is also convenient (breast milk doesn't have to be bought, stored, mixed, warmed, or sterilized), and it promotes close mother-infant bonding.

I usually suggest that all mothers who have some interest

in breastfeeding try it. The most critical time to breastfeed is in the first six weeks of life, when the immunity the mother can give to her baby is most important. After this initial period, if the interaction is satisfying to both mother and infant (which it usually is), it can be continued until the baby shows signs of losing interest, or it ceases to be convenient or enjoyable for the mother. Some babies nurse until the age of three years, although most stop by age one.

MYTH: *Breastfeeding mothers should not eat chocolate or spicy foods.*

Frankly, because there is such a variation from child to child, any type of food could provoke an abnormal reaction in a particular baby. One of the most persistent beliefs, though, is that chocolate must be avoided by breastfeeding mothers. Most of the folklore associated with chocolate claims that its consumption by mothers will cause diarrhea in their infants; but ironically, some people attribute constipation to this food as well. *No* evidence, however, exists in the medical literature that clearly links chocolate to adverse effects in the nursing baby.

In the *Journal of Pediatrics* (1977), a team of researchers at the State University of New York in Buffalo reported that chocolate contains significant levels of a substance called theobromine, which produces the same pharmacologic effects as caffeine and theophylline—specifically, stimulation of the central nervous system, increased urination, and stimulation of the heart. But even though theobromine passes freely into mother's milk after chocolate is consumed, a mother would have to eat four six-ounce chocolate bars to accumulate even a low dosage of this substance. Although it is conceivable that very sensitive babies could exhibit some reaction to theobromine, *none* of the infants studied by the Buffalo researchers displayed any of the common side effects attributed to chocolate. In summary, then, if you consume moderate amounts of chocolate, it is extremely unlikely that your breastfeeding baby will experience any negative side effects.

And what about spicy food? Although any food substance, spicy or not, can be rapidly assimilated into your breast milk, there is no reason to presume that it will automatically have a detrimental impact upon your baby. If you enjoy a particular food, continue eating it after the delivery of your baby, and see what happens. If it seems to cause some undesirable symptoms in your infant, then it would be advisable to eliminate it from your diet for several weeks before reintroducing it. At that time, if the side effects again occur in your baby, then permanently exclude that food for the duration of your breast-feeding.

MYTH: *Breastfed babies need supplemental water.*

Many nursing mothers believe that water must be added to their infants' diets, in order to maintain a proper water balance. Particularly in hot climates, breastfed babies are given water several times a day.

But most pediatricians believe this practice is unnecessary. The volume of liquid in breastmilk can fulfill all a baby's water needs, even in the hottest weather.

This issue was explored at Children's Hospital in Corrientes, Argentina, where researchers checked the urine concentration of babies at both hot and cool times of the day. Despite excess fluid loss during periods of extreme heat, the babies' kidneys were able to adjust, maintaining a normal bodily water balance without the babies' being given extra water.

Despite research indicating that supplemental water feedings are not necessary, they may still provide some benefits, particularly if the local water supply contains fluoride, a trace metal that can minimize dental decay. Also, for babies ill with fever, or who have gastrointestinal ailments, additional water may be desirable.

Even so, I advise that nursing mothers do not begin giving

water to their newborns until breastfeeding is well established. The sucking action required for bottle feeding is different from—and easier than—that for breastfeeding. When exposed early to both breast and bottle, babies may choose only the easier, artificial nipple. Once a breastfeeding pattern has stabilized, usually by three weeks of age, then water can also be introduced without problems.

MYTH: *Whole milk is healthier than formula; nonfat milk is preferable to whole milk; goat's milk is as nutritious as human breast milk.*

See pages 204–205.

MYTH: *If a mother is consuming fluoride in her diet, it will be passed on to her breastfed baby in adequate amounts.*

Fluoride is an important trace mineral that is more effective than any other agent in strengthening your child's tooth enamel and resisting the acid that causes decay. Adequate fluoride consumption in the first year of life can significantly reduce dental problems later in childhood.

Unfortunately, even in mothers who drink fluoridated water, almost no fluoride passes through the breastmilk. Consequently, because small amounts of fluoride are recommended beginning at two to four weeks of age, I suggest that all breastfed babies (who are not also drinking fluoridated water) receive fluoride supplementations. Consult your pediatrician or dentist for recommendations. See also "Babies don't need fluoride," pages 134–135.

MYTH: *Your breastfed baby must have supplements of vitamin D and iron.*

For decades, many pediatricians have been telling parents that breastfed babies require vitamin D supplements, particularly in regions where sunshine is not always prevalent.

Recent studies, however, appear to contradict this belief.

Drs. Lakadawala and Widdowson tested the watery part of the breast milk and discovered a vitamin D compound there, equivalent to the accepted standard requirements for vitamin D. Although more research is necessary to determine just how readily babies can make use of this storehouse of vitamin D, those early findings suggest that the breastfed baby probably does not need a vitamin D supplement.

As with vitamin D, supplements of iron have long been prescribed for breastfeeding infants. But we now believe that this, too, is unnecessary. Although the iron content of breast milk is certainly below that of iron-fortified formulas, special carrier proteins in the breast milk allow the baby to utilize these small levels extremely effectively, thus providing all the iron the baby needs.

MYTH: *Breastfed babies never have colic.*

Colic, the severe, spasmatic crying unique to infants, typically begins two to four weeks after birth and continues for up to twelve to fourteen weeks. Colicky babies seem to be bothered by abdominal discomfort; they typically pull their knees up to their chest, clench their fists, and scream for hours.

Although colic is more common in formula-fed babies than in their breastfed counterparts, it does exist in some breastfed infants. An interesting study reported in *Lancet* (1978), conducted by Drs. Jakobsson and Lindberg, revealed that when cow's milk was removed from the diet of eighteen mothers, colic promptly ceased in thirteen of the breastfeeding babies. True, the study itself had certain technical weaknesses. But there now appears to be some validity to the belief that cow's-milk protein, which some infants are sensitive to, can be passed to the child through breast milk. If you have a colicky breastfed baby and have tried everything else to make him or her comfortable, you might put yourself on a diet free of cow's milk. When you do, however, be sure to replace the cow's milk with another dietary source of calcium.

MYTH: *Too much gas in the stomach causes colic.*

Colic is often attributed to gas or cramps, but this relationship has never been proved. In fact, various studies have revealed that total gas production in very colicky babies is identical to that in nonfussy infants. Other researchers have speculated that colic is caused not by gas but by a prolongation of the time it takes for food to pass through the intestinal tract, as well as an abnormal pain response to expansion of the gut.

Intestinal gas, as you might guess, has been studied rarely. (There's not much glamour associated with researching gas, even if it's dignified by medical terminology like flatulence or borborygmi). Even so, discomfort from gas is a common cause of physical distress among both children and adults, although its exact relationship to infantile colic remains unclear.

MYTH: *Babies must be fed on a regular schedule.*

The advocates of scheduled feedings have been battling for generations with those who support feeding on demand. Both regimens have advantages and disadvantages, and a compromise between the two seems like the most reasonable route to pursue.

If your baby feeds solely on demand, for example, you'll find yourself controlled by a newborn's primitive instincts, which are usually completely incompatible with your own everyday living. Some parents report that their demand feeders have quickly manipulated them into snacking once an hour, with naps in between. Such a routine becomes chaotic for the family. By contrast, the scheduled feeder is ruled by the clock, with no consideration given to the infant's particular needs, and no room for flexibility or for parental interaction, which is particularly important in this essential mother-infant relationship.

I advocate a modified demand feeding, whereby the baby is fed no more frequently than every 2½ hours and during the day is not allowed to sleep for more than 4 to 4½ hours without being fed. I recommend that at night the child never be awakened for a feeding. Not only does this program help establish an eating routine, but it also encourages the baby to develop night sleeping habits.

MYTH: *Bottles must be sterilized.*

Because of dramatic advances in recent years—including the hygienic, sanitary procedures to which municipal water supplies are subjected—sterilization is no longer as critical as it once was. As a general rule, if bottles are cleaned in the dishwasher, or if they are washed carefully by hand, sterilization is probably unnecessary. Some parents, particularly during the first month of their infant's life, feel more comfortable boiling at least the nipples. But when measures for ordinary cleanliness are followed, even this is not essential.

MYTH: *Bottled milk must be warmed before feeding it to a baby.*

Breast milk is naturally warm, and consequently most parents warm cow's milk before giving it to their infants. Actually, babies will drink whatever they're used to, whether it be cool, warm, or room temperature, and thus it's not necessary for milk to be warmed. However, if milk is ice cold, your child will need to expend extra calories to bring the milk to body temperature after consuming it. For that reason, I tell parents that ice-cold milk (or any other icy liquid) is probably not a good idea.

MYTH: *Tap water must be boiled before feeding it to a baby.*

In the days when plumbing and sanitation techniques were inadequate or contaminated, water supplies were often a source of infection. But today almost all tap water has been adequately treated for both infant and adult consumption. Tap water in almost all American cities is safe to drink without boiling. Check with your physician about your municipal water supply if you have any doubts.

MYTH: *Begin feeding solids to your baby as early as possible.*

Until recently, there was a trend in the United States to introduce solids to babies at an increasingly early age, often to babies as young as two weeks old. Although this practice has been widely encouraged by baby-food advertisements and parts of the popular press, a growing number of pediatricians are changing their recommendations because of recent scientific findings.

Today, there is *no* medical evidence to support the introduction of solids for breastfed babies earlier than ten to twelve months of age and for bottlefed babies only a few months sooner. Admittedly, more research is necessary in the field of nutritional science, and until it is accomplished, many pediatricians are compromising on this subject, recommending that formula-fed babies start solids at four months of age (but no sooner), and that breastfed infants begin at about six months old.

The evidence *against* introducing your baby to solids before four months of age is impressive. Laboratory analysis of stool samples indicates that much of the solid food that an infant eats passes through the body undigested. An infant's intestines are simply too immature to process the food molecules properly, particularly protein. Rice cereal, which is the most common solid food given to newborns, is a starch that can only be broken down by an enzyme called amylase. But amylase is not fully present in the intestinal tract until almost four months after birth, and thus the cereal (like many other solids) is passed partially digested through the stool.

If your child is prone to an allergy to a particular food, the allergy might be avoided if the food is introduced when your baby is older. The risk of an allergy is increased when a baby absorbs nonhuman protein without it being sufficiently broken down. As the infant grows older, the digestive and the intestinal defense system against allergies matures, making the youngster less vulnerable to possible allergy-provoking foods. So when there is a family history of allergies, it usually makes sense to begin solids later, not earlier.

Until the age of four months, the highly coordinated skill of swallowing is still maturing, and until it is properly mastered, newborns experience a higher incidence of choking than older children. Also, all newborns are equipped with the "extrusion reflex"—that is, if a solid object touches the front one-third of their tongue, they instinctively push it out. Louis Barness, a prominent pediatric nutritional expert, quips that this is God's way of keeping out flies! A more plausible explanation is that this primitive reflex may be an instinctive way of preventing solid objects (food, spoons) from being placed in the mouth.

Babies introduced to solids before the age of four months have a higher incidence of childhood obesity than those who receive their initial solids later in their first year of life.

Despite such evidence, the advocates of solid foods argue endlessly about their benefits. The most familiar argument is that early solid feedings prevent night awakenings. But in fact, study after study indicates *no* correlation between sleep patterns and the age at which solids are started. Solids do not fill up a baby for a longer time period than does milk.

Not surprisingly, the loudest advocates of the early feeding of solids are the baby-food manufacturers themselves. Their advertising campaigns have influenced both pediatricians and parents, but fortunately, their unsubstantiated biases are now being questioned. Introducing solids before four months of age simply doesn't make sense.

MYTH: *Breastfed babies are never obese.*

See pages 215–216.

Umbilical Cord and Umbilical Hernia

MYTH: *The way your baby's navel will ultimately look was determined by how the umbilical cord was tied at birth.*

While in the mother's uterus, the growing fetus is nourished through the umbilical cord. In the first few moments immediately after birth, blood continues to flow through the cord, which is soon cut by the doctor or midwife close to the newborn's body, with a clamp placed on it about ½ inch to 1½ inches from its base. The cord itself is not *tied;* if an attempt were made to do so, it would probably unravel on its own because of its slippery texture. The eventual appearance of the navel is unrelated to how the cord is cut—whether close to or far from the stomach—or whether the clamp used is plastic, metal, or a stringlike material. Each baby's own unique healing process, more than anything else, determines how the navel will look.

Interestingly, although the clamping of the umbilical cord is traditional and recommended, the blood flow through it would soon cease on its own, and the cord would promptly begin withering anyway. With mammals in the wild, the rush of blood terminates even without the aid of a clamp, because of the dryness and cold temperatures of the extrauterine environment and the high levels of stress hormones and oxygen in the animal's blood after the initial few breaths, which induce a spasm and constriction of the blood vessels.

MYTH: *Babies should not be allowed to sleep on their stomachs until the umbilical cord has fallen off.*

Many parents are apprehensive about touching the delicate-appearing cord, fearful that bleeding may occur or that the cord could rupture or burst. To avoid any friction to the stomach area, newborns are placed on their backs to sleep.

But there is no need to take such precautions. Friction is

part of the process that helps the cord fall off, and thus sleeping on the stomach is not only harmless, but probably beneficial.

MYTH: *Blood from an umbilical cord is abnormal.*

In the first few days of life, a small amount of bleeding from the healing umbilical cord is normal. A mild, unpleasant odor may eminate from it as well, because of the accumulation of bacteria on it. As long as the bleeding is minimal and the area is kept clean and dry, no danger exists. However, if the bleeding is excessive, or redness is noticed around the base of the cord (a probable sign of infection), contact your pediatrician.

MYTH: *Babies should not be bathed until the umbilical cord falls off.*

Some parents actually fear that when their baby's body is submerged in a bath, water will rush into the body's insides through the umbilical cord. That's simply not possible—no water can enter the body this way.

Even so, many pediatricians recommend that a child not be given a tub bath until the cord has fallen off, in order to keep the cord dry and minimize the risk of infection. Shortly after birth, the remaining stump of the umbilical cord begins to dry and shrivel, and through bacterial action it falls off in seven to fourteen days. Until it does become detached, and for three days thereafter, cleanse your baby's cord with alcohol. Also, fold the diaper below the cord to keep moisture from reaching it. The rest of the newborn's body can be cleaned with a sponge for those first few days. Keep in mind, however, that it's quite unlikely that submerging your child in bathwater is harmful, particularly if the cord is dried off afterward.

MYTH: *All umbilical cords fall off by two weeks of age.*

Though most cords have fallen off when a baby reaches two weeks of age, some stay on through the first month, often in those children who do not sleep on their stomachs.

Some research suggests that if the umbilical cord is still on beyond four weeks of age, there is a slightly higher risk of infection in the area. If the cord of your child has not detached by the end of the fourth week, notify your pediatrician.

MYTH: *All babies need belly binders.*

As recently as the 1930s, all babies were wrapped up to four months in a so-called "belly binder"—a tight strap of cloth encircling the baby at the naval—applied in the belief that it protected the cord from rupturing and infection. We now know, though, that this wrap prevents neither and may, in fact, increase the chances of infection. Some ethnic groups still continue this nonproductive practice, but its use should be discouraged.

MYTH: *Taping a coin over an umbilical hernia will cause it to heal faster.*

An umbilical hernia is a protrusion of the abdominal contents around the navel, caused by a midline weakness in the abdominal wall. It typically measures from one-quarter inch to nearly a full inch in diameter (.5 to 2.5 cm) and is frequently not detected until the first to third month of life.

Although umbilical hernias are a common defect, occurring more often in females and among premature infants, their exact frequency seems to vary widely, depending on the study being cited. Research in England revealed that the condition occurred in one out of every six babies there, or about 17 percent of the infants studied. In a study of American blacks, the incidence was as high as 40 percent.

Because of the concern over these anatomical variations, taping them has long been practiced, usually with a coin over the hernial sac itself, in an attempt to flatten the protrusion. But today most pediatricians reject the use of tape, coins, and other devices, because they may irritate the skin and obstruct normal muscular development. In most cases, umbilical hernias correct themselves, usually by age one, and almost always by age five and there is no evidence to show the healing is in any way helped by use of these devices. In fact, taping a hernia may be more detrimental to its healing than if it were left alone. In a ten-year study conducted by L. J. Halprin on premature black infants at Chicago's Michael Reese Hospital and Medical Center, small umbilical hernias (a protrusion less than half an inch or 1 cm.) all healed by themselves, without taping or other intervention. When larger protrusions were left untaped, there were three times as many that healed spontaneously as those that didn't. By contrast, when the hernias were taped, less than one-half of them healed.

Parents tell me that they often fear that umbilical hernias could become caught in a zipper or other device, or simply not go back in place, causing a rupture and blockage of the intestinal tract. Yes, this is possible, but it happens so rarely that it is an unreasonable fear. When such blockages occur, they tend to materialize in small hernias rather than the large ones that usually produce this anxiety. As a general rule, if through gentle pressure you can push the contents of your baby's hernia into the abdominal cavity, no blockage exists.

MYTH: *Crying can cause an umbilical hernia.*

Because the hernial sac frequently protrudes when a child is crying, some parents believe that excessive crying has caused the hernia itself. Not true. The increased abdominal pressure produced by crying is minuscule in comparison to the force that would be necessary to actually cause a hernia.

MYTH: *Surgery is usually necessary to correct umbilical hernias.*

Most umbilical hernias heal themselves as the abdominal muscles mature. Surgery is rarely necessary to correct them and is probably relied upon more than it should be. If by the age of five, however, healing hasn't occurred spontaneously, it probably won't on its own, and surgery may be advisable at that time to prevent your child's psychological trauma of entering school with a protruding belly button.

Sleeping and Sleep Positions

MYTH: *Turn your newborn's head periodically while he or she is sleeping or it will become lopsided or flattened.*

If your baby is healthy and full-term, there is no risk of the head being malformed during sleep. Your baby will rapidly develop enough strength to move his or her head, eliminating any risk of this problem.

Premature babies have extremely moldable skulls and as a result occasionally develop a narrower shape to their heads. In some hospital nurseries premature infants are placed on water beds, usually to provide constant, subtle stimulation, which helps prevent transient stopping of breathing (apnea). The flexibility of these beds also allows the head to round out.

Head shape, incidentally, is determined primarily by genes. If you want to know the ultimate head shape of your child, the most reliable indicator is to look at your own or that of the baby's other parent.

MYTH: *During the first three months of life, babies should sleep only on their backs.*

This myth apparently has its basis in the fear of harming the umbilical cord while the child sleeps. But as I discussed earlier, there is no risk of infection or other harm to the cord in the tummy-down sleeping position.

In fact, for newborns lacking the skill to roll over, sleeping on the back is probably the most dangerous sleep position for them. If they vomit while on their back, they are more likely to choke on the vomitus than if they were sleeping on their side or stomach. This is one reason that I recommend that babies sleep on their stomachs or right side. Sleeping on the right side is preferable to sleeping on the left, since this position aids digestion as gravity will help empty food from the stomach (which is on the left side of the abdomen) into the small intestine.

Placing babies on their stomachs to sleep has received further support from Y. Brackbill and her associates. In the *1973 Journal of Pediatrics*, she reported that infants in the prone position slept significantly longer and cried less than those who sleep on their backs. According to Dr. Brackbill, infants on their backs cry about five times longer and sleep 26 percent less than stomach-sleepers.

The prone position, then, reduces crying, promotes sleep, and decreases the risk of choking. What more could parents ask for?

MYTH: *Most babies sleep through the night by three months of age.*

For any parent who has been awakened from a deep, late-night sleep by a crying baby demanding immediate attention, I need not provide any explanation of why night awakenings are a major concern to parents. Until recently, little information has existed on night sleeping, and the few studies that had been conducted caused anxiety in some parents who read about them. A 1957 study in England, for example, indicated that 70 percent of infants slept through the night by three months of age, 83 percent by six months, and 90 percent by nine months. Imagine how distraught this study might make you feel each time you are aroused by your shrieking eleven-month-old baby,who has made the late late TV movie an unwelcome way of life in your household.

Actually, as encouraging as those statistics may sound for most parents, they are not as clear-cut as they seem. In that same British study, half the babies who were sleeping through the night began waking again during the second half of the first year of life, perhaps because of teething, the onset of dreaming, or excess psychic energy accumulated throughout the day. No wonder so many parents complain to their pediatricians, "I don't understand it; my baby used to sleep at night so well, and now he's waking up again."

To date, the most thorough observations of infant patterns have been conducted by Thomas F. Anders at the Stanford University Medical Center. He monitored two groups of babies—some two months old, the others nine months old—by videotape-recording their sleep habits in the natural settings of their own homes. At age two months, the children averaged twenty-eight minutes to fall asleep; at nine months, sixteen minutes. The study showed that 44 percent of the two-month-olds and 78 percent of the nine-month-olds either slept through the night or awakened so briefly that they were not removed from their cribs. Not surprisingly, parents paid more attention to the awakenings of the two-month-olds than those of the nine-month-olds.

MYTH: *You can't "teach" your baby to sleep through the night.*

Can your baby be taught or trained to sleep through the night? Probably, yes. If an infant over four months of age awakens crying—and if a safety pin, a wet diaper, or hunger is not the culprit—the baby eventually will stop crying and do so sooner on each successive night if you do not rush to the crib. But if you pick up and/or feed the baby, you reinforce the crying behavior by "giving in." Also, you can help break the nighttime feeding habit by progressively diluting the formula in the bottle with water.

If, as with many new parents, it is more painful for you to let the baby cry than to get up with him or her, then do so. But at least recognize that you are contributing to this unwelcome nighttime behavior. As your baby grows older, your own frustration with these late-night awakenings will probably overpower your guilt, making it easier for you to tolerate the crying, if that is what is necessary to change the sleep patterns.

General Care

MYTH: *Babies who are only a few days or a few weeks old should not be taken outdoors.*

Many parents are convinced that the worst possible place for their babies is the outdoors. Although there is no evidence to connect colic with swallowed air, some people believe that a baby who inhales windy air will develop this crying disorder. Others are afraid that a newborn will be exposed to harmful bacteria or infection outside. But in fact, there is generally less chance of catching illness, unless transmitted by people, when outdoors, because concentrations of potentially injurious germs are probably reduced in the free circulation of outside air.

So the mere act of taking your baby for a walk, or even letting your baby sleep in the carriage in your own backyard, does not present any danger in itself. Even in very cold weather, babies can be taken outside if they are properly bundled.

MYTH: *Newborns should be handled by others as little as possible.*

Because of the potential seriousness of childhood illness in the first few weeks of life, some parents feel extremely uncomfortable having friends and neighbors handle their newborn. While some caution may be reasonable, it need not be carried to extreme. However, if you feel strongly about this, but don't want to offend people, simply tell them that you're only following doctor's orders—that your pediatrician suggested you not let others hold the baby to minimize inadvertent transmission of infectious agents. Even if your doctor never actually offered such advice, you will take the burden of guilt off yourself by saying so. (See page 81 of the cold chapter for further discussion of this matter.)

MYTH: *Newborns are immune to colds.*

See page 64.

MYTH: *Always dress a baby warmly.*

Although it's only natural for you to want to protect your baby as much as possible, there's no need to dress an infant warmly except in cold weather. Many parents, however, keep their babies bundled, indoors and outdoors, in warm, comfortable temperatures. Even in particularly cold areas, babies are still sometimes overdressed, often after coming indoors wearing several layers of clothing.

On a sunny day outside, your baby will be just as eager as you to stay cool. If you are wearing shorts and perspiring, it's foolish to dress your baby any more heavily than yourself.

Keep in mind, however, that a baby's temperature-regulation mechanism is much more susceptible to change than an adult's. For example, after a bath, a baby's body temperature can sink quite rapidly as the moisture evaporates from the skin. So, dry and dress your baby quickly after a bath.

MYTH: *To encourage your newborn to suck on a pacifier, dip it in honey.*

True, your baby will probably be more interested in a pacifier brimming with honey. But it could be dangerous to coat its tip with this sweet substance. In recent years, researchers have discovered that honey contaminated with the bacterium *Clostridium botulinum* directly causes one-third of the cases of infant botulism. About 10 percent of all commercially prepared honey found in the supermarkets contains this particular bacterium, which for unknown reasons, seems to affect only children six months old or younger.

Infant botulism in itself can be a serious disorder. It can produce a muscle-weakening disease in babies and has even been implicated in some cases of the Sudden Infant Death

Syndrome (the unexplained death of a baby under one year of age; see pages 242–243). Consequently, many pediatricians now insist that no child take any form of honey in the first year of life. The old practice of dipping the pacifier in honey must cease.

MYTH: *A string can be attached to a pacifier to keep it from slipping away.*

Some parents have told me that they have tied a string onto their baby's pacifier, with the other end of the string tied around the child's neck. This prevents the pacifier from slipping away from the infant when it falls from his mouth. But even though this procedure may prevent the temporary displacement of the pacifier, some cases of babies strangling on the string have been reported. As an alternative, try the following: If your baby's pacifier has a ring attached to it, pull a diaper through the ring itself, which will stabilize the pacifier, preventing it from dropping out of the infant's mouth.

MYTH: *If you touch the "soft spot" on your baby's head, you can easily poke a hole in it.*

The fontanelles, or "soft spots," are the soft areas on the head where the bony plates of the skull have not yet fused together. These areas of unfused bone allow for molding and repositioning of the head as it navigates the birth canal during birth.

The larger of the two fontanelles is at the top of the head near the front and may take up to eighteen months to close. The smaller, posterior fontanelle usually closes within four to six months. Because these soft spots are anatomical variations that clearly differentiate infants from adults, much mysticism and fear surround them. The most common fear is that the baby can be injured just by touching the skull at this "open" point. But you can touch your baby's soft spots without any worry. "Soft spot" is really a misnomer. In fact, this area is covered by a sturdy membrane as strong as canvas, which protects the baby's head from damage.

MYTH: *Never pull a nipple or pacifier too quickly out of a baby's mouth, or it could "pop" the soft spot.*

Some individuals believe that a connection exists between the fontanelles and the top of the child's mouth and that a blow, a fall, or a sudden withdrawal of an object (like a nipple or a pacifier) from the mouth can suck the fontanelles into the head. This belief, fortunately, is pure fiction.

Although this particular myth may seem rather unusual, it is strongly rooted in Mexican-American folklore. The condition is referred to as *caida de mollera,* or "fallen fontanelle." In a recent survey, 97 percent of the Mexican-American women interviewed were familiar with this belief. The primary danger of the myth is that some of the commonly accepted home remedies for *caida de mollera* are potentially risky in themselves.

Perhaps you've noticed that your own baby appears occasionally to have a sunken or softly pulsating fontanelle. In almost all cases, there is no need for concern. This is only the normal pulsation of the veins situated in this region. However, this may sometimes be a sign of severe dehydration, perhaps because of repeated diarrhea and vomiting episodes. In such cases, dehydration is accompanied by dry mouth, sunken-appearing eyes, loose or dough-like skin (like the skin on the back of an elderly person's hand), and a marked decrease or absence of urination.

MYTH: *Children who are tongue-tied at birth need to have their tongues clipped.*

See pages 138–139.

MYTH: *Sunlight is good for jaundiced newborns.*

Jaundice is a condition characterized by yellowish skin, caused by the bilirubin pigment in the blood. In the first few days of life, almost 50 percent of all babies experience some jaundice until their liver (the organ that aids the body in excreting bilirubin) begins functioning at full capacity.

Some years ago, nuns in a hospital nursery in Essex, England, noticed that the newborns closest to the window, and thus exposed to the most sunlight, were less jaundiced than those receiving smaller amounts of light. Studies soon documented that the visible, blue-range component of sunlight is, in fact, helpful in reducing jaundice in newborns.

However, the situation is more complicated than that. The sun also emits ultraviolet rays that can cause severe sunburn. There have been reports of parents, eager to ease their baby's jaundice, exposing their newborn to sunlight, causing severe— and, in some cases, life-threatening—sunburn of the baby's sensitive skin.

If sunlight treatment is used, your baby should only be exposed to it behind a glass window, which filters out the potentially damaging ultraviolet rays. A much preferred alternative, however, is an artificial, phototherapy light, like those now universally used in hospital nurseries, which are free of ultraviolet rays. Your pediatrician is the best guide as to the necessity and type of treatment necessary.

MYTH: *Bluish hands and feet in a newborn indicate the presence of heart disease.*

In adults, particularly the elderly, blueness in the extremities may indeed indicate a circulation disorder. But in the first few hours and even weeks of life, blueness of the hands and feet (acrocyanosis) is quite normal. It is usually caused by immature, sluggish capillary circulation in the skin, which improves as the baby ages. Because the blood passes through these tiny capillaries slowly, more oxygen is removed, causing a chemical change in the hemoglobin molecules (the red coloring matter of the blood), giving the blood a bluish discoloration. When acrocyanosis occurs in older infants, it is usually after exposure to cold temperatures and does not necessarily indicate that heart disease is present.

MYTH: *A noticeable bump in the middle of your baby's chest may be a tumor.*

Very often, parents feel a tiny round or triangular protuberance at the tip of their baby's breastbone (sternum), and their anxiety level immediately skyrockets. But there's really no cause for concern. This bony structure is called the xiphoid process, and everyone—children and adults—has one. But because babies have an extremely thin abdominal skin wall, it is much more noticeable in them. This protrusion is normal and does not indicate a tumor or a hernia.

MYTH: *Cradle cap is an infectious disorder.*

"Cradle cap," or seborrheic dermatitis, is a common, mild condition in babies, characterized by an oily, waxy, yellowish substance on the scalp. It occurs most often when a baby's head is improperly cleaned, usually because parents are afraid to scrub the soft spot vigorously.

Although cradle cap may appear unsightly, it is not infectious, but just the normal skin secretions of your baby's scalp. The suggested treatment is simply to wash daily with soap and water, or special "antiseborrhea" shampoo, scrubbing energetically until the yellow buildup has been gradually removed.

MYTH: *Babies must have a daily bath.*

Did you grow up with the notion that your baby would be happiest with a fixed and established daily routine that included a bath? Despite this widespread belief, some infants dread taking a bath, no matter how routine it has become, making the experience miserable not only for baby but for parent as well. If that's the situation in your household, there's no need for your infant to be bathed daily. Cool washcloths applied to the face and regular cleaning of the diaper area are all that's normally necessary. For fussy babies, a thorough bath need only be given once or twice weekly.

MYTH: *Tickling a newborn can cause stuttering in later life.*

About 250,000 children in America stutter, and although many factors have been suggested as provoking this disorder, only psychological stress has been well documented as a cause. No association exists between tickling and stuttering, although this myth may have evolved because tickling does produce a staccato-sounding laugh in children. Still, there is no evidence that tickling and laughter are anything but normal, healthy behaviors.

Most often, stuttering seems to occur in three- and four-year-olds whose capacity to express themselves verbally is inadequate to meet their needs. This type of stuttering usually vanishes on its own unless parents overreact to it.

MYTH: *All babies need one bowel movement a day.*

The way some parents talk, a daily bowel movement is as American as apple pie and Fourth of July picnics. Many parents become upset when their babies vacillate from such regularity, yet almost all infants do. One stool per day just isn't on the agenda of most newborns.

Breastfed babies, especially during the first month, may have as many as ten bowel movements a day, as though the mother's milk itself were a laxative. These stools are often loose in consistency and may have a yellowish or greenish appearance. Then for reasons not really known, at about six weeks to two months of age, the frequency of bowel movements reverses. Rather than having three to ten stools a day, a breastfed baby may only have one or two per week. Despite this significant change, there is no cause for alarm. It's all quite normal.

Bottle-fed babies can range in frequency just as dramatically. They may have more than one bowel movement a day or can go several days without one. Both circumstances are normal. As a pediatrician, I am not concerned so much by the number of stools but more by any abnormal consistency. If your baby's bowel movements are too hard (constipation) or watery (diarrhea), consult your doctor.

MYTH: *It is impossible to toilet-train a child under fifteen months old.*

You might be surprised to find a discussion of toilet training in the newborn chapter. After all, in American culture, most parents wait until their child is between 1½ and 2½ years old to begin toilet training. They believe that, before this age, the youngster is simply not intellectually or physically able to follow instructions. Many parents and physicians also feel that early initiation of toilet-training techniques could lead to psychological problems, though this has never been proved.

While I am not advocating a cultural shift in which toilet training begins at a much earlier age in the United States, studies of other cultures show that more than half of the world's societies start toilet training at age six months, while about 26 percent begin even before that. Consider, for example, the Digo tribe, who live in eastern Africa along the Indian Ocean. Bladder and bowel training is started there in the first few weeks of life, and by age four to six months most children are relatively dry during both day and night.

Here is how the Digos approach toilet training: Whenever parents sense that their babies need to urinate, the children are placed in a pre-established position, while mother or father makes a "shuus" noise that the baby learns to associate with urinating. Each time the infant actually urinates, the parent again makes this "shuus" sound, as well as reinforcing the behavior further with rewards like feeding, affection, or other pleasurable activities. As the children become older, they eventually urinate on command upon hearing the "shuus" sound from the parents. Bowel training is done a little differently, but the general principles are the same.

Diaper changes in the Western world tend to be done at the convenience of the parents, rather than at the time excrement is passed; thus, unlike the Digo infants, babies here do not learn to quickly associate the physical sensations of having a bowel movement with the actual passage of a stool. Also, the site of toilet training in many other societies is outside, while in the United States the process is much more complicated, with bathrooms, toilets, unzipping, unsnapping, and unpinning—all of which make early toilet training a much more complicated process. Both cognitively and mechanically, the procedure is clearly more complex.

The early training of the Digos and other tribes indicates that bladder and bowel control is due primarily to sociocultural patterns and not necessarily the readiness of children. For the reasons mentioned in the previous paragraph the Digos techniques are less adaptive to Western culture. However, I do think that parents and pediatricians can be more flexible in both reacting to the physical and psychological needs of each baby as well as increasing their understanding of divergent individual or cultural ideas on "the best time to start" a child's training.

MYTH: *If parents have allergies, their babies will inherit them.*

Parents sometimes warn me, "I'm allergic to penicillin, so you'd better not give it to my baby." But although *tendencies* toward allergies (from hay fever to asthma to eczema) can be inherited, the specific allergies themselves are not transmitted from one generation to the next. The antibodies that create allergies do not cross over the placenta from mother to child.

Thus, while your newborn may have inherited the tendency for allergies, only repeated exposure to common irritating substances (pollen, dust) can provoke the allergy itself. Even though you may have a particular allergy—to penicillin, for example—your child will not necessarily develop it, too.

MYTH: *Babies cannot begin rolling over until four to five months after birth.*

For most parents, rolling over is one of the milestones of their baby's development. It most frequently occurs in the four- to five-month age range, usually beginning with a roll from the stomach to the back.

Not all infants, however, read the same growth and development books as their parents and pediatricians. Don't count on your baby rolling over at a particular age. In fact, some babies can roll over at *two weeks of age,* although it is not as controlled and sophisticated as it will be later. This extremely early rolling, although uncommon, is made possible by a phenomenon called the "tonic neck reflex," in which one of the child's arms becomes bent while the other is straight, as the baby gazes in one direction or the other. If the child is lying prone when the bent arm ultimately straightens out, the arm may push against the bed with a force strong enough to flip the baby over. This tonic neck reflex usually disappears by the third month of life. But because it can occur unexpectedly in newborns, don't leave your baby unattended for even a moment on a bed, changing table, or other raised platform.

MYTH: *A blue discoloration on the back is usually a bruise contracted during the delivery of the baby.*

Once the baby is home, many parents notice a bluish-gray discoloration, usually at the base of the newborn's spine, and presume that it is a bruise that will disappear quickly. True, these irregular spots are only temporary, but they are not bruises. These large, benign patches are called "Mongolian spots," and in a major study by Alvin Jacobs at Stanford University, they were found on the bodies of 9.6 percent of the white babies examined, 70.1 percent of those of Latin origin, 81 percent of those of Asian origin, and 95.5 percent of the black babies.

Despite the name "Mongolian spots," they are unrelated to Mongolism; they are caused by accumulations of pigment under the skin and usually disappear by the age of four years. Don't be concerned by them.

MYTH: *All birthmarks are permanent.*

Because birthmarks are common and prominent in newborns, their importance tends to be exaggerated by parents, and many erroneous beliefs and superstitions are based on their size, shape, and appearance. Some mothers even blame themselves for their baby's blemishes, believing that the spots were caused by a stressful occurrence during pregnancy or delivery.

But even though Madison Avenue has convinced most of us that a baby's skin is perfect, it is not. During the first few weeks of life, a newborn's skin goes through many changes, including peeling, cracking, shedding, and even an acnelike disorder called acneneonatorum, which may be caused by the baby's withdrawal from maternal hormones. Most of the "unsightly" birthmarks and skin disorders that disturb parents so terribly eventually fade or disappear completely on their own.

Mongolian spots, one of the more familiar types of birthmarks, is discussed above. There are two other common variations that you may notice on your baby:

- Salmon patches (or nevus simplex) are present in 40 percent of all newborns, usually on the neck, forehead, or eyelids. These light-red areas, sometimes called "stork bites" or "angel's kisses," generally disappear in six to twelve months, particularly those on the face. Although the lesions present on the nape of the neck may not fade completely, they are eventually covered by hair and become undetectable.

- Strawberry marks are noticeable, red skin lesions, often resembling a strawberry. They are raised and rough-surfaced and most commonly appear in the first few weeks after birth in about 8 to 10 percent of all babies, particularly premature ones. About 75 percent of all strawberry marks occur in the head region, grow in size until about eight months of age, and then eventually disappear, almost always by the age of seven years. I tell parents that the best treatment for these strawberry marks, unless they're extremely large or critically located (like around the eyes, nose, or mouth), is to leave them alone. They will heal perfectly well without surgical removal or other invasive treatment.

MYTH: *You can't spoil a child under six months of age.*

According to Jeff Levine, child psychiatrist at the University of California at Irvine Medical Center, a "spoiled child" personality may develop in a child "who has become used to the constant gratification and attention of his parents, and then is deprived of this continuous parental attention at a critical time in his life."

A child cannot become truly spoiled by six months of age. However, parents' actions can lead to spoiling, particularly when parents believe all needs of their infant, no matter how unrealistic, must be met. Eventually, they recognize the impossibility and undesirability of immediately satisfying every desire of their baby. Amid their own frustration, they may begin feeling angry toward the child and may often react with a sudden and infuriated withdrawal of attention. The child, accustomed to having all desires fulfilled, frequently responds in an angry behavior pattern that is typically referred to as the spoiled-child personality. The child's aggressive reaction to this sudden decline of attention can occur at any age, whether the child is six months or sixteen months old.

The world we live in is not always gratifying, and this inevitable realization is often learned more easily in small stages, beginning at infancy, rather than having it suddenly thrust on an older child during a time of parental frustration.

As a parent, you should set reasonable, consistent loving limits that are acceptable to you and sensitive to your baby's needs. Children who confront and adjust to these limits will proceed through a healthy psychological growth process, with minimal risk of becoming "spoiled."

MYTH: *Newborns are too young for car restraints.*

Always place children in car seats or other restraints. Once children are beyond the critical first few days of life, the leading cause of death among them is automobile accidents. And according to the National Center for Health Statistics, babies are the most vulnerable. Infants under six months of age—even though they travel in cars less often than older children—have an automobile death rate twice as high as children one year old, and three times as high as six-to-twelve-year-olds.

The proper time for babies to start using approved auto restraints is on the initial drive home from the hospital. Even though babies may slouch in the car seat, and their heads may appear very wobbly, no damage can be done to their back or other parts of their body. To stabilize your baby's head in the car seat, place rolled-up towels on either side of your infant's head. See also "Babies don't require car seats after the first year of life," page 238.

MYTH: *Never put an infant in front of a mirror during the first year of life.*

There are many variations of this old superstition, most notably, "Don't put a child in front of a mirror before the first tooth appears." According to the proponents of this belief, children may become vain, or thieves, or even never learn to talk if they see their own image so young. Many primitive tribes believe that a mirror can actually steal a baby's soul.

As intriguing as these stories may be, I'm sure you won't be surprised to learn that no scientific evidence exists to substantiate any of them. In fact, playing in front of the mirror can be an enjoyable, stimulating experience for babies. Let them look to their heart's content.

2

FEVER

At two in the morning you shakily reach for the telephone and dial your pediatrician's number. "I'm sorry to bother you so late," you anxiously explain, "but Billy's temperature has climbed to 102.8° [39.3°C]. I'm worried. What should I be doing?"

This is perhaps your first health-related crisis as a parent. Your child has a high fever, his face is flushed, and he is shivering with the chills. And you can't remember ever being quite so nervous.

Fortunately, most fevers do not require emergency advice. But parents still become alarmed each time their child's temperature rises. About 30 percent of all visits to pediatricians' offices are to evaluate and treat fevers.

Many centuries ago, fever was considered a major disease. It was universally feared and aggressively treated, particularly after the thermometer became widely employed by physicians in the mid-1800s. Although the clinical thermometer had been invented in the seventeenth century by Santorio Santorio, professor of physiology at an Italian medical school in Padua, it was not widely accepted, largely because physicians, such as the influential eighteenth-century British surgeon, John Hunter, claimed that oral readings were inaccurate because they were altered by the cool air of the breathing process. However, James Currie helped the thermometer gain medical approval by suggesting that when the bulb is inserted under the tongue, and when the lips are closed, "the effect of respiration may be disregarded, as I have found from many hundred experiments."

In more recent times, some physicians regarded fever as an ally, even using "fever therapy" to treat many ailments. Before antibiotics, as late as the 1930s, patients with syphilis and gonorrhea were treated in "fever boxes," where their temperatures were raised as high as 107.6°F (42.°C) for up to eight to ten hours, without harmful effects but with questionable benefits. These ailments, along with other serious disorders, were treated in this manner on the assumption that bacteria could be "burned out."

Today, we know that a fever is not an illness or the *cause* of illness but a symptom. Fevers are most commonly disease- or injury-related but may also result from other factors, such as prolonged drug use (including penicillin and antihistamines).

If you're like other parents, you've probably tried lowering your child's fever with methods ranging from bedrest to alcohol sponging to ice-water baths. Not all these common techniques are either helpful or necessary.

I believe that fevers are a misunderstood phenomenon, possibly a beneficial mechanism of the body's defense system, and certainly a source of more parental anxiety than they warrant. This chapter is intended to acquaint you with the purpose, cause, treatment, and mythology surrounding elevated temperatures in your child.

The Nature and Causes of Fever

MYTH: *98.6°F (37°C) is the normal body temperature; anything above or below is abnormal.*

We all grew up with the magic number of 98.6° (37°C) as the undisputed indicator of a healthy physical condition. Any variation signified trouble.

But that's not necessarily the case. Body temperatures above 98.6° (37°C) are not always a sign of illness. In fact, normal temperature levels can differ considerably from one child to another. Using 276 healthy students as subjects, a Northwestern University School of Medicine professor found that their individual normal oral temperatures ranged from 96.6° to 99.4°F (35.9 to 37.4°C), with the group average at 98.1° (36.7). Only 19 of the 276 students registered the traditional 98.6° (37°C).

In general, temperature readings are a less exact science in children than in adults. Under the age of two, youngsters normally have relatively high rectal temperatures. In one study, the average, healthy rectal temperature at 18 months was 99.8°F (37.6°C), with half the subjects registering 100°F (37.8°C) or higher. Although this "normal" reading gradually decreases, beginning at the age of two, it does not stabilize until the teenage years.

Not only can the specific set point differ from one child to the next, but the "normal" body temperature varies in each youngster during the day. Your child can have a 98.4°F (36.8°C) temperature in the morning, and a 100.4°F (38°C) reading in the late afternoon, without any reason for concern. In my practice, I receive most phone calls from parents about high temperatures from 5 to 7 P.M., which, not surprisingly, is also the time of day when the body temperature normally peaks. (Body temperatures reach their lowest levels between 3 and 6 A.M.) Don't become anxious over such a variation; a daily swing of as much as 2 degrees (about 1 degree Celsius) can be expected in your youngster.

During or immediately after periods of active exercise or play, a child's thermometer reading could temporarily rise as high as 104°F (40°C) and still be within the "normal" range. Exercising in 80° (27°C) weather at 75 percent of one's capacity can cause an increase in body temperature of 2 degrees (1.1°C).

Many parents also worry when their child's temperature is *below* 98.6° (37°C), but their concern is almost always unwarranted. "Normal" readings can dip to 96°F (35.6°C), while extreme body temperatures as low as 74°F (23.3°C) have been reported without causing death. Low temperatures (down to 96°F or 35.6°C) are almost never due to illness, with the rare exception of certain bacterial intestinal infections, deficient thyroid activity (hypothyroidism), and rare ailments unique to newborns. Aside from these infrequent disorders, only exposure to extreme environmental coldness may cause troublesome marked decreases (hypothermia) in body temperature.

With so many factors at play, no wonder 98.6° (37°C) cannot be considered normal for everyone at all times. Taking your child's temperature during a healthy period will tell you what his or her own normal reading is. As a general guideline, a thermometer reading above 100.4°F (38°C) rectally in a child who is quiet, not overheated from exercise, and not bundled or overdressed usually signifies a fever.

MYTH: *You can determine if your child has a fever by placing your hand on his or her forehead.*

A child with a fever feels warm to the touch, or at least that's what most of us believe. But placing your hand on your youngster's forehead is far from the most dependable method of detecting an elevated temperature.

In a study at the Comprehensive Child Care Clinic at Johns Hopkins Hospital, three nurses trained in working with children were asked to feel the foreheads and/or chests of 1149 children (from newborns to age eighteen) to determine whether a fever was present. After the nurse's estimate was made, each child's temperature was verified with a thermometer.

These skilled health professionals, despite their training, often made inaccurate evaluations. Of the 138 children whose fevers were established by thermometer readings, 58 (42 percent) of them were erroneously judged to have normal temperatures by the nurses using the hand on the forehead (or chest) method.

Interestingly, near the end of the study, the nurses became more accurate in their determinations of fever. This may indicate that with repeated experience, as parents may obtain with their own children, proficiency can improve.

Nevertheless, don't rely solely on hand readings to judge your child's body temperature. If your youngster doesn't feel well, has chills, or acts sick, take his or her temperature with a thermometer. It's the only consistently accurate method of determining the presence of fever.

A plastic fever detection strip has emerged onto the marketplace in recent years. It contains a thermophototropic ester of cholesterol that changes color when body heat changes. According to its manufacturer, the instrument can identify the presence of a fever when placed on the forehead for sixty seconds.

The concept behind this device is excellent, since in the majority of common childhood illnesses it is more important to determine if a fever is present than what the precise temperature is. Knowing whether the temperature is 101°, 102°, or 103°F (about 38.5 to 39.5°C) will rarely change the course of treatment, and this detection strip not only indicates that a fever is present but can save the child the annoyance of having his or her temperature taken rectally.

However, since a recent study has questioned the reliability of the device, noting that it did not properly identify some fevers, I suggest that you rely on the old-fashioned thermometer as your most dependable tool, at least for the initial determination of your child's temperature.

MYTH: *All fevers are caused by infections.*

Statistically, infectious diseases, particularly those of the upper respiratory tract, produce most childhood and adult fevers. But fevers can have many other causes, ranging from the expected temperature increases due to exercise, digestion, ovulation, pregnancy, or a warm environment (like a sauna) to significant, noninfectious disorders such as rheumatoid arthritis, gout, physical injuries, and burns.

Sometimes, when particular drugs are taken, a fever may be a side effect. These drugs include the sulfonamides, penicillin, quinidine, salicylates, bromides, antihistamines, and streptomycin. Exposure to various industrial materials, ranging from raw cotton to zinc oxide, can induce elevated temperatures as well.

Essentially, fever is an indication that tissue or an organ has suffered damage, to which the body has reacted with an inflammatory response. For instance, during an infection, your child's white blood cells (leucocytes) will attempt to cleanse the body of damaged tissue and foreign substances, while also trying to engulf and destroy bacteria or viruses (phagocytosis). In the process, the body will release heat-generating substances (pyrogens) that raise the body temperature.

Here is a summary of the more common childhood causes of fever (temperatures over 100.4°F or 38°C rectally):

Newborns (birth to 1½ months): In this age group, fever is usually caused by infection, which may be related to the delivery process or even the intrauterine experience. An elevated temperature may also be caused by a common cold or by overdressing. Whenever a fever occurs in a newborn, it is *essential* that your doctor be notified immediately.

Infants (1½ to twelve months): Respiratory infections—including colds, tonsillitis, and ear infections—most frequently produce fever in this age group. Also, some childhood immunizations, most commonly the pertussis (whooping cough) component of the DPT shot, can cause fevers.

Preschoolers (one to five years): Respiratory infections most frequently induce fever in this age bracket, particularly sore throats, ear infections, bronchitis, and tonsillitis. Bladder infections, vomiting, diarrhea, and measles are also often accompanied by fever.

Schoolchildren (six to fourteen years): While respiratory infections are again the most frequent cause of fever in this age group, infections of the urinary tract, bladder, and kidney may also be responsible, particularly in younger girls.

MYTH: *Teething can cause fever.*

See pages 139–140.

MYTH: *The higher the fever, the sicker the child.*

Despite myths to the contrary, the height of a child's fever is usually *not* an indication of the severity of the illness. A temperature as high as 105°F (about 40°C) may accompany an illness that is not serious, while, conversely, many dangerous ailments are associated with low-grade temperatures.

Consider the viral infection called roseola, a rose-colored rash that afflicts children primarily between six and eighteen months of age. Although it is not a serious illness, it often produces a high fever, from 103° to 105°F (about 39.5 to 40.5°C). Usually the child appears much happier and more active than you would expect for this high temperature. In this case, as in many others, the intensity of the fever is not a faithful barometer of the ailment's severity.

In 1975, William Tomlinson (in the *American Journal of Diseases of Children*) evaluated the records and histories of 1500 children in his practice to determine whether a high fever was necessarily an indication of serious illness. Interestingly, the illnesses experienced during high fevers (104°F or 40°C or above) were no different from those producing milder fevers, with the exception of a slightly higher incidence of pneumonia in children with persistently elevated fevers. During thirteen years of medical practice, Dr. Tomlinson encountered only two cases of 106°F (41.1°C) temperatures, and none higher. No deaths occurred among the children with high fevers.

I constantly receive calls from concerned mothers who say things like "Doctor, my child's temperature was 102.4°

(39.1°C), and it just went up to 103.1° (39.5°C). What should I do?" In most cases, I advise parents to stop taking their youngster's temperature. The actual reading doesn't matter any longer. We know the child has a fever. The primary concern is the seriousness of the child's condition, which is more often reflected in how sick the child appears, not the precise reading of the thermometer.

As a pediatrician, I am much less disturbed about a child with a 104°F (40°C) temperature who is alert and appears well than I am about one who has a 101°F (38.3°C) temperature but looks ill and is weak and weary. *A youngster's overall condition and appearance must be considered, not solely temperature. The level of sickness and discomfort should determine how aggressively you try to lower the temperature, how much you should worry, and how quickly you should call your doctor (despite the hour).*

MYTH: *Fevers are dangerous.*

Children do not die from illness-induced high fevers. Nor is there a single well-documented case of any part of the body being damaged by a high fever caused by an infectious illness (see also "High fevers cause brain damage," pages 48–49.) But most of us have believed for years that fevers are potentially dangerous and harmful. No wonder we take every reasonable step available to us to lower an elevated temperature.

Extremely high fevers (over 106°F or 41.1°C) are actually quite rare. Eugene F. Dubois, in the *American Journal of the American Sciences,* reported his study of 357 patients suffering from diseases typically characterized by high fever. Of 1761 separate temperature readings, only 4.3 percent were above 106°F (41.1°C). None exceeded 107.8°F (42.1°C).

Dr. Dubois discovered that there were about twice as many readings in the 104° to 105°F (40 to 40.6°C) range than in the 102° to 103°F (38.9 to 39.4°C) range. He and other physicians have concluded that a body mechanism exists that raises the temperature to 104°–105°F (40 to 40.6°C)—perhaps for protective reasons—but rarely allows it to reach or exceed 106°F (41.1°C).

Yet even when temperatures rise to high levels, they are not only generally safe but probably are playing an important disease-fighting role.

MYTH: *All fevers should be treated.*

Some medical clinicians make a strong case for not treating moderate or low-grade fevers (under 102°F or 38.9°C) in any way. After all, not only human beings but every warm-blooded animal experiences fever. Thus, goes the reasoning, it must serve a useful function or it would have become extinct over many millennia of evolution.

Some studies suggest that elevated temperatures create an unfriendly environment that discourages the survival of the infecting organism. In the laboratory, many childhood viruses stop growing at the temperature levels generally associated with fevers, although these same findings have not yet been substantiated *within* the human body. An Indiana University researcher has shown that fever temporarily reduces the blood's level of trace metals, particularly iron; because iron enhances the infecting properties of bacteria, lowering the serum iron would make it more difficult for the invading microorganism to multiply.

Some reptile research focusing on fevers may be particularly relevant to people. For instance, in one study, a group of lizards was innoculated with bacteria that raised their temperatures to 105°F (40.6°C). A second group also received the same bacterial infection, but researchers took measures to prevent their temperatures from rising above 100°F (37.8°C). Interestingly, many more lizards in the second group died than in the group allowed to develop fever. For these reptiles, fevers appeared to be a beneficial rather than a harmful phenomenon.

Does this mean we are wrong to treat fevers in human beings? No one knows for certain. But Elesea Atkins, in her authoritative look at the controversy in the *New England Journal of Medicine,* observes, "[T]he role or purpose of fever in disease remains unexplained. Clearly, under normal circumstances of infection, the raised body temperature does not destroy the micro-organisms directly. In the subtle balance between host and invader, fever may eventually be shown to confer a greater advantage to the defense mechanisms of the host than to the invasive properties of the micro-organism."

While the debate continues, most parents still consider fevers to be a negative side effect of infection. They routinely try to reduce their child's fever through means ranging from aspirin to sponge baths. I am constantly asked by mothers and fathers to "do something" for a feverish youngster.

But because a fever is usually a self-limiting phenomenon, and perhaps a beneficial one, should a parent or a pediatrician always "do something" to reduce the temperature? I am rarely overconcerned about a child who may have a 103°F (about 39°C) temperature, but who is comfortable and doesn't act ill. By contrast, lowering the temperature and having the child checked by a physician may be advisable for even a low-grade fever in a youngster who looks and acts miserable, with a headache, chills, or muscle aches.

As general guidelines, I ask parents to call me about a feverish child under any of the following circumstances:

- Any fever exceeding 100.4°F (38°C) in a child up to two months of age, because of the potential seriousness of illnesses in babies.
- In older infants and children, a fever of 104°F (40°C) or higher that can't be lowered within six hours by aspirin, acetaminophen, or a cooling method like sponging with water and when the child appears very ill or uncomfortable.
- A fever, even if only a moderate one, that persists for three days or more. You can watch for the first forty-eight

to seventy-two hours without concern if the signs of illness are mild, especially if your youngster is old enough to describe any complaints.

- Diarrhea, vomiting, abdominal pain, or ear pain accompanying the fever.
- Difficulty in breathing (fever alone will cause breathing to be more rapid but not labored).
- Increase in the frequency of urination, pain accompanying urinating, or recurrence of bed wetting once the child is toilet-trained.
- A fever that is accompanied by twitching of the face, arms, or legs, or by other unusual movements.
- A change in the child's activity level.
- An observation that the child is unusually sleepy.
- A complaint by the child of a headache or back pain when bending the knees up to the chest or lowering the chin to the chest.
- The parents are frightened by the child's appearance.

MYTH: *High fevers cause brain damage.*

No evidence exists that an infection-related high fever, in and of itself, can cause brain damage—or any other serious injury—to a child. Yes, some youngsters with severe fevers have suffered brain damage. But this injury was caused by the infection itself (usually encephalitis, meningitis, or other infections of the central nervous system), not the fever, which is only a symptom.

Brain damage may occur with a condition called heat stroke. It is an overheating illness that sometimes occurs in individuals who vigorously exercise without having the salt and water lost through perspiration replaced. Sweating ceases, and the internal mechanism for regulating body temperature fails, leaving them no means of keeping themselves cool. Extreme brain damage is sometimes the result.

In general, however, high fevers themselves, when activated

as a bodily defense mechanism against an infecting agent, do not cause brain damage, although they can be a symptom of an illness that might.

MYTH: *High fevers are likely to cause seizures in children.*

More than 2300 years ago Hippocrates introduced the concept that teething caused both fever and convulsions. Consequently, the belief evolved that because seizures were sometimes seen in those who had high fevers, they were caused by these severely elevated temperatures.

However, most children will *never* have a fever-related (febrile) seizure or convulsion. Only about 3 percent of all children ever experience one; even when they occur, although frightening, they are generally harmless. These seizures usually materialize only when the temperature has risen above 103°F (about 39°C) rectally, often within the first twenty-four hours of the illness. When they happen, the fever has usually been produced by a common childhood illness, such as tonsillitis, pharyngitis, or an ear infection. Roseola has also been connected with a high rate of febrile seizures.

Most of these attacks are brief, some lasting less than a minute, with few extending more than twenty minutes. As the susceptible child's body overheats, the brain's electrical impulses begin misfiring, causing involuntary muscular movements. Initially, the body may become rigid, followed by rhythmic head, hand, or foot jerking. The eyes may roll back, and saliva may drool out of the mouth. When the seizure ends, the child is usually relaxed, and often appears soundly asleep.

How can you tell if your child is prone to febrile convulsions? Youngsters, especially with a family history of seizure with fever, are susceptible primarily between six months and five years of age, with the first attack rarely occurring after the first three years of life. Such seizures manifest themselves more frequently in boys than girls. After age five, even in children who were once at risk, seizures with fever are rare.

If your child is in the most susceptible age range, and if there is a family history of these convulsions, your pediatrician may suggest trying to control the height of your child's fever (e.g., with aspirin, sponging) to minimize the chances of seizure. Because convulsions usually occur when the level of the fever is climbing, there is a chance that if the temperature isn't effectively controlled, it could swing upward again and again, thus *increasing* the risk of seizures. So with these few children, the fever should be carefully controlled.

Don't panic if your child has a febrile convulsion. The following suggestions should be helpful:

- Place your child on his or her side to prevent choking on saliva.
- Keep your child's head away from hard objects and surfaces, which can be banged against.
- Make certain that your child's breathing passage remains open by removing vomit or other matter from the nose or throat. Use your finger, or for an infant use a bulb syringe. (Do not try to pry open your child's mouth with your fingers during a seizure. You may get bitten. Instead, gently insert a soft, unbreakable object like a wallet between the teeth.)
- Call your doctor and explain what is happening.
- Don't give your child anything to eat or drink immediately after the seizure.

Just as there are appropriate times for a parent to be sensitive to the possibility of febrile seizures, there are also worry-free times as well. If your child is over the age of five and has never had a seizure and there is no family history of them, no great risk of convulsions exists. Even in a child of five or under there is no significant danger of convulsions when a fever has persisted beyond two days, if it is not above 103°F (about 39°C) and if the youngster looks good and feels comfortable.

MYTH: *Seizures from a high fever cause brain damage and epilepsy in young children.*

If seizures occur in your child, keep in mind that they are usually benign phenomena. No serious aftereffects develop from them. A study reported in *Pediatrics* (1978) showed that among 1706 children who experienced febrile seizures, no deaths or motor defects occurred as a result. Almost all children who have them outgrow the tendency for seizures completely. Also, despite a myth to the contrary, children who have had only a single febrile seizure are not more susceptible to epilepsy later in life. The study cited above concluded that unless a child has high-risk factors for epilepsy (like pre-existing neurological abnormalities), she has no greater chance of developing epilepsy because she has had a febrile seizure.

MYTH: *Sweating means the fever is climbing.*

Most parents become distressed watching their feverish child sweat, usually because they believe that the excessive perspiration is a sign that the youngster's temperature is worsening. But in fact, the converse is true. Sweating is really an indication that the temperature level has started *decreasing.*

Here's how the process works:

The hypothalamus, an area at the base of the brain, acts as a thermostat, maintaining the body temperature at around 98.6°F (37°C). But with an infection, chemical substances called pyrogens are released that elevate this thermostat's set point so that the body may be tricked into believing that 103°F (about 39°C) is its most desirable temperature. In turn, the body, in an attempt to raise its reading to this 103°F (about 39°C) level, generates heat through vigorous muscle contraction (chills) and a decrease in the surface circulation that inhibits heat loss. The body temperature thus rises, and during the illness your temperature may be maintained at this "desired" 103°F (about 39°C).

Once the infection is conquered, the "thermostat" is set back to 98.6°F (37°C). The body, recognizing now that "I am too hot" at 103°F (about 39°C), begins sweating to stimulate heat loss, bringing the temperature down to 98.6°F (37°C).

Thus, sweating indicates that the fever is falling. Conversely, chills mean that the temperature is climbing. In the days before antibiotics, when the primary mode of "treatment" was sitting by the bedside, the physician and the family would feel relieved when sweating occurred, recognizing this as an indication that the condition was improving—the fever had "broken."

The Treatment of Fevers

MYTH: *Feed a cold, starve a fever.*

Should you feed a cold and starve a fever? Or starve a cold and feed a fever? The debate is endless and heated, but neither is entirely correct.

The metabolic needs of a child with a fever (but also with a cold) may be increased as the body may then consume calories more rapidly to combat the invading organism. The high temperature of a fever rapidly burns up the body's excess supplies of proteins, carbohydrates, and fats, making it necessary to replenish the body through caloric intake.

But unfortunately, many children lose their appetite when they're sick. The most important guiding principle, then, is to make certain that your feverish youngster is at least drinking fluids, particularly those with some caloric benefit like fruit juices. A sign that your child is not consuming enough fluids is a decrease in the rate of urination. Encourage him or her to drink more. Most children have a reserve storage of calories, which makes it unnecessary to eat solids during the relatively short period of an illness. However, if the child's appetite remains normal, there is no need to inhibit it.

MYTH: *High fevers should be treated with antibiotics.*

Antibiotics can be extremely effective as a treatment for illnesses caused by bacteria, like strep throat and most urinary tract and ear infections. However, probably 90 percent of childhood fevers are produced by *viral* illnesses, including most respiratory infections. These infections do not respond to antibiotics, and thus it is unproductive and potentially harmful to prescribe them in such instances.

Even so, antibiotics are administered for many viral illnesses, primarily because parents request them. However, I believe that pediatricians have the responsibility to educate parents about the appropriate uses, misuses, and dangers of antibiotics. Antibiotics are suitable for specific *bacterial* diseases; they are not effective in lowering viral-induced temperatures. (See page 72 for a further discussion of antibiotics and the common cold.)

MYTH: *Liquid aspirin should be used to treat feverish children.*

There are two types of nonprescription drugs that can control temperature: (1) aspirin, or acetylsalicylic acid (ASA), marketed under an endless number of brand names, and (2) acetaminophen, sold under names like Tylenol, Tempra, and Liquiprin. Aspirin is one of the safest drugs in use, with more than 27 million pounds consumed yearly in the United States. But it does not exist in liquid form, and in fact, all so-called "liquid aspirin" is actually acetaminophen. Technically, because of aspirin's instability in solution, there is no such product as "liquid aspirin."

Both acetaminophen and aspirin are equally efficient in lowering childhood fevers. Aspirin is usually less expensive, but because acetaminophen can be administered in liquid as well as tablet form, many pediatricians and parents prefer it. Also, acetaminophen is generally considered less risky than aspirin, but both are very safe if properly administered. Overdoses of either substance, of course, can be fatal.

Your pediatrician can prescribe the recommended dosage of aspirin or acetaminophen for your youngster, based upon age and weight. Interestingly, these substances can be given simultaneously, since they work in slightly different ways within the body. So if your child's temperature does not respond to acetaminophen, you can also concurrently try aspirin in the normal dosages. It is important for parents to be aware that there is a difference between these commonly used preparations. Doctors have sometimes been unintentionally misled, while diagnosing and treating cases of overdoses, when parents have mistaken acetaminophen for aspirin and vice versa.

MYTH: *A child with the chills should be wrapped in blankets.*

Chills are often a component of fevers (see page 47). As one's body temperature rises, the hypothalamus may temporarily believe that the elevated temperature is "normal" and operating at the most efficient level possible. Thus, as it attempts to maintain this fever, messages are communicated to the skin's blood vessels, causing constriction that inhibits heat loss. As muscles contract, goose bumps develop, which decrease surface heat loss. The abnormally high "set point" in the brain makes the individual feel cold, so the body develops shakes and chills, which are mechanisms for generating heat by muscular activity.

Thus, when your child has the chills, his or her body temperature is actually rising. Wrapping your child in a heavy blanket will not make the already heated body more comfortable, nor will it help "break" the fever. Instead, it will cause the fever to rise even more rapidly.

Wrapping an infant under three months of age in a blanket is more than counterproductive; it may be life-threatening. Physicians in England have reported cases where excessive wrapping of feverish babies—which is an improper way to manage elevated fevers—has led to fatal heatstroke. Infants are particularly vulnerable to overheating because of their high metabolic rates and unstable body temperatures. Also, babies do not have the strength or mobility to toss off tightly wrapped blankets.

Therefore, during an illness with chills, blankets and clothing should be light rather than heavy.

MYTH: *Sponge a child who has a high fever with alcohol.*

Sponging a feverish child is certainly one means of reducing the fever. The liquid evaporating on the skin cools it, and in turn lowers the child's overall body temperature.

Alcohol as a sponging agent may work well. However, it is a poor and potentially dangerous choice. Although alcohol is only absorbed in minuscule amounts through the skin, your child can inhale its vapors. Some cases of near-fatal coma have been reported after sponging with alcohol in poorly ventilated areas.

Because of the danger of using alcohol, I recommend instead that parents sponge their children with tepid water. Some mothers and fathers believe that ice water must be used for this procedure, because its coldness will reduce the fever more quickly. But tepid water is just as effective as cold water in lowering the body temperature, because it is the evaporation of the water from the skin (as with sweating), and not the temperature of the water, that causes the fever to fall. Furthermore, the already ill-feeling, feverish child is made additionally miserable by the ice water and may fight against it, actually leading to an *increase* in temperature rather than the desired decrease.

MYTH: *Ice water, tea, cornstarch, or soapsuds enemas should be used to reduce high fever.*

Giving (or receiving) enemas is no one's beloved pasttime. But because they can lower body temperature and because of our historical preoccupation with bowel catharsis as a health remedy, parents have traditionally used various enema preparations to reduce their children's fevers.

Cool enemas are, in fact, no more effective than other methods described earlier (aspirin, sponging). And they have the disadvantage—and serious risk—of causing the dilution of essential body chemicals called electrolytes, which are necessary for normal metabolism. Consequently, enemas have no place in the treatment of childhood fevers.

MYTH: *Don't allow a feverish child to go outside.*

There is no problem in allowing a child with a fever to venture outside, assuming the weather is pleasant. There are probably more germs inside the house than outside, so the health danger of going outdoors is minimal and the child may, in fact, feel cooler or more comfortable being outdoors. Of course, keep your child away from other people to avoid putting them at risk. But if your youngster would like to sit in the backyard or even go for a walk, let him or her do so.

3

COLDS

The cave man and woman had colds. This ancient ailment is also the most common of all human illnesses, afflicting the average child three to eight times a year. Over 100 million colds are reported in the United States annually, and about 60 percent of all children's visits to the pediatrician are for colds and cold-related illnesses.

But despite the fact that we're all familiar with the runny or stuffy nose, sneezing, sniffling, coughing, sore throat, chills, low-grade fever, and general malaise that accompany them, we still don't understand colds. There have been many advances in our understanding of respiratory diseases, often raising more questions than they answer. How and why do children contract colds? What is the best treatment for them? Can colds be prevented?

We are now certain that viruses are the villains behind colds. Scientists have identified more than 200 different cold viruses, each with its own unique properties. The most common cold virus, the rhinovirus (in Latin, *rhino* = nose) was not clearly identified until 1960, when an electron microscope first photographed it. This virus is just one-millionth of an inch (20 billionth of a meter) long and is an extremely durable piece of genetic material. Scientists have isolated many other types of cold viruses, including the respiratory syncitial virus, the adenovirus, the coronavirus, and the picornavirus, but still others have not yet been clearly identified, despite continual studies.

Unfortunately, the development of a vaccine that is effective against all 200-plus of these cold viruses is unlikely.

Research into the common cold is difficult and slow-moving, largely because most animals that are usually used experimentally in the laboratory don't develop colds. Besides human beings, only chimpanzees suffer from colds. Also, variations in cold symptoms from person to person, and the similarity and confusion between cold and allergy symptoms, have made controlled studies of the illness complicated.

The term "cold" is clearly a misnomer. True, colds do occur more frequently during the cooler months of the year. And some people say they feel chilled when they have the infection. But even so, there is nothing inherently and universally "cold" about the illness.

Much of our current knowledge about colds has emerged from the Common Cold Research Unit in Salisbury, England. During the early stages of World War II, Harvard University and the American Red Cross established a hospital in Salisbury, ninety miles from London, to study the epidemics that were expected to occur as the aftermath of the bombings of Britain. Fortunately, these epidemics never materialized, and the hospital was used instead to investigate the effect upon health of close contact among individuals. At the end of the war, the hospital was donated to England's Ministry of Health. The Common Cold Research Unit was established there in 1946, and studies have continued ever since.

As scientists try to solidify their own knowledge about colds, a swarm of folklore, superstition, and misinformation still persists about the ailment. In fact, there are probably more myths and misinformation surrounding colds than any other single illness. Everyone, it seems, has some advice to give to the parent of a cold-ravaged child, and most of it is simply inaccurate. Drafts, wet hair or feet, and improper diets have generally been accepted as causes or perpetuators of colds, yet there is no evidence to substantiate these beliefs. Many of the most common cold treatments have, at best, doubtful value. Even so, the mythology is religiously passed on from one generation to the next and has a greater influence upon parents' treatment of children's colds than the most informed advice provided by their pediatricians.

Actually, medical science still knows relatively little about the cold. Most pediatric textbooks devote only a few pages to this ailment, despite the large amount of patient-care time eventually spent dealing with the problem. In my own medical school training, I recall only one day of instruction devoted to colds. No wonder, then, that physicians probably base much of their cold treatment on the fifteen to twenty years of maternal indoctrination that all of us receive.

Let's explore and dispel the myths surrounding the common cold, and in the process discover the best ways to treat and prevent this universal illness.

The Cause and Nature of Colds

MYTH: *Colds are most commonly spread by sneezing and coughing.*

A single sneeze can cast millions of droplet particles into the air, spreading them as far as twenty feet away, where they will remain for up to an hour. If your child is unfortunate enough to inhale one or more that may be carrying an infectious virus, he or she *may* develop a cold.

But according to research at the University of Wisconsin, even if your child is directly sneezed upon, his or her chances are only one in ten of catching a cold. A study reported by Jack M. Gwaltney at the University of Virginia School of Medicine showed that he could not recover the cold virus from a natural sneeze. In a study by J. Owen Hendley at the same university, only two of twenty-five cold patients expelled viruses in a sneeze or a cough. The common-cold virus is apparently absent or occurs in only low concentration in human saliva, and since most material in a cough or a sneeze is from the mouth and not the nose, neither sneezing nor coughing is a major cause of cold virus dispersal. Repeated studies at the Common Cold Research Unit in England indicated that even when special nose drops—composed solely of nasal secretions from cold victims—were given to volunteers, only one-third of them developed colds, despite this very direct exposure to the virus. Even if infectious cold material were to be swabbed on your child's throat, it would rarely lead to a cold (kissing, then, is probably not a major mode of transmitting colds, although I don't encourage it at the time of maximum illness).

The most common means of spreading colds among both children and adults is not through sneezing or coughing, but rather by the hands. Mucus from the nose containing the cold virus is transferred from the fingers of one child to the fingers of another, either by direct contact or through an intermediary inanimate object that both of them touch. The virus can live on such objects for about three hours. A child, picking up the germs with his or her fingers, easily transfers them to the points of entry to the body, the nose or eyes.

In Dr. Gwaltney's study, reported in the *Annals of Internal Medicine* (1978), the cold virus was detected on the hands of 65 percent of the individuals with colds, and hand contact was clearly the most frequent means of transmitting the virus. Colds were transferred in 11 of 15 hand-to-hand exposures, compared with only 1 of 12 when susceptible volunteers, found to have low antibodies before the test, were subjected to coughing or sneezing instead. Dr. Hendley found that when a cold virus was placed on the hands of his research subjects, 40 percent of them developed a cold simply by touching their eyes or nose.

We tend to rub these parts of our face more often than you might believe. In one study, Dr. Hendley observed the behavior of 124 adults, including physicians at a medical convention and churchgoers at a Sunday school class. He found that one of three adults picked his nose or rubbed his eyes in a single hour (the physicians picked their noses more often than the churchgoers).

Even when presented with all this evidence, many are still surprised that the eyes serve as a site for the introduction of infectious material into the body. But keep in mind that tears from the eyes drain through the tear ducts (the nasolacrimal ducts) directly into the nose, which is how the virus eventually arrives in the nasal passages.

Therefore, teach your children to keep their own fingers away from their eyes and nose when they are playing with another child who has a cold until they have had a chance to wash their hands. Naturally, a child shouldn't share towels with another family member who has a cold.

MYTH: *Cold weather, chills, and wet feet cause colds.*

In one public opinion poll, 64 percent of those surveyed believed that colds were caused by chilling. Cartoons typically show a cold sufferer soaking his feet in a tub of hot water, on the premise that since cold feet produced the cold, warming them up will cure it. In reality, colds are caused by contact with *people* who have a cold—not by drafts, chills, wet weather, cool air temperatures, or any similar environmental factor. Even if your child comes home from school or play totally drenched by a fierce rainstorm, he or she will *not* catch a cold—unless your youngster has been sharing an umbrella with a friend who already has one, since viruses are the cause of colds.

Colds tend to peak in frequency in the cool autumn months, decrease in number in the early days of winter, peak again after the New Year, and then decline once more. Such data would certainly seem to support the myth correlating cold weather and colds. However, no evidence exists to support this relationship. In study after study, drafts, chills, and cool temperatures have *not* induced colds. At the Common Cold Research Center in Salisbury, England, volunteers took hot baths and then stood undried in a drafty hallway in wet swimsuits for thirty minutes. By the end of the half hour, the subjects felt chilled and terribly uncomfortable; in some cases, their teeth were chattering. For the rest of the morning, they were instructed to wear wet socks. Despite this chilling, not one of the subjects contracted a cold, leading the researchers to conclude that drafts and chills in themselves do not induce colds.

In a related experiment at Salisbury, volunteers went for a walk in the rain and were not permitted to dry themselves until thirty minutes after their return. Even though the heating in their rooms had been turned off, no evidence was found that chilling increased their frequency of colds. Similar studies at the University of Illinois Medical Center and the Baylor University College of Medicine have arrived at the same conclusion.

Christopher Andrewes, director of the Salisbury studies, has offered the following hypothesis about why people continue to connect dampness with colds:

> It may be that in the early stages of a cold before the nose has begun to run, a person is abnormally sensitive to feelings of chill. There is then a confusion between cause and effect. Because your socks are wet and you feel chilly, you think the wetness causes the cold which shortly develops. You do not consider the possibility that you felt chilly because the virus already had a grip on you. Plenty of people get their feet wet and get no cold and forget all about it. It has been recorded that soldiers in terribly cold and wet conditions in the trenches in the First World War showed no tendency to develop colds then, but were very apt to do so when back in comfortable billets.

Still unanswered is the question of why autumn and winter are the seasons for colds. Why are there more colds during the periods of coldest and wettest weather, if environment does not play a role in the illness? Some researchers have suggested that the increase of colds during cold and rainy weather may result from the closer contact among people, as they are driven indoors by the elements. Also, the cool weather may create an environment that increases the survival rate of the viruses on your hands or on an inanimate object, also improving the chances of transmission.

MYTH: *A sneeze is a clear indication of a cold.*

For most people, a sneeze is as closely related to a cold as a runny nose or a cough. Yet a sneeze may have absolutely no connection with an upper respiratory infection.

Sneezing is merely a reflex action, behavior established by the body to expel foreign matter from the upper breathing passages. When the linings of the nasal passages are irritated by an unfamiliar substance, a sneeze ensues. But as with a baby (see page 5), sneezing in older children and adults can be provoked not only by cold-related mucus but also by dust, pollen, or other irritants in the air. So when your child sneezes, a cold may not be the reason at all.

MYTH: *Don't give children baths when they have a cold.*

I am asked by many parents about giving baths to children suffering from colds.

R. Gordon Douglas of the Baylor College of Medicine subjected volunteers with colds to an 89.6°F (32°C) bath at various stages of their illness. At no time did bathing increase the severity of their colds, their chances of developing a secondary infection, or the quantity of the virus they eventually spread. Thus, the popular belief that "bathing with a cold may be hazardous to your health" appears to be unfounded. In fact, most ill children (and adults) feel better and refreshed after a cleansing bath.

MYTH: *Children with colds should not have their hair washed.*

There is no evidence that wet hair can aggravate a cold or cause a middle-ear infection. However, if your youngster has an ear infection, don't allow the child to submerge his or her head deeply, as in a swimming pool, in order to avoid possible changes in pressure upon the eardrum.

MYTH: *Air conditioners cause colds.*

Because of the cool room temperatures that air conditioners produce, some parents are convinced that they stimulate colds. But let me emphasize once again that colds are caused only by viruses, not by any other environmental factor.

However, air conditioners can be accurately blamed for symptoms very similar to those of colds. For instance, if your child comes from warm outdoor weather into an air-conditioned room, the rapid drop in temperature and the change in humidity may cause a reaction called vasomotor rhinitis, in which the mucous membranes in the nose swell, resulting in sneezing, coughing, and other symptoms that are also associated with colds. A similar reaction can occur with an air conditioner that hasn't been used for a while. When it is turned on, dust and mold spores from the appliance can be blown throughout the room, causing allergy symptoms that mimic those of a cold.

MYTH: *Newborns are immune to colds.*

For about the first four to six months of life, babies are less susceptible to many of the contagious illnesses, including specific cold viruses, that their mothers have already had. However, newborns are as vulnerable as their mothers to *new* cold viruses that the mother has not been exposed to and thus has not produced any protective antibodies against. Because newborns can more easily develop secondary infections and other complications from colds, a special effort to minimize your infant's exposure to cold viruses might be worthwhile, particularly during the first six weeks of life.

A common cold is no more serious an ailment in a newborn than in an adult, but when such symptoms surface, the pediatrician must aggressively determine whether they are signs of a cold or of a more complicated infection.

In the first few weeks after birth excessive drowsiness, a failure to eat, diarrhea, persistent vomiting, or a fever may be a cold symptom, but any of these may also be an indication of a dangerous illness.

To make the proper diagnosis, certain tests must be conducted, and because there are risks, discomfort, and costs to these diagnostic procedures, and considerable parental worry when a baby is ill, newborn exposure to the cold virus should be avoided as much as possible. I encourage mothers and fathers to minimize the handling of their babies by strangers. Although immediate family members and close friends should be involved with the infant, restrict young children, except for siblings, from holding the newborn. (Siblings might feel slighted if they are kept at a distance, and possible psychological damage to them may be worse than a baby's cold. You will be the best judge of your other children's feelings.) Before *any* visitors touch the baby, be certain they have washed their hands.

MYTH: *Some children have a greater weakness and susceptibility to colds than others.*

Many mothers are insistent that their child's nose "never stops running." I often hear the complaint that a youngster has "one cold after another," or that "this is his fourth cold in two months." The question is then usually raised, "Why is my child more susceptible to colds than other kids?"

However, a child who seems to have an above-average number of colds probably does *not* have a "lowered resistance" or a greater susceptibility to them. Instead, the frequent infections can usually be explained by the child's level of exposure to the cold viruses involved and the absence of previous experience with them. A child in constant contact with other children will almost certainly have a greater number of colds than more reclusive companions. A child with older brothers and sisters already in school will be exposed more frequently to the cold viruses spreading through the neighborhood, as the siblings carry them home.

In almost all cases, children will have progressively fewer colds as they become older, except for a slight increase at around age six or whenever they begin school. While they may seem to have more than their share during the first year or two of school—as they are exposed to a large number of children with colds—eventually children develop a short-term immunity to certain types of viruses. Thus, a nine-year-old will probably only have half as many colds as he or she did at six, and a twelve-year-old only half as many as at age nine.

This issue of susceptibility becomes further muddled since, as discussed earlier, allergies can masquerade as colds, especially in young children. The symptoms of these two disorders can be so similar as to confuse even pediatricians. A child who is sneezing, with a dripping nose and a sore throat, may be having an allergic reaction to food, animal hair, house dust, plant pollen, trees, grass, or occasionally milk. But many of these children are diagnosed as having an infection when they have an allergy, and their parents then complain that they are overly susceptible to colds.

MYTH: *Your child can have a cold that lasts for several weeks.*

Parents often tell pediatricians, "My child has had the same cold for a month." But as we currently understand the course of the common cold, we know that it cannot possibly last for a month.

Scientists at the Common Cold Research Unit in England have clearly defined the course of the typical cold. It begins at the moment of exposure and "inoculation," even though symptoms will not surface for another two to three days. The acute stage begins when the cold symptoms first appear and lasts three to four days. The virus grows rapidly in the nose and throat, and the cold becomes even more contagious. The nose runs, the youngster may feel tired, a mild fever may develop, the appetite may disappear, and coughing may begin.

After the acute period, the virus disappears, but the symptoms may linger on for another three to ten days. During this less contagious stage, the swollen linings of the nasal passages gradually return to normal, but they may still produce some excess mucus as the recovery proceeds. The nose eventually stops running, the fever subsides, the appetite returns, and the child's energy level is revitalized.

If your child's cold symptoms linger on for more than two weeks, several explanations are possible. A new cold may have replaced the original one, and the symptoms of the second overlapped with those of the first. Or an allergic reaction that imitates the characteristics of a cold may be the problem. Or your child may have developed a secondary infection—like an ear infection, sinusitis (inflammation of the sinus), or tonsillitis—that appears to prolong the cold symptoms.

MYTH: *Your child can have a cold in only one nostril.*

See page 121.

MYTH: *Psychological influences frequently play a role in childhood colds.*

Stress can be as prevalent in a child's life as in an adult's. Even a preschooler can have fears, tensions, and anxieties that may provoke disease symptoms. In school, apprehension over an impending exam or worry over being confronted by the class bully can be transferred to the body.

However, there is no specific medical evidence that children are particularly susceptible to cold viruses during periods of stress. A 1977 study by W. Thomas Boyce and his colleagues at the University of North Carolina revealed that in a group of youngsters between ages one and eleven, the number of colds actually *decreased* during times of stress. More research is certainly needed in this area, but as yet, the "stress causes colds" theory is in doubt.

MYTH: *Some children's colds are so severe that they always settle in their chest.*

Most childhood colds run a similar course. Usually two or three days after the virus has been transmitted, the first symptoms surface. The nose begins running, and a cough, which is an irritative response to these secretions, may develop if the nasal secretions drip back into the windpipe. These secretions may make the breath sound rattly but the noises originate not from the lungs but rather the upper airways. When a physician listens with a stethoscope to the lungs of a child suffering from a cold, the lungs almost always sound clear since, in fact, there usually is no infection in the chest. The best treatment for this postnasal drip and its ensuing cough is a decongestant (not an antihistamine), which may reduce the volume of nasal secretions.

When asthmatic children develop a cold, their asthma-related symptoms usually worsen and are accompanied by a cough. But here again, the cold itself has *not* moved into the chest; instead, the added stress on the body has increased the severity of the asthmatic condition. The best treatment is medicine that relaxes muscle spasms in the airways (bronchodilating medicine), thus opening the air passages into the lungs.

A cough can also be caused by an allergic runny nose (allergic rhinitis); in such cases, antihistamines may decrease the level of secretions. Finally, in those rare instances when a cold becomes quite severe, the defenses of the upper respiratory tract may become weakened, thus leaving the child more susceptible to pneumonia. In fact, some of the same viruses that cause colds can also cause pneumonia. Although pneumonia is one of the greatest fears of parents, the word itself usually sounds worse than the disease really is. Most cases of pneumonia are caused by viruses, and the treatment for mild cases differs little from the proper care of a cold. Only occasionally does bacterial pneumonia develop, which requires an antibiotic to treat it. Alert your physician if any of the three following signs of serious pneumonia is present: difficult or rapid breathing (forty to sixty breaths per minute in older children); increased prominence of the ribs while inhaling; or any degree of blueness.

Cold Treatments

MYTH: *Aspirin can cure the common cold in your child.*

No cure exists for the common cold. Doctors can suggest ways to ease the discomfort and keep the infection from spreading, but no effective antidote for the cold has been developed.

Aspirin is the most useful medication that you can give your child to alleviate the muscle aches and fever often associated with colds. However, this is only symptomatic relief; aspirin is powerless to cure the cold itself.

MYTH: *Antihistamines can hasten your child's recovery from a cold.*

Antihistamines, prescribed by most pediatricians to alleviate sneezing and watery eyes, account for a large portion of the $843 million spent each year on cold remedies. For many decades, antihistamines have been used effectively to ease the symptoms of allergies. But thirty years ago drug companies boisterously claimed that antihistamines were also useful in curing colds, and drugstores began selling them by the millions, even though the Council for Pharmacy and Chemistry of the American Medical Association expressed concern over their indiscriminate use.

Very few well-controlled studies have supported antihistamine use for the treatment of colds. A recent review of antihistamine research at the Johns Hopkins Medical Institution conclusively found this medication useless for colds, even when dispensed as early as three days before a cold virus was placed directly into the noses of volunteers. True, a few studies have validated antihistamine use, but these investigations were conducted on patients who may have had various diseases, including allergies, for which antihistamines are known to provide symptomatic relief, and therefore their conclusions are questionable.

So if the effectiveness of this medication is doubtful, why do many pediatricians continue to recommend antihistamines? Richard B. Goldbloom, M.D., has suggested, "Too often, these shotgun [antihistamine] mixtures are prescribed principally as a result of advertising pressure and as a means of dealing with parental pressure to 'do something.'" Some parents—and physicians—claim success with antihistamines but overlook the facts that a cold's duration may vary and that the body's own defenses sometimes terminate colds in their early stages. In such cases, the antihistamine often receives the undeserved credit for "curing" the cold.

Various side effects can accompany antihistamine use, from drowsiness to hyperactivity, making the administering of this medication for colds even more unacceptable. Despite such evidence, one survey shows that in 94 percent of all office visits for colds, patients receive prescriptions, of which one-third are for medications containing antihistamines.

MYTH: *If you give your child a decongestant at the first sign of a cold, you can prevent an ear infection from developing.*

Decongestants are effective in reducing nasal secretions during a cold. Not only do they make your child feel more comfortable, but your child's cold may also become less contagious, since there are fewer mucous discharges that can be transmitted via the hands to other children.

Because of their usefulness, decongestants are widely recommended by pediatricians. Although many decongestant medications are combined with antihistamines when sold over the counter, their cold-related benefits are probably produced solely by the decongestant component, unless allergy symptoms accompany the cold.

Decongestants, however, are ineffective in preventing ear infections. An ear infection is not "caught" the way a cold is, but rather is caused by the improper functioning of the eustachian tube (the tube connecting the back of the nose to the middle ear cavity) during a cold. Despite the logic to the theory of their use, decongestants won't remedy this imperfect performance of the eustachian tube.

John E. Randall and J. Owen Hendley, in a study in 1976–77 involving 104 preschool-age youngsters in New York and Virginia, treated some of their colds with a decongestant-antihistamine mixture and others with a placebo (sugar pill). Of the 234 colds treated over a one-year period, about 6 percent of them developed ear infections, no matter which of the two treatments (decongestant-antihistamine or placebo) was prescribed.

Medicated nasal sprays and nosedrops, when administered to reduce mucous secretions, may be effective, but should be used with caution, and only as directed by your pediatrician. For children up to age two, nasal decongestants may cause irritability and even a rapid heartbeat; a safer preparation for infants is several drops of a salt-water mixture (made by dissolving one-half teaspoon salt in a cup of water) in each nostril and then suctioning it out with a bulb syringe. Medicated nose drops are safer for youngsters over two, but their continued use for more than three or four days can cause a rebound effect—that is, even after the cold is gone and the medication has been discontinued, the nasal passages will swell and remain swollen, giving the impression of a worsening cold. Consequently, parents will often put their children back on the spray, when it is the medication itself that is the cause of the symptoms.

MYTH: *Antibiotics can be helpful in treating colds.*

At the first sign of a runny nose in their child, many parents ask their doctor to prescribe an antibiotic. Or (and even worse), they rush to the medicine cabinet, and grab a bottle of antibiotics remaining from an earlier illness and have their child take one.

We've come to rely on antibiotics to treat our most common illnesses. However, antibiotics have absolutely *no* effect in combating colds, and they shouldn't be prescribed for that purpose. True, there is some preliminary, although not conclusive, evidence that a sulfa drug called Gantrisin (sulfisoxazole) may be effective in preventing bacterial ear infections in children suffering from colds if they have a history of severe and frequent ear inflammations. And antibiotics may also be appropriate to protect against bacterial complications in youngsters with colds who previously have had rheumatic fever (a serious inflammation of the body joints and the heart), had their spleen removed, suffer from cystic fibrosis, or have certain congenital heart anomalies. But in the overwhelming majority of cases, antibiotics are worthless in treating colds.

Studies show that antibiotics do not shorten the length or severity of colds, nor do they prevent complications. When E. H. Townsend and J. F. Radebaugh treated 781 children with colds, most of them received drugs like tetracycline and penicillin, while some were given only placebo. Complications developed in 12 percent of those receiving placebo and in 11 percent of those given antibiotics. In a separate study by L. M. Hardy and H. S. Traisman, the colds of 217 children under the age of fourteen were treated with drugs; these antibiotics did not decrease the number of complications or quicken recovery.

Because antibiotics are designed to eradicate or prevent the spread of bacteria, it is really not surprising that they are of no value in treating viral infections like colds. So although a drug like penicillin may be effective for treating a bacterial infection like a strep throat, caused by the streptococcus bacterium, it is useless against colds, which are all caused by viruses.

Even so, one survey reveals that physicians prescribe antibiotics (tetracycline, penicillin) for about 60 percent of the colds they treat. Their action is often in response to a parental plea, "I'd sure appreciate you prescribing an antibiotic, just in case." However, this kind of reasoning can be harmful to your child, simply because of the side effects of *all* drugs. Some children react to penicillin and ampicillin with vomiting, skin rashes, fever, kidney disorders, and loose bowel movements. In about 2 percent of the cases, these reactions are severe. Tetracycline should not be prescribed for children under age ten and pregnant women because it can cause permanent dental staining in a growing fetus or child.

Additionally, the more contact your child may have with a single antibiotic, the greater the chance of developing an allergy to it. It would be tragic if later in your child's life, a serious infection couldn't be treated with a particular antibiotic because of an allergy that evolved when it was improperly prescribed for a simple cold years earlier.

Just as sobering is the real possibility that when drugs are used needlessly and repeatedly, bacteria may develop a tolerance to them. Thus, when a bacterial infection does occur, the antibiotic may have little or no effectiveness. The *Journal of Infectious Disease* (1976) reported that on one entire hospital ward, a large number of common infections were resistant to even the strongest antibiotic after that drug was used frequently on the ward.

One final—and perhaps hopeful—note about drugs: Researchers at the University of Illinois have recently developed a drug called propanediamine. It can apparently induce the body to manufacture large amounts of interferon—a component of the body's own natural defense network. When administered immediately after exposure to the cold virus, the new drug has significantly reduced cold symptoms. However, despite such encouraging findings in Illinois, other researchers have been unable to duplicate these results. The verdict is still out on propanediamine.

MYTH: *Feed a cold, starve a fever.*

See page 52.

MYTH: *A child ill with a cold should drink as many fluids as possible.*

Children with colds are often given a steady diet of fluids—usually fruit juices or tea—as a means of combating their illness. But colds *can't* be cured, eased, or shortened by a constant intake of liquids.

Of course, if your child's cold is accompanied by a fever, then a valid argument can be made for giving fluids, in order to replace the moisture lost as the youngster breathes rapidly and perspires. However, in the absence of fever, fluids are neither necessary nor helpful. Even so, they cannot cause harm, and if your child feels comfortable drinking liquids rather than eating solid foods, let him or her do so. Particularly if your youngster has very little appetite, fluids may be his primary source of nutrition.

The origin of the myth linking colds and liquids is unknown. However, one Salisbury researcher has speculated, "This was apparently based on the fact that no one ever saw a fish sneeze."

MYTH: *Alcoholic beverages can terminate a cold.*

An eighteenth-century British physician once proposed the following advice at the first sign of a cold: "Hang your hat on a bedpost, drink from a bottle of good whiskey until two hats appear, then get into bed and stay there."

For centuries, alcohol has been perceived as a cure for colds, coughs, and even pneumonia. This belief may be based on the long association of wine with religious festivals, family celebrations, and other happy events. According to the mythmakers, if alcohol can instill a sense of well-being at these jovial festivities, it should make the cold sufferer feel better, too.

Even if alcohol could be substantiated as a cure for colds (which it hasn't been), it's still doubtful that parents would encourage their children to recklessly guzzle whiskey or wine just to alleviate a few sniffles. So even though this myth may seem unusual in a book on child health care, it is nevertheless included here primarily for parents who may believe that alcohol has some value as a cold cure.

MYTH: *Hot chicken soup can cure the common cold.*

Ask any Jewish mother, and she will swear that nothing works better than chicken soup as a cure for colds. Generations of children have grown up convinced that bowls of hot chicken soup have pulled them through some of childhood's most harrowing moments.

Not surprisingly, few studies have devoted themselves exclusively to the medicinal value of chicken soup, and as yet, its effectiveness as a cold remedy remains to be verified. One interesting study with only fifteen volunteers, conducted by M. A. Sackner, concluded that the hot vapor inhaled from the chicken soup increased the flow of mucus through the nasal passages, more than simple hot-water vapor could. Although more research is necessary before chicken soup can finally be vindicated, its psychological benefits certainly cannot be denied.

MYTH: *Eating cold food and drinking cold liquids will worsen a cold.*

Considerable folklore, particularly among certain Latin subcultures, focuses on the temperature as well as the color of the food being consumed. Eating and drinking cold substances, they claim, further irritate a cold, while warm items have a healing effect. The basis of this myth is unknown.

Eating only warm foods cannot worsen a cold. So if keeping cold foods away from your ill child makes you happy, then feel free to continue doing so. However, this practice will not influence the severity or duration of the cold.

MYTH: *Milk makes cold symptoms worse.*

Many parents believe that when milk is consumed by a child with a cold, the amount of mucus he or she secretes will increase, aggravating the cold and making the child more uncomfortable. But it isn't true. There is nothing in milk to increase mucus production, and thus there is no reason to keep milk away from a child with a cold.

This myth may have evolved from the fact that milk has a consistency similar to that of mucus when felt in the back of the throat, or perhaps from the observation that the symptoms of milk allergies are similar to those of the common cold. At two to four weeks of age, from 1 to 7 percent of all children begin showing signs of sensitivity to cow's milk, with symptoms such as nasal dripping or stuffiness, sneezing, and coughing. This infrequent problem probably led to the belief that milk can cause increased mucus secretion in *all* children, not just in those with milk allergies. But in fact, children without this allergy can drink milk freely, even when they have a cold.

MYTH: *Children with colds should be kept indoors, particularly at night.*

For centuries, the night air has been unfairly blamed for worsening many illnesses. Even in *Julius Caesar,* Shakespeare questioned whether the ailing Brutus would "steal out of his wholesome bed, to dare the vile contagion of the night and tempt the rheumy and unpurged air to add unto his sickness."

Actually, exposure to the air, whether during the day or

night, poses no danger for sufferers from colds or several other diseases. In fact, one treatment for a harsh, raspy cough called croup, which is also caused by a virus, is to take the coughing child out into the night air, where the cold moisture can help shrink swollen upper air passages.

The night-air superstition probably dates back to ancient Greece, when malaria (meaning "bad air") was thought to be spread in the nighttime air. Noxious vapors from swamps and lowlands were suspected of contaminating the air, which then circulated the disease to nearby neighborhoods. The only effective means of avoiding the night air's "poisons" was to stay indoors.

Today, despite the pollutants in the air, there is no benefit derived from keeping your cold-suffering child indoors. Particularly if your child plays alone during the contagious period, there is no reason not to allow him or her outdoors. Frankly, children may even be safer playing outdoors, since their chances of catching other viruses in the open air are less than they would be in an enclosed room, where there is more immediate contact with others.

MYTH: *Bed rest can shorten the severity and duration of your child's cold.*

R. A. J. Asher wrote in the *British Medical Journal* (1947),

> It is always assumed that the first thing in any illness is to put the patient to bed. Hospital accommodation is always numbered in beds. Illness is measured by the length of time in bed. Doctors are assessed by the bedside manner. Bed is not ordered like a pill or a purge, but is assumed as the basis for all treatment.

In fact, there is no evidence that bed rest will ease or end your child's cold. Obviously, if he or she has a high fever and feels more comfortable resting in bed, then encourage your youngster to do so. But every parent knows the struggle of trying to keep a child in bed who doesn't want to be there. Let your child's feelings be your guide to bed rest. Some light exercise and fresh air will not worsen the cold and in fact may make your child feel better, at least psychologically.

While bed rest is indeed essential for the proper healing of certain diseases, there is growing evidence that it can cause serious problems as well. The phenomenon of bedsores on the skin is well known to most people, as are heartburn and constipation. When an individual is confined to bed for an extended period, the absence of leg movement can cause blood clots. Muscle and joint stiffness can also occur, as can the weakening of bones as calcium drains from them.

One study tested American soldiers in Vietnam who said they felt fine but were found to have liver disease from infectious hepatitis. They were placed on a strenuous exercise program and recovered just as quickly as a second group of soldiers recuperating in the traditional, sedate manner.

Although the following verse offered by Robert Asher may contain some exaggeration, there is also a degree of validity to its advice:

> Teach us to live that we may dread
> Unnecessary time in bed.
> Get people up and we may save
> Our patients from an early grave.

MYTH: *Chest rubs can help ease the discomfort of colds.*

No one can refute the physical and psychological benefits of a loving massage. But the over-the-counter chest-rub ointments that purport to alleviate chest colds are—in a word—useless. To begin with, colds rarely settle in the chest (see page 68–69); thus, there's no rationale for applying an ointment to an area of the body that is in no way involved with the illness. In those infrequent cases where a true lung infection such as pneumonia does develop, treatment more potent than a chest rub is necessary.

If a chest massage is pleasing to your child, feel free to oblige. But the ointment that you've bought for this purpose will not help end the cold.

MYTH: *Vaporizers can make a child suffering from a cold more comfortable.*

Although vaporizers have been recommended by pediatricians for decades, their effectiveness is doubtful. Vaporizers are supposed to dampen the air and thus keep your child's nasal secretions moist, so they will drain away easily. But the small amount of steam produced by a bedside vaporizer is rarely enough to moisten the air adequately, and a vaporizer heats up the room, sometimes making the child even more uncomfortable. Additionally, medications placed in vaporizers have not proved to be of any benefit in treating colds. In short, a vaporizer is not worth the expense and effort.

A better alternative, though still controversial, is a cool-mist humidifier. Rather than blowing steam into the room as a vaporizer does, it sprays out tiny droplets of cool water, which moisturizes the room and effectively counteracts the dryness of a heated room. The cool-mist humidifier is particularly helpful for croup, the dry, tight, barking cough that frequently occurs at night.

Some people claim that humidifiers are especially beneficial for colds in the winter months, when homes are usually drier because of artificial heating. But no firm evidence yet exists that humidifiers are always useful for colds.

Cold Prevention

MYTH: *Each time your child has a cold, he or she is building up resistance against getting another one.*

Preventing a cold is not only preferable to curing it, but it is also more feasible. However, the issue of natural immunity is generally misunderstood. After your child has a cold, he is protected in the future against just that particular strain of the cold virus (there are more than 200 varieties), and even then, only strongly protected for about two years. However, when your youngster is exposed to a different cold virus, he probably has no protection at all against it.

In one study, individuals who had recently recovered from a cold were exposed to a cold virus unlike the one they had just overcome. Forty percent of them caught another cold. But when another group of volunteers were subjected to the identical virus that they had recuperated from, only 10 percent caught the cold. The researchers concluded that immunity to the same virus may well have been 100 percent, since the 10 percent who were afflicted probably had picked up still another type of cold virus randomly encountered.

Isolating your child from all cold viruses in the environment not only is impractical but may also be impossible. The best protection against colds is good hygiene habits. Encourage your child to avoid other children who are in the contagious stages of colds and to wash his or her hands periodically—particularly before rubbing or touching his or her eyes or nose.

MYTH: *The members of your family can give each other the same cold back and forth for weeks.*

Pediatricians often hear stories from parents like, "My child gave her cold to me, and just as I was getting over it, I gave it back to her, and a week later, I caught it again." That's highly unlikely, since once an individual has had a cold, he or she can't catch the same cold virus again for at least two years. More than likely, your child was exposed to another strain of the virus, which caused the "relapse."

As you might surmise, when a group of people is totally isolated—for example, on a remote island—colds tend to completely disappear, because there are no new strains of the virus to which they are introduced. On the Norwegian island of Spitsbergen, colds almost vanish during the seven coldest months of the year, when visitors are rare. But with the arrival of the first ship each May, an epidemic of colds breaks out. The island's storekeeper, who has immediate and constant contact with the outsiders, often is the first to catch the viruses. There are similar reports of Arctic explorers who remain cold-free during their lonely expeditions through uninhabited, icy terrain but immediately upon reentering civilization come down with colds.

MYTH: *A child who avoids people with colds will never catch one.*

As logical as this belief may seem, keep in mind the course of the typical cold. As each cold begins, it proceeds through a so-called incubation period lasting two to three days, in which symptoms are *not* present even though the illness is contagious and nasal secretions contain high levels of cold virus. Thus, your child may be in close proximity to a friend who has a very contagious cold but not know it because of the absence of a runny nose, a cough, and other common symptoms.

Children, incidentally, are the main spreaders of colds. Were it not for children, colds would still exist, but in lesser numbers. Adults in families with school-age children typically have 2½ times as many colds as adults who do not live with children.

MYTH: *Periodic injections of gamma globulin can help prevent colds in children.*

Gamma globulin is a protein in the blood that has antibody properties responsible for fighting off some of the most common childhood diseases. Although the amount of gamma globulin in the newborn is equal to or higher than that of his mother, it rapidly decreases, and from the ages of one to three months it is at only one-third of its birth level. Its concentration then begins to increase gradually but attains adult levels no earlier than the age of two.

On this basis, many physicians have given repeated injections of gamma globulin to young children who seem to have an unusual number of colds. Although these injections have proved effective in the prevention and weakening of some infections—measles, hepatitis, chicken pox, rubella, mumps, rabies, for example—repeated studies show them to be useless for protecting youngsters from childhood colds.

K. C. Finkel, in a study reported in *Pediatrics,* gave gamma globulin in various doses to 102 children under the age of two. He found that the amount of the substance given made no difference in the number of colds the children contracted.

Some children suffer from the extremely rare condition of partial or complete absence of gamma globulin. Those who suffer from this syndrome, called agammaglobulinenemia or hypogammaglobulinenemia, are susceptible to a variety of infections, including colds, but can lead a near-normal life with monthly injections of gamma globulin. However, except in those individuals affected by this unusual, immunological disorder, the injections have *not* proved useful against colds. In fact, a regular regimen of injections is potentially dangerous, since children could become sensitized to this blood component, and when it is critically needed under emergency circumstances, the body may not be receptive to it.

It seems best to stay away from gamma globulin. In the long run, it could do your child more harm than good.

MYTH: *Vitamin C can prevent colds.*

Everyone has a favorite preventive measure against colds. Some people claim that taking a cold shower every day will keep the colds away. Others insist that a teaspoon of cod-liver oil will kill colds before they ever surface.

Although most such methods are useless, one approach gained instant respectability in 1971 with the publication of

Linus Pauling's book *Vitamin C and the Common Cold*. Pauling presented an impressive case that vitamin C might not only prevent the common cold but could also minimize the symptoms and the number of sick days associated with it.

Studies of the benefits of vitamin C have been difficult to conduct, simply because of the subjective nature of cold symptoms. But the initial studies seemed to support many of Pauling's contentions. In 1974 John Coulehan found that children in a Navajo Indian boarding school were able to decrease significantly their sick days from colds, by 28 to 34 percent, by consuming 1000 to 2000 mg of vitamin C daily. A separate study in Dublin in 1973 revealed that school-age girls with colds benefit more from vitamin C than boys do.

But more recent research has not been nearly as encouraging. A 1976 study by Dr. Coulehan has not substantiated his earlier findings. About half of 868 students, ranging in age from six to fifteen, were given one gram of vitamin C a day. The other half received a placebo (sugar pill). After fifteen to eighteen weeks, those who had taken vitamin C did *not* have any fewer or any shorter colds than the non-C children.

When Henry Pitt and Anthony Costrini conducted an eight-week study with 674 Marine recruits in South Carolina in 1978, the group that received 2 grams of vitamin C daily had just as many colds as the group that was given placebo, and no difference existed in the severity of the symptoms.

So should you give your own children high dosages of vitamin C daily? Based on the inconclusive and conflicting evidence, there seems to be no reason to do so. In addition, there may be harmful side effects from large amounts of vitamin C. In some studies, high doses of the vitamin have been potentially linked with diarrhea, abnormal childhood bone growth, and kidney stones. The risks may not be worth the benefits.

The medical profession has been attacked in recent years for not leaping more enthusiastically aboard the vitamin C bandwagon. The critics claim that physicians have reacted with scientific snobbism to Pauling and his colleagues, as though doctors had a vested interest in minimizing the use of vitamin C.

These accusations, however, are unfair. As in other areas, the medical establishment is moving conservatively and cautiously with respect to vitamin C. Until all the data are in, it would be unwise—and perhaps even dangerous—for pediatricians to recommend sweepingly that vitamin C be consumed by children in large quantities. After all, in such high doses, the vitamin becomes, in effect, a medication, with various side effects. After reviewing all the evidence, Thomas Chalmers does not consider "the very minor potential benefit that might result from taking ascorbic acid [vitamin C] three times a day for life worth either the effort or the risk, no matter how slight the latter might be."

MYTH: *Disinfectants can kill cold viruses and thus prevent children from catching colds.*

Supermarket shelves are lined with products that promise to kill all the germs in a room with their disinfectant vapors and mists. With one spray, viruses are supposed to be zapped into harmless oblivion.

The advertising claims have been effective, as reflected by the sales of these air purifiers. If only the products themselves were as potent. However, tests have clearly shown that these spray mists are ineffective against cold microbes and other undesirable organisms. To have any impact at all, these products would have to be manufactured in concentrations that would harm not only the cold viruses but also the people who occupy the rooms in which they are sprayed.

So if you would like your house to have a pleasant smell, these spray mists are fine, but don't expect them to protect your children from colds.

A recent study released by the Center for Disease Control in Atlanta revealed that phenolic compound, a common hospital disinfectant detergent, was linked with an epidemic of jaundice in a newborn nursery. Safe levels of the chemical for adults proved to be dangerous for infants. Here, again, is an example of a seemingly beneficial product that deserves cautious analysis when used around children.

MYTH: *Foul-smelling items like garlic can prevent the spreading of colds.*

For centuries, many Europeans have believed that eating garlic sandwiches, or wearing a bag of garlic around your neck, can keep away colds. Even today, heirs to this cultural myth still believe there is some medicinal value in strong-smelling substances, and consequently, their children are periodically placed in proximity to garlic, asafetida (a lumpy gum resin), salted herring, or burning leaves—all on the assumption they can prevent colds.

About sixty years ago, the *London Chronicle* advised that onions could be used effectively to fight the prevailing influenza epidemic. A raw onion, eaten along with a cucumber, was supposed to provide protection against infections and still leave a pleasing smell to the breath. Also, an onion cut in half and sitting in a room supposedly attracted germs to its surface, thus leaving the air in the room free of these contaminants.

As you have probably guessed, there is no scientific validity to any of these beliefs. True, the smell of garlic on the breath may be so offensive as to keep your child's playmates—including those with colds—at a safe distance, thus minimizing the risks of transmitting the infection. But the garlic itself possesses no known cold-preventive qualities.

4

EYES AND VISION

The eyes are a marvel of mechanical, optical, and biological engineering, delicately cushioned in their sockets, necessitating only minimal care in order to provide efficient, lifetime vision. Despite the incredible demands upon them, they generally function well, without undue strain or defects.

Even so, children are not exempt from eye disorders. Despite the proliferation of medical information, too many vision problems are almost universally misunderstood. Parents are more concerned than necessary about some eye disorders, while falsely minimizing the gravity of others. In many cases, eye ailments are never properly diagnosed, because parents doubt that their youngsters will submit to an ophthalmologist's examination. This is further complicated by the fact that myths and misconceptions about eyes and vision are perpetuated. I will concentrate on this misinformation in the present chapter.

The Ability to See

MYTH: *Babies see very poorly, if at all, at birth.*

Despite myths to the contrary, a solid body of evidence now substantiates that newborns can respond to reasonably sophisticated visual stimuli, certainly not as well as older children or adults can, but much better than was once generally believed. All parts of your infant's eyes that are required for seeing are fully developed shortly after birth. A newborn often stares intensely at surrounding objects and can start following the movement of large objects at about six to eight weeks of age. By the age of six months, the eye is mature enough to see with 20/20 vision. However, because the interaction between the eye and the brain is not yet refined at that age, the baby is not able to recognize and distinguish subtle differences between objects, even though his or her eyes may see them well.

The face of the baby's mother often is the first stimulus that the child actually recognizes. Soon thereafter, the infant will begin to differentiate between colors and patterns. One study showed that as early as the first few days of life, newborns became so familiar with their own mother's appearance—as well as her odor and behavior—that they became distressed and slept and ate poorly when their mothers wore masks when attempting to feed them.

No one knows for certain why newborns respond to the sight of the human face more quickly than to other stimuli. But at the moment of birth, they seem to be programed to recognize the face, turning their own heads to follow it more frequently than they do other multidimensional forms. A study of forty newborns, conducted by a team of Los Angeles researchers, revealed that they all visually followed a facelike pattern more often than a scrambled arrangement of similar brightness and complexity. The researchers concluded that the newborn does not have to learn to recognize the human face; this seems to be an instinctive behavior.

You may notice that newborns sometimes imitate their mother's actions during the initial few hours of life, only to suddenly discontinue doing so for several months. In the first twenty-four hours after birth, this imitative behavior of babies may include sticking out their tongues, protruding their lips, opening their mouths, and moving their fingers—all mimicking the motions of their mothers. But just as suddenly as this started, it may stop, not to resume again until the end of the first year of life. Researchers believe that this early imitation may be an instinctive bonding behavior, improving the chances that babies will survive by making them more lovable to their mothers.

MYTH: *The term "20/20" describes the ability of the eyes to see in relation to each other.*

In visual examinations, each eye's capacity for sight is measured separately, and each is assigned its own visual ratio. Thus, during your child's first ophthalmological exam, vision may be found to be 20/20 in one eye and 20/30 in the other.

In essence, the visual ratio is a measurement of each of your child's eyes in relation to a normal eye, not to each other. If your child has 20/20 vision in one eye, it means that the eye sees at 20 feet what a normal eye sees at 20 feet—thus, that eye has normal vision. If the eye has 20/80 vision, it would be capable of seeing at a distance of no more than 20 feet what a normal eye can see up to 80.

As the eyes develop through early childhood, 20/20 vision is not usually observed in the normal child until about the age of five. At age two, visual acuity is usually about 20/70; at three years old, most children test between 20/30 and 20/40; and at age four, about 20/25. However, there is some controversy among the experts about these figures. The normal inability of the young child's brain to distinguish the subtleness of visual stimuli may account for these imperfect scores on eye tests. Thus, the measurement of 20/70 in your two-year-old may not indicate an optical abnormality at all but rather an inability of the brain to differentiate details at that age. One study, in fact, purports that a six-month-old baby can demonstrate 20/20 vision using a specially conceived brain-wave, eye-testing technique that compensates for the brain's relative unsophistication and the difficulty of accurately monitoring the infant's responses to the test.

MYTH: *Both nearsightedness and farsightedness are signs of eye disease or eye weakness.*

Eyes that see poorly up close (farsightedness) or at a distance (nearsightedness) are usually neither diseased nor weak. These disorders are caused by a variation in the structure of the eye. Most commonly those who are myopic (nearsighted) have an eyeball that is longer than normal—that is, the distance from the front to the back of the eyeball is too long. Consequently, light passing through the lens focuses in front of the retina instead of on it. Conversely, if a child is hyperopic (farsighted), the distance is too short, and thus the light focuses *behind* the retina.

Children who are nearsighted or farsighted may need corrective lenses to sharpen their vision, but their eyes are *healthy*. The eyeballs may have an irregular shape, but they are not diseased or weak; nor are they predisposed to eye disease in the future.

To a large extent, both nearsightedness and farsightedness are hereditary. Although farsightedness may be present in toddlers, nearsightedness usually does not develop until later in childhood. By age seven or eight, about 10 percent of all youngsters suffer from near- or farsightedness that is serious enough to require corrective lenses. Farsightedness usually does not worsen through adolescence and may actually diminish at age nineteen or twenty. However, nearsightedness, the most common of these disorders in children, can worsen progressively until the age of about twenty-one, when the condition will stabilize. During the years of the child's most rapid growth, a change in glasses may be needed as often as every six months.

Incidentally, although many parents are distressed over their child's poor eyesight, there may be a silver lining to this condiion as well. A study reported in the *British Medical Journal* (1977) indicates that nearsightedness may be associated with higher intelligence—that is, myopic children usually perform better in reading, arithmetic, and general academic tests than their peers with perfect vision. The youngsters who were studied underwent a significant intellectual gain just before their nearsightedness first manifested itself, which a group of children with normal vision did not experience. Throughout the remainder of their schooling, the myopic youngsters had more than a one-year academic advantage over the normal group. While the nearsighted children read more in their leisure time, they also participated in outdoor sports as frequently as other youngsters.

This study may provide answers to some unresolved questions about myopia. For instance, since nearsightedness is usually hereditary, why is it still so prevalent among human beings today—that is, shouldn't most nearsighted people (and thus the trait for nearsightedness) have been eliminated in the era of sabertooth tigers and other predators, when the inability to see clearly to avoid such deadly plunderers could have proved fatal? The researchers speculated that perhaps the only nearsighted survivors were those who also possessed the desirable trait of intelligence. This intelligence could have helped compensate for poor vision in the individual's battle for survival in a hostile environment.

MYTH: *Eating carrots will improve a child's vision.*

During World War II, carrots were fed to American military pilots as a means of improving their vision. But this practice, however well intentioned, was probably useless. In normal, balanced diets, the body (and the eyes) receive all the vitamin A that is needed. Although carrots, egg yolks, and sweet potatoes are particularly high in vitamin A, consuming extra amounts of these foods won't enhance your child's vision, because the body cannot utilize the excess vitamin A. In fact, it may do more harm than good, since extravagant amounts of the vitamin can be detrimental to health. One of the most common but nondangerous effects of eating an excessive num-

ber of carrots is that the body will accumulate carotene pigment, which frequently causes a yellow discoloration of the
skin. This is most commonly seen during the first year of life.
In Germany fifty to a hundred years ago, this discoloration
was considered a sign of a healthy baby. Today, although it
is not regarded as dangerous, most pediatricians recommend
that the consumption of carrots be reduced to return the skin
color to normal.

Eye Structure and Functioning

MYTH: *Eye color is fixed at birth.*

The color of your newborn's eyes is *not* necessarily the
color they will be later in life. Almost always, the irises of an
infant's eyes are blue or gray at birth, indicating nothing more
than a scarcity of pigment on the back surface of each iris.
As the amount of pigment increases, the iris tends to become
darker, and by six months of age you should be able to tell
whether your baby's eyes will remain blue or become brown
or green. A large amount of pigment means brown eyes, less
pigmentation will result in lighter-colored eyes. So although
the ultimate color of your youngster's eyes is genetically determined at birth, you'll have to wait a few months to find out
what that color is.

MYTH: *Only blue-eyed parents can produce a blue-eyed child.*

Each person possesses two genes for eye color—one
inherited from the mother, one from the father. For a child
to have blue eyes, a blue (recessive) trait gene must be inherited
from each parent. Thus, two brown-eyed parents *can* have a
blue-eyed offspring, but one of the two genes for eye color
that each of them possesses and passes on to the child must
be a blue gene. If the baby inherits one brown gene from
one parent and one blue gene from the other, the brown will

always dominate, and the child will have brown eyes. Two brown-eyed parents, each of whom possesses a recessive blue trait, statistically have a 25 percent chance of having a blue-eyed baby.

If you have brown eyes, there is no way to determine if you have a blue or green gene to pass on to the next generation. However, if you have a close relative—your mother, father, sister, or brother—with light eyes, you *may* possess this recessive trait.

As with all inherited characteristics, there are subtle factors at work with eye color, and thus forecasting it is essentially impossible. For instance, if you look at your child's irises closely, you'll see many color specks rather than a uniform blanket of color. Although these granules help explain the existence of various shades of blue, green, or brown, geneticists do not yet fully understand every variable involved in eye color.

MYTH: *Blue eyes are more sensitive to light and irritation than brown eyes.*

The principal function of the iris is to allow more or less light to enter the eye, primarily by altering the size of the central opening, the pupil. However, children who have light-colored eyes have less pigment in their irises than brown-eyed youngsters. Consequently, with less absorbing pigmentation, blue eyes may be slightly more sensitive to bright lights. But they are not more susceptible to irritation or any other eye condition.

Albinos are individuals who lack pigment in not only their iris but in the retina as well. Their eyes appear pink, because the red wavelengths of light, which are usually absorbed by the retinal pigment, are reflected, giving the eyes this pinkish appearance. With absolutely no pigmentation, the iris cannot act as effectively as a filtering agent, and thus the retina is more fully exposed to external bright lights. Lack of retinal pigmentation is usually accompanied by an increased sensitivity to light.

MYTH: *Bright lights, including those from camera flashbulbs, are bad for the eyes of newborns.*

For centuries, mothers and fathers have falsely believed that strong lights are bad for babies. But this belief is based on the shakiest of premises. Because of the unusual strength of the closure muscles of newborns' eyelids, parents have difficulty opening their babies' eyes. To explain this phenomenon a mythology developed purporting that the tightly shut eyes were an indication that infants have an aversion to bright lights.

Though it is true that continued, direct exposure to the infrared component of bright sunlight can cause retinal damage, this is no more true of newborns than it is of any other individual. Everyone, whether young or old, should avoid gazing directly into sunlight.

Exposure to ultraviolet light can damage the cornea of the eye. Interestingly, the structures of the eye behind the cornea, such as the retina, are protected from ultraviolet light damage by the cornea itself, just as a plate of glass between you and the sun will protect you from sunburn. But there is no evidence at present that artificial light, including flashbulbs, has any detrimental effect on the eyes. You can safely expose your child to normal environmental light, including flashbulbs, without fear.

Some parents are particularly concerned about the possible negative effects of phototherapy (bilirubin light) on their babies' eyes. Healthy newborns often have a yellow tint to their skin—an indication of jaundice. This condition usually lasts only a few days and is partly caused by an immature liver that has not yet been able to metabolize the bilirubin pigment, thus permitting its buildup. The most effective treatment is phototherapy, in which the body is exposed to light rays, particularly the blue wavelengths. Unfortunately, animal studies show that in addition to lowering the bilirubin, prolonged direct exposure to blue wavelengths can cause retinal injury. Although this same finding has not been duplicated in human studies, most pediatricians still recommend that your newborn's eyes be protected by being covered during phototherapy.

MYTH: *A dust particle or other foreign substance in your child's eye should be removed before it becomes lost inside the head.*

Any foreign body in your child's eye is uncomfortable and might scratch the transparent tissue at the front of the eye (the cornea). Thus, anything in the eye should be removed as quickly and gently as possible. However, there is *no* danger of the substance moving from the front of the eye to the inside of your youngster's head. The front, visible portion of the eyeball is completely separated from the internal part of the eye and the socket by the conjunctiva, a clear membrane that lines the eyelids and spreads over the surface of the eyeball. The conjunctiva creates a closed cavity that prevents a dust particle (or a contact lens) from floating to the inside of the head.

In fact, the only open passage from the outer eye inward is the lacrimal duct, which allows tears to drain from the eye into the frontal portion of the nose. This explains why your nose "drips" when you cry. To see the opening of this duct in a mirror, pull the lower eyelid slightly down, away from the eyeball; the duct is the tiny hole near the inner nasal corner on the rim of the eyelid.

MYTH: *Your child's eyes reveal whether he or she is telling the truth or lying.*

There are many literary references to the eyes as a source of insight into an individual's character. Poets have even called the eyes "the windows to the soul."

Although I consider such hypotheses to be speculative at best, in the mid-1960s some University of Chicago researchers decided to study the relationship between pupillary size and a person's emotional state. They already knew that the pupil, the black opening at the center of the iris, contracts and dilates in response to the intensity of light directed at it. But they sought to determine whether varying emotional conditions could alter the size of the pupil. After all, throughout history, magicians have allegedly been able to detect which of their subjects have been holding hidden objects by looking for clues in their eyes. Could there actually be some truth to their claim?

The Chicago group discovered that, in fact, provocative stimuli (for example, a significant or suggestive word or photograph, such as a nude female photo shown to a male college freshman) caused the pupils to dilate. In contrast, noxious stimuli induced pupillary constriction. This study has led to speculation that the pupils might function in the capacity of a lie detector—dilating when a child is agitated or aroused. But this is presently only a theory; don't expect such evidence to be admissible in court.

Eye Defects

MYTH: *Intentionally crossing the eyes may cause them to stick or permanently hook together.*

From the time your youngster begins focusing on specific, close objects, his or her eyes may occasionally appear crossed. After all, if you were to hold an object close to your own nose and look at it, your eyes would converge, just as your child's do. But there is *no* risk of them ever sticking.

The muscles of the eye are meant to be used. They are designed to move the eye in all directions, and there is really no way to misuse or abuse them. Six muscles—the superior, inferior, medial, and lateral rectus muscles, and the superior and inferior oblique muscles—control the movement of the eye and connect the eyeball to various parts of the socket. None has hooks or sticky substances on it. Crossing or rolling the eyes is not particularly attractive, and it may even cause fatigue, but the eyes will never hook together or be damaged in any sense.

Even so, many parents cling to the unfounded fear that when eyes are crossed, no matter how briefly, irreversible injury will result. Adults have told me about the unnecessary anxiety they experienced as children because of this myth. Accurate information can spare your children from this worry.

MYTH: *Some children outgrow crossed eyes.*

This belief has only a germ of truth to it. Babies often appear to have crossed eyes (strabismus) when they really don't. This parental concern about crossed eyes usually begins when parents observe what they interpret as a crossing of the eyes when their baby gazes to the side. In fact, this "crossing" is only an illusion. There is a prominent flap of skin (epicanthal fold) in the newborn that covers the white portion of each eye closest to the nose. When the baby gazes to the side, one eye seems turned in too far, because part of the white of that eye is hidden by the epicanthal fold. In fact, this so-called pseudostrabismus is the most common reason that ophthalmologists are asked to evaluate infants.

As the bridge of the baby's nose develops with time, the inner corners of the eyes are stretched toward the center, and the excess skin becomes less prominent. More of the white of the eye nearest the nose is visible, and the illusion of crossed eyes is "outgrown."

Crossed eyes are, of course, a real phenomenon as well, affecting about 5 percent of all children. In the first few weeks of life, even the healthiest eyes will not always focus perfectly on the object being viewed. However, if the eyes have not steadied by the age of three months, and if they appear crossed more than just occasionally at that age, an ophthalmologist should have a look at your baby. If one eye (or sometimes both eyes) is *continuously* crossed, even before three months of age, your child may suffer from strabismus and should be checked.

Imagine how confusing this must be to the brain if the eyes consistently fail to sustain parallel visual images. The "fixing," or straight, eye is sending a clear, normal visual message to the brain. But the "deviant," or turned-in, eye is seeing something different. The child experiences double vision, and the brain soon learns to discard and suppress the image transmitted by the turned-in eye. In short, the deviant eye shuts down, the child learns to see with only one eye, and the condition called "amblyopia," or lazy eye, may result. Lazy eye is actually a misnomer, inaccurately intimating that the eye is weak and too sluggish to function correctly; in reality, the eye is anatomically healthy but does not see properly because the brain will not accept and process its visual messages.

What happens if amblyopia (defective vision in an eye) is not diagnosed and properly treated? Despite what the perpetuators of medical myths would have you believe, your child will not automatically outgrow this syndrome, and vision will progressively deteriorate. In addition, if your youngster's strabismus is not corrected by the age of eighteen months, the child will never develop vision in which images are properly fused and depth is accurately perceived, even if the eyes become correctly aligned at a later age.

Unfortunately, in some cases of amblyopia the deviant eye may be turned so subtly as to be difficult for the parent to detect. But you should make the effort to judge your baby's vision early, asking for the assistance of your pediatrician if necessary. When a defect is present, early treatment is absolutely essential to avoid permanent visual impairment. The best time to begin treatment is at the earliest possible age that the diagnosis can be made, usually between three and six months of age, but may be as soon as the first month of life in the child with eyes continuously gazing inward or outward.

If amblyopia is detected in your youngster, an ophthalmologist will usually decide to place a patch on the fixing eye, thus compelling the brain to use the "bad" eye exclusively. Or less frequently, the doctor may administer drops in the good eye, temporarily blurring its vision and thus forcing the use of the deviant eye. If amblyopia is diagnosed at six months of age, the eye drops or the patching treatment may return vision in the weakened eye to normal in just one week. However, if care does not begin until the age of eighteen months, the therapy may be required for one or more months before satisfactory results are achieved. Treatment that begins at six years of age usually must be continued one year or longer before vision returns to normal, although when a management program begins that late, it may be less effective. When amblyopia is diagnosed in a child older than nine years, the affected eye will probably *never* achieve good visual acuity, since the brain will no longer be able to learn to interpret the information transmitted from that eye.

For this reason, I recommend a visual screening test for all children at as young an age as possible, and certainly by the age of four.

MYTH: *Conjunctivitis (pinkeye) is always contagious.*

"Pinkeye" is the average person's term for conjunctivitis, the reddening of the white part of the eye. It can have literally thousands of causes, although the public is most concerned when it involves an infection.

Infectious conjunctivitis can usually be blamed on a virus; however, the inflamed eye can sometimes become secondarily infected with bacteria. This bacterial infection is characterized by a mucous discharge and swelling of the lids. Often the mucus dries on the lashes during the night, and when the child awakens, the parents may be horrified at finding their youngster's eyes seemingly glued shut. (Washing with warm water will alleviate the stickiness.) The bacterial infection is treated with antibiotic drops or ointment, but the original virus remains very contagious.

However, the reddened eye can be produced by conditions other than infections—an allergy, foreign bodies in the eye, exposure to a variety of irritating chemicals, smog, or a chlorinated pool. None of these is contagious. A red eye is also a factor in many serious but noncontagious diseases of the eye's inner structure, including the cornea, lens, and iris. Thus it is necessary to accurately diagnose the condition in order to exclude the potentially serious causes of reddened eye, as well as to determine whether a contagious condition exists.

Generally, only bacterial and viral conjunctivitis are contagious, and precautions should be taken to avoid their spread. For instance, children with these infections should be discouraged from rubbing their eyes. They should wash their hands frequently and wipe them dry on disposable towels. Physicians can minimize their own role as a carrier of the disorder by washing their hands thoroughly both before and after examining each patient.

MYTH: *Children who are color-blind see only in black-and-white.*

Color blindness is found in 5 to 10 percent of the world's population, mostly in males. It is present at birth and continues throughout life. Although the condition prevents the child from differentiating between some colors, particularly red and green, it is more of an inconvenience than a serious, life-disrupting disorder. Sometimes, color blindness is never diagnosed, and it can usually be compensated for by learning to recognize colors through other visual cues.

Despite myths to the contrary, a child (or an adult) with color blindness seldom sees only in black-and-white. There is an extremely rare inherited color vision defect called achromatopsia in which only black-and-white is perceived, but the inherited form occurs in only one of every 100 million individuals.

MYTH: *Children with the measles should be kept in a darkened room to avoid damage to their eyes.*

Measles, or rubeola, is a viral disease that was once a common and contagious childhood illness. But now, with the recent development of an effective vaccine, measles can be avoided. In communities where immunizations are commonplace, some pediatricians never see a case of the illness.

The most identifiable symptom of measles is a red rash on the body. Simultaneously, the conjunctival membrane of the eye is infected for from one to three days and shows redness, swelling, and a discharge. There may also be a corneal inflammation called epithelial keratitis.

An intolerance to light (photophobia), long associated with the measles, is a result of this inflammation of the cornea. The eyes become hypersensitive to light because the light rays to the eyes disperse, as if they were passing through a prism, increasing their intensity on the retina. If corneal irritation has occurred, exposure to bright lights is *not* dangerous or damaging to the eyes during the measles. Keep your child in a darkened room only if the youngster feels more comfortable in a dimmer environment, since in no way can it alleviate the corneal inflammation.

On rare occasions, measle-related eye problems can deteriorate to a more serious state. So if your child complains about severe eye discomfort, or if the inflammation is prolonged and seems to be worsening, your pediatrician should have a look.

MYTH: *Vitamin A deficiencies can cause eye problems.*

Insufficient amounts of vitamins seldom cause eye disorders. True, inadequate levels of vitamin A can promote a condition called xerophthalmia, a dryness of parts of the eye, but this malady is extremely rare. In the United States, no matter how unbalanced a child's diet may be, it almost always contains ample levels of vitamin A.

Even so, there are some rare circumstances in which a vitamin A deficiency can occur, resulting in eye ailments. For instance, some children on prolonged, severely restricted diets for food allergies might not be consuming enough vitamin A. Or a gastrointestinal disorder may be restricting intestinal absorption of vitamin A. Likewise, some types of liver disease, in which metabolism is altered, can cause a vitamin A deficiency. But all these situations are extremely uncommon.

If your child suffers from a true vitamin A deficiency, the earliest sign of this disorder is night blindness—an inability to see well in dim light. Other symptoms include the absence of luster in the white portions of the eyes and a decreased sensitivity of the eye. In such cases, the U.S. Food and Nutrition Board recommends 1500 units of vitamin A per day, permitting slow recovery from the ailment.

Ironically, in the health-conscious society in which we live, children are much more likely to suffer from *excessive* levels of vitamin A than a deficiency. A child who consumes very large amounts of vitamin A may experience itching, irritability, and a loss of appetite. Hard lumps on the arms, legs, and head may surface in the more extreme cases.

Eyeglasses and Contact Lenses

MYTH: *If your child's vision is not 20/20, then glasses or contact lenses will be needed for correction.*

Children with eyesight of 20/30, 20/40, or worse do not have perfect vision. But that in itself is not reason enough to have your child fitted for glasses. Experts concur that young children can function very adequately in the world with vision no better than 20/40 or 20/50.

Serious problems could arise, though, particularly in young children, if each eye has a *different* visual acuity. For example, one eye may see at 20/20 and the other at 20/40. This is potentially more health-threatening than if both eyes see at 20/50, because the difference in acuity could lead to, or be a sign of, amblyopia, in which the brain shuts down one of the eyes to avoid double or blurred vision. If amblyopia is not detected or treated early, by patching the stronger eye and forcing the brain to use the suppressed one, proper vision may never be regained (see 97–98).

However, if both of your child's eyes have identical visual acuity, which deviates only slightly from a 20/20 measurement, then glasses are not necessarily required. Instead, the youngster's ability to operate in the world is a better gauge of the need for corrective lenses. For instance, can your son follow the path of the baseball while playing in the Little Leagues? Does he squint at the blackboard at school? Does he always sit in or near the front row in movie theaters? Once the quality of life is adversely affected by a child's vision, then glasses should be seriously considered.

MYTH: *If your child learns how to squint properly, then glasses need not be worn.*

Some children, particularly teenagers who are cosmetically conscious, decide to go through life squinting rather than wearing glasses. In fact, squinting can improve the vision of a nearsighted person. But it's doubtful that it is ever as effective in correcting optical deficiencies as glasses are.

Glasses, of course, do not change the structure and the internal optics of the eye. Instead, they compensate artificially for the eyes' shortcomings by properly directing light rays onto the retina. In a sense, when a myopic individual squints, a similar effect occurs. Squinting narrows the aperture through which light is allowed into the eye, eliminating some of the more poorly focused light rays that create a blurred image on the retina. This works on the same principle as a pinhole camera, in which the tiny hole permits the light to enter at only one angle in its path to the back of the camera, thus eliminating the need for a lens to refract the light. In the same way, looking through a pinhole will allow you to see better if you are near- or farsighted, by circumventing the deficiencies of your eye's lens and cornea.

MYTH: *The wearing of glasses will strengthen your child's eyes.*

Eyeglasses cannot provide a cure for conditions like nearsightedness or farsightedness. They cannot change the distortions in the shape of the eyeball and the curvature of the lens and the cornea—the two causes of these conditions. They improve the ability to see only by bending and focusing the light more clearly, and only when they are actually being worn.

One exception to these rules occurs with accommodative esotropia, a type of strabismus (crossed eyes) in which, in the farsighted child, one eye tends to deviate inwardly while trying to focus upon an object. In this case, glasses worn for a period of time can assist the deviant eye muscles in learning to coordinate with the brain. The eye is strengthened and the condition is corrected, permitting many of these children to have straight eyes without glasses.

MYTH: *It is better to postpone fitting your child with glasses for as long as possible, because the eyes will become dependent upon them and even be weakened by them.*

A surprising number of parents adhere to this myth, avoiding glasses for their child in the belief that their youngster's eyes will become habituated to the glasses, will not work as hard, and consequently will become weaker. According to this hypothesis, when glasses are not worn, the eye will be forced to work harder and vision will improve.

But that simply isn't the case. Glasses are like a hearing aid, in that they are an artificial device that can compensate for a physical defect, while neither enhancing nor worsening the deficiency itself. Eyes work just as hard whether glasses are worn or not, and no physical dependency can develop. A child who needs glasses will simply be able to see better with the glasses than without them.

An argument can be made, though, that a child may become *psychologically* dependent on glasses. After all, it's desirable to be able to see better, and once the brain becomes accustomed to seeing sharp rather than fuzzy images, it would prefer to continue doing so. In that sense, your child can become emotionally dependent on glasses—or more specifically, dependent on seeing well—which is a desirable form of dependence.

Parents have frequently told me that after they've stopped wearing their glasses for some time, their scores on an eye chart test improve. Isn't this proof, they ask, that vision can be enhanced when glasses are put aside for good? Well, it is true that a person with, say 20/80 vision—correctable to 20/20 with glasses—may score 20/40 or 20/60 on an eye chart after stopping wearing glasses. But this change is *not* due to improvements in the mechanical functioning of the eye but rather to the increased ability of the brain to interpret the blur. In essence, the individual's eyes become attuned to the more subtle qualities of light and dark.

You could argue that this situation has some benefits. But even at its best, this uncorrected vision cannot match the clarity of sight offered by properly fitted lenses. Therefore, the decision to have your child fitted for glasses when needed should not be postponed.

MYTH: *Children must be over the age of two years before they can wear glasses, and much older to wear contact lenses.*

This is a misconception that has been propagated by many physicians, including some old-school ophthalmologists. In fact, in rare cases, children as young as three weeks old can be fitted for contact lenses, and if necessary, with glasses by one year of age. To correct specific types of eye disorders, which must be treated at as early an age as possible, glasses or contact lenses are prescribed, no matter how old the child is. Immediate treatment can often prevent or eliminate amblyopia (lazy eye) in the weakened eye; in some forms of strabismus (crossed eyes) it can eliminate the need for surgery to straighten the eye.

If the eye does not learn to see in the first few weeks of life, it may never see normally. For instance, in certain rare eye ailments like congenital cataracts, *no* focused light can reach the retina. If the obstruction is not surgically removed by one to two months of age, and a corrective contact lens program and patching therapy started, the child's vision with correction in that eye will probably never be better than 20/200, the visual ratio of one characterized as legally blind. There is a critical time period of less than three months of age in which normal vision must begin in order for the child to develop it. In a study of newborn cats, their eyelids were sewn shut during the first month of life; after the eyes were reopened, and for the rest of the cats' lives, they were functionally blind—that is, they could see light, but could not discriminate between shapes.

If your child has an eye disorder, I cannot overemphasize the need to treat it early.

MYTH: *Contact lenses are not safe.*

In the early days of contact lens development, the thought of putting a foreign object in the eyes frightened some people, and many misconceptions grew out of these fears.

In reality, contact lenses can be as safe as glasses, for children as well as adults. Although nothing in life is free of all hazards, millions of people wear contacts every day without problems. If they are properly fitted by an eye specialist and are cleaned, handled, and worn according to instructions, there is no reason why they can't be used without risk or discomfort.

MYTH: *If your child uses someone else's glasses, or wears a pair of dime-store prescription glasses, permanent eye damage can occur.*

At some variety stores, you can choose from an array of inexpensive prescription glasses, without a physician's guidance and advice. The thought of placing a pair of these glasses on a child makes some people shudder. All their lives, they've heard about the serious harm that the eyes can suffer by wearing improperly fitted prescription lenses.

I, too, recommend that children avoid wearing glasses not made specifically for them. Only an ophthalmologist or optometrist can prescribe the glasses that can give the best possible eyesight. But my advice is *not* based on any concern over possible permanent eye damage. While someone else's glasses may make your child uncomfortable, they will not damage the eyes themselves. Yes, eyestrain and headaches may occur as the eyes futilely attempt to see clearly. But once these glasses are removed and the eyes rest, even these minor symptoms will disappear.

The greatest danger of inexpensive, store-bought glasses is that most of them are not shatterproof. Because children are so active physically, it's critical that their glasses be resistant to shattering. For that reason, avoid these low-priced lenses.

Eyestrain

MYTH: *Eyestrain is the leading cause of headaches.*

Headaches are probably our most common affliction. Although ophthalmologists disagree on the relative number of eyestrain-induced headaches, there is a consensus that eyestrain is not a principal cause of headaches. Childhood headaches can be produced by many other factors, and, as with adults, tension is the most common provocation.

Although eyestrain is uncomfortable and may cause headaches, it cannot induce damage to the eye structure. Instead, it is a sign of eye fatigue, much like when any other muscles of your body become tired with overexertion. Even though the retina (the receptor of light) and the optic nerve (which transmits visual impulses from the eye to the brain) never become fatigued, the focusing mechanism (the lens and muscles) can tire from overuse and cause the sensations of eyestrain. As the eyes become tired and the muscles of the brow and forehead experience weariness as well, a headache can ensue.

Children suffering from eyestrain do not necessarily need glasses. Their eyes may simply be tired and should be rested for a few minutes. However, any persistent complaint related to the eyes should be checked by an ophthalmologist before being considered harmless.

MYTH: *Reading in poor light can damage your child's eyes.*

Most parents become frustrated and anxious when their youngsters read in dim light, since they are convinced that eye damage can result.

However injurious this activity may seem, it *cannot* damage your child's eyes, either temporarily or permanently. Eyes cannot wear out. True, the eyes may become tired in poor light (see eyestrain discussion, above) but not because they have to work harder. The fatigue results from the additional strain put on the brain as it tries to interpret what the eyes are seeing. This can cause tension in the temples and the muscles around the eyes, provoking eye fatigue and sometimes headaches. But aside from this temporary discomfort, reading in poor light has no effect on the eyes.

MYTH: *Too much reading or close work will damage your child's eyes.*

Eyestrain or headache will be the only result of excessive reading or other close work. After a period of rest, the eyes will recover without any harm, as do any other fatigued muscles.

Many parents are convinced that excessive close work will hurt the eyes and create a need for glasses or even cause blindness. But keep in mind that optical deficiencies like nearsightedness are not caused by overtaxing the eye but rather by structural defects within the eye that have nothing to do with how the eye is used. Reading cannot impair visual health.

Hypnotists capitalize on the eye muscle fatigue that occurs in an individual when an object is held close to and above the line of vision. By carrying out this common hypnotic induction maneuver, while *telling* the subject that "your eyes are getting tired," the hypnotist is able to convince the person of a supernatural control over his mind.

MYTH: *Sitting too close to the television is bad for your child's eyes.*

The average American youngster watches more than six hours of TV each day, most often perched on the floor or in a chair, no more than perhaps three or four feet from the set. That's enough to send many parents into a frenzy, convinced that each hour in front of the TV is forever weakening their child's vision—not to mention boggling the youngster's mind with an onslaught of outlandish cartoons and other violence.

I'll reserve comment on the quality of the programing for the TV critics. But concern over sitting too close to the TV is a leading complaint heard by ophthalmologists. Your child has probably chosen to be close to the set in order to feel more involved with the action on the screen, and this close proximity will *not* damage your child's eyes. Neither is it a sign of eye weakness. True, a nearsighted child may sit close to the TV because of a visual deficiency, but if that's the case, the youngster will show signs of this disorder not only in front of the TV but also in everything else in life.

If your child is watching the set at an awkward angle, eyestrain might occur, but that's not going to cause any permanent visual damage. If the eyestrain were extremely fatiguing, your youngster would probably turn off the TV or move to a different chair. A child who continues to sit close to the TV is probably not experiencing any visual tiredness.

One final note: Some parents are concerned about the radiation that may be dispersed from their TV, particularly as it may affect their child sitting close to the set. The verdict is still out on this matter. But TV manufacturers, sensitive to this problem, have made special efforts in recent years to improve the radiation safety of their sets.

In 1968, the Bureau of Radiological Health noted that 6 percent of all the sets it tested leaked x-rays above the recommended maximum levels, with color TVs being the biggest culprits. But since the Radiation Control for Health and Safety Act was passed by Congress in 1968, the TV industry has taken steps to rectify these shortcomings. New circuits have been developed to reduce high voltage, and components have been redesigned to minimize x-ray emissions. In addition, protective shielding for TV tubes has been improved, and service technicians have been trained to adjust the x-radiation capability of TV sets.

Over the past twenty years, the federal government's allowable level of TV x-rays has been reduced more than twenty times. While 50 millirems per hour was once permissible, now the limit is one-half a millirem per hour. The U.S. Public Health Service thus reports that on TV sets manufactured since mid-1968, radiation levels are too low to present a health hazard. A 1970 survey by the U.S. Bureau of Radiological Health revealed that in the TV sets it tested, none of the x-ray emissions exceeded the federal limit of 0.5 millirem per hour. The TV industry's own research showed that in a five-month period ending in March 1970, none of the 48,400 sets tested had emission rates above the maximum-allowable levels.

The Surgeon General doubts that TV x-rays have much potential for biological damage, and in fact no case has ever been reported of TV radiation causing human injury. Even so, no one knows the effects of low-level TV radiation exposure over many years, and thus some caution should be exhibited until such studies are concluded.

5

EARS

Not only are ears one of the body's most noticeable features, but they are also a common site of childhood infection. No wonder, then, that they are a source of considerable parental attention.

Some parents insist, for instance, that their child's hearing organs are either oddly shaped, too prominent, or too small. But although everyone seems to have an opinion on what an aesthetically perfect ear should look like, there is actually a wide range of ear sizes and configurations that fall within the range of "normal." The shape of a child's outer ear, most often an inherited characteristic, in no way affects hearing ability.

The human ear develops from six small elevations that initially surface during the sixth week of fetal life. These elevations gradually fuse together to form the characteristic outer ear, which attains a complete adult configuration by the twentieth week of development in the mother's uterus. When ear malformations are detected after birth, they can alert the pediatrician to possible problems in other organs, like the kidneys, which develop in the fetus at the same time as the ear.

The ear's visible outer portion, called the auricle, is connected to the middle ear by a canal. The skin lining this canal also forms the outer layer of the eardrum, separating the middle ear from the inner ear. The middle ear itself is a cavity containing three tiny bones called ossicles. The ossicles are the smallest bones in the body, reaching their full adult size prior to birth.

Hearing becomes possible when sound vibrations that have struck the eardrum are transmitted across the middle ear by the ossicles. As they travel into the inner ear, they are received by the specialized nerve receptor mechanism there. Mechanical sound waves are then changed into nerve impulses, which are communicated to the brain instantaneously.

There are many interesting little-known facts about the ear. For instance, unlike other structures in the human body, the outer ear actually continues to grow, although at a slow rate, for an individual's entire life. (No wonder, then, that so many elderly people seem to have large ears.) Some people have a diagonal crease on their earlobes, a trait that some preliminary studies have connected to a higher incidence of adult heart disease.

Also, you may have noticed that your child coughs when an object (like a doctor's speculum) is placed in the ear. This cough is caused by stimulation of Arnold's nerve, a branch of the tenth cranial nerve located in the ear canal. This nerve can also provoke a slowing of the heart rate, and in some cases, a crying child will calm down while the ear is being examined.

In this chapter, the most familiar myths surrounding phenomena like ear infections, "swimmer's ear," and earwax will be disspelled.

Ear Infections

MYTH: *Ear infections, like the colds that often cause them, are contagious.*

When pediatricians are awakened by a middle-of-the-night phone call from a concerned mother, they are frequently told, "My child is just getting over a cold but woke up at midnight crying with terrible ear pains and a 102° (39°C) temperature." In most instances, this is an indication of a bacterial middle-ear infection, or *otitis media*. (Not all ear infections, however, occur in the middle ear.)

Here is what typically happens: A viral infection like a cold causes the eustachian tubes (the channels connecting the middle ear to the upper throat) to narrow and eventually block. Normal drainage from the middle ear is obstructed and a vacuum is created in the middle ear chamber into which mucus can still be secreted. Eventually, the trapped fluid becomes colonized with bacteria, and when the bacteria multiply, pus forms in the middle ear chamber, resulting in an ear infection. The concentrations of pus may eventually become so large as to apply pressure on the eardrum, often causing severe pain and sometimes even rupturing it.

Antibiotics are typically prescribed to combat a middle ear infection when it is believed to be caused by bacteria. The type of antibiotic depends on which specific bacterium your doctor feels is probably causing the infection.

If you're like most parents, you may try to keep playmates away from your child until the ear infection disappears so as not to spread the illness. But in fact these earaches are *not* contagious. Your child probably became vulnerable to an ear infection when a cold weakened the ear's drainage and defense systems. Most of the bacteria that can ultimately cause ear infections are probably already present in the nose and throat, awaiting the viral cold that can create the proper conditions for them to settle and thus infect the middle ear.

MYTH: *Children of any age are susceptible to ear infections.*

In their practices, many pediatricians diagnose ear infections more frequently than any other illness. The peak age for the onset of ear infections is between six and twenty-four months, with a gradual decline in frequency thereafter. At this young age, the eustachian tubes are particularly short, narrow, and inclined horizontally, rather than being more vertical and longer as in the older child. These characteristics make infection more likely. By the time a youngster reaches age seven, the ear drainage system has become more adultlike, and middle ear infections are much rarer.

Some families have more ear infections than others, probably having inherited specific anatomical features in the ear that make them more susceptible to inflammations. A large research program in Boston in 1973 showed that children with episodes of otitis media were likely to have siblings with a history of frequent infection.

Another recent study showed that by age five, 75 percent of all children have had at least one ear infection. About 14 percent of the youngsters contracted an infection during their first year of life, and 50 percent of this vulnerable group experienced six or more episodes in the ensuing two years.

Although no child is completely immune to ear infections, some racial groups (like American Indian and Eskimo children) seem to have higher rates of infection. Black youngsters, however, tend to have less ear disease than their white counterparts.

If you suspect an ear infection in your child, a visit to the pediatrician's office is suggested within about twelve hours, if possible. This infection most often surfaces between the third and seventh day of a cold, frequently when a child's cold symptoms are starting to improve. Even the mildest case requires medical attention. If left untreated indefinitely, serious damage could result, including hearing loss. In the pre-antibiotic era, ear infections sometimes caused severe complications, including brain infections.

MYTH: *Your child's ear infections will always cause pain.*

Persistent pain in the ear of a youngster under age five is almost always due to a middle ear infection. (The primary exception is painful "swimmer's ear," which will be discussed on page 116–117.) But the *absence* of pain certainly does not eliminate the possibility that an ear infection still exists. In fact, I often unexpectedly detect pus or fluid in the middle ear of a youngster who is being routinely examined during a "*well*-child" visit.

When pain does accompany an ear infection, it can vary in intensity, depending on the type of bacteria present. For instance, the bacteria *Streptococcus pneumoniae,* accounting for 40 percent of ear infections, generally produces more severe discomfort than *Haemophilus influenzae,* which causes 20 percent of the cases but generates only mild pain.

MYTH: *Don't wash the hair of a child who has an ear infection.*

Wet hair does not cause or worsen an ear infection. True, fully submerging the head of a child who has a perforated eardrum should be avoided. But even then, a shower, or a bath in which the head is not immersed, will not pose any danger.

MYTH: *Exposure to cold weather, or leaving ears uncovered in the wind, can cause ear infections.*

Some parents believe that ear infections are caused and exacerbated by exposure to cold weather and wind. But here again, no direct connection exists. Although some individuals develop transient ear pain when exposed to the cold, this discomfort is probably caused by a muscle spasm and is not related to a middle ear infection.

MYTH: *If you give your child a decongestant at the first sign of a cold, you can keep an ear infection from developing.*

See pages 70–72.

MYTH: *A child whose eardrum bursts will suffer permanent hearing loss.*

The eardrum, the thin membrane separating the external ear canal from the middle ear, sometimes bursts under the stress of an ear infection. As pus accumulates, the buildup within the middle ear can become intense enough to rupture the eardrum, thus relieving the pressure. As with a pimple that pops, once this ear pressure is alleviated and the ear begins to drain, the pain will subside. This is one of nature's ways of healing the infection.

Lasting hearing loss occurs only occasionally with ruptured eardrums, and even then only when the ear becomes infected repeatedly, without proper medical treatment. Burst eardrums usually heal without complications. As a general rule, the potential for hearing loss is more dependent on the frequency, severity, and duration of an infection and less on whether or not the eardrum ruptures.

When I detect an ear infection that is causing considerable middle ear pressure and pain, intentional perforation of the eardrum is sometimes the treatment of choice. A pediatrician or an otolaryngologist (an ear, nose, and throat specialist) can use a sterilized surgical blade to puncture a small hole in the eardrum, choosing the best site for the drainage to occur.

When children have recurring or persistent ear infections, I occasionally recommend that polyethylene tubes be inserted into their eardrums. These tubes maintain a permanent opening in the eardrum, which permits any new accumulation of fluid to drain, thus averting a buildup of pressure and the ensuing infection. Though the tubes themselves can provide routes of escape for the fluid, their primary purpose is to allow air to enter the middle ear space, thus promoting more normal drainage through the eustachian tube. This process operates not much differently than punching a second hole in the top of a beer can so the liquid can flow out more easily.

The Ear Canal

MYTH: *"Swimmer's ear" is caused by dirty swimming pools.*

External otitis is a painful inflammation of the outer ear canal. It does not involve the middle ear chamber and thus is *not* related to the classic ear infection discussed above.

Because of the commonly held belief that external otitis is contracted from bacteria in swimming pools, this infection is often
called "swimmer's ear." Studies do show that the incidence
of this infection increases after water gets in the ear. But dirty
pool water is not the real culprit here. Instead, the infection
is traceable to the outer ear's weakened defenses, caused when
swimmers constantly immerse their heads in water, leaving
some liquid in the ear canal.

If your child is experiencing an earache, here is a simple
method to help decide whether your child's infection is of the
middle or the outer ear. Simply tug on your child's ear lobe,
which will place stress on the outer ear canal and cause pain
if an outer ear infection exists. Were it a middle ear infection
instead, this maneuver would not provoke any additional discomfort.

How should external otitis be treated? Instead of administering oral antibiotics, as you would with a middle ear infection,
your doctor will prescribe medicated eardrops to combat the
ailment. As a preventive measure for children frequently in
the water, some pediatricians suggest earplugs or administering
eardrops containing peroxide after each swimming session.
These drops stimulate evaporation of the water, encouraging
ear dryness.

MYTH: *Earwax is unsanitary.*

For millions of people, there is a certain sacredness
about bodily secretions. A comedian once observed that as a
general trait of human nature, almost no one is capable of
removing any substance from a crease or opening in his or
her body without closely examining it.

A special aura certainly surrounds earwax. Although it is a
normal bodily secretion of the sebaceous and the ceruminous
glands of the external ear canal, earwax is the source of considerable parental anxiety. Despite the valuable protective and
cleansing functions of this substance, many parents tell me
how "dirty" and "unsanitary" they think it is and ask me to

remove it regularly from their child's ears as a hygienic measure.

But there is nothing unhealthy or unclean about earwax. Individuals differ in the amount of wax they produce, but whether your child's ears have a little or a lot of the substance, it represents no hygienic problem and is no reflection of how well you clean your child.

The texture of earwax can vary considerably among racial groups. Both whites and blacks have predominantly a wet, sticky, honey-colored earwax that may darken on exposure to air. By contrast, the Oriental and American Indian populations manifest a dry, rice-like wax, sometimes referred to as "rice-brand" type. Studies have not yet revealed an explanation for this difference in earwax texture, or any obvious benefits of one type over the other. But an epidemiologist, Nicholas Petrakis of the University of California at San Francisco Medical Center, in researching the higher incidence of crystalline, flaky wax in both Asians and American Indians, believes that this phenomenon may be a further indication that these races shared a common ancestry before the people we now call "American Indians" migrated across the Bering Strait many centuries ago.

MYTH: *Earwax impairs hearing.*

An excessive accumulation of earwax can produce a blockage of the ear canal, which may hinder normal sound vibrations from reaching the eardrum. But this condition is uncommon in adults and rare in children. It is one of the least common causes of impaired hearing in youngsters, ranking far below middle ear infections.

MYTH: *Earwax must be periodically removed.*

I have no objections to parents using cotton swab sticks to remove small amounts of earwax that may be visible on the fleshy outer ears of their children. However, I strongly discourage using them to clean the ear canal itself. This practice tends only to push the wax farther into the canal, which risks impacting the wax, injuring the sensitive canal, and possibly rupturing the fragile eardrum.

Earwax is removed from children's ears not for hygienic or auditory reasons but to permit a doctor to clearly examine the area, particularly when a middle ear infection is suspected. If, however, a parent has repeatedly used swabs and impacted the wax, the process of removing the substance is made more difficult.

The Outer Ear

MYTH: *If a baby's ears protrude, they should be taped down.*

Throughout history, devices like straps, bands, and even bubble gum have been used to press an infant's ears inward toward the head, in the hope that as the ears grow they might become situated closer to the skull. But although there may seem to be some common sense supporting such action, ear position is determined either genetically or by the degree of compression in the uterus. No type of intervention after birth is going to change ear appearance.

Not surprisingly, protruding ears worry parents much more than the child or his or her peers. For anxious mothers and fathers, current hair styles can conceal the "unattractive" ears of their youngsters. In extreme cases, plastic surgery is an available option, although I rarely recommend it. Most people consider only their own ears, or their children's ears, to be "funny-looking." But if you glance around, you'll notice that so-called "oddities" are quite common and actually fall well within the range of normal.

MYTH: *It is safer to pierce a child's ears than an adult's.*

Some physicians have compared the piercing of ears to skin tatooing. The greatest danger with both is a risk of infection because of unsanitary instruments. A study in Seattle found that instruments used in jewelry stores often were insufficiently sterilized between each ear piercing. In the same city, a later and separate investigation studying 702 cases of viral hepatitis discovered that some of the victims were women who had no exposure to the typical causes of this illness (like contaminated hypodermic needles), but their ears had been recently pierced. Some of these women had apparently been exposed to the hepatitis virus during the ear-piercing process.

Despite the myth to the contrary, the dangers of skin infection may actually be greater in a child than an adult. After all, an adult's cleanliness habits may be more sophisticated than a child's, and proper hygiene is particularly important in the critical healing period after the piercing in order to reduce the risk of infection. To further complicate matters for both adults and children, the skin of some people reacts to the ear piercing with the formation on the lobe of unattractive, thick, fibrous scar tissue. Safety is further threatened by a squirming child, who can make the proper positioning of the hole difficult.

For these reasons, many physicians discourage the piercing of young children's ears. But if you are still certain you want your young child's ears pierced, at least have it done at a physician's office rather than at a jewelry store, in order to minimize the risks of infection.

6

NOSE

The nose is a multifunctional organ of the body. It is an important part of the body's breathing apparatus, warming, moistening, and even filtering the inhaled air, and it is the site of the nerve endings that perceive smell.

The most frequent nasal disorder—the common cold—is discussed in depth in a separate chapter. This section will focus primarily on other nasal problems, ranging from nosebleeds to hay fever. The record will be set straight on the most frequent nose-related misinformation I hear from parents.

MYTH: *Your child can have a cold in only one nostril.*

Occasionally, it will appear that your child has a cold that drains more from one nostril than the other. When this drainage has an unpleasant smell, is filled with pus, and persists for more than a week, then your child may actually have a foreign object in the nose, not a cold.

Youngsters are known to try to stick everything from peanuts to tissues into not only their nose but any other opening they can find in their bodies as well. When an object blocks nasal drainage, pus may form. If this happens with your child, you may need a doctor's help in removing the object(s). Physicians are well aware of the need to look for a second or third foreign body where the first one is found. Children are just as apt to put several beads in their nose as just one.

MYTH: *Broken noses in children must be set as soon as possible.*

Injury to the face, and particularly to the nose, is common in children. Often, as soon as this occurs, parents rush their child to a pediatrician or an emergency room, anticipating a broken nose. There may certainly be good reason to have a doctor examine the area, but even if the nose is diagnosed as broken, it's doubtful that it will be set until several days have passed.

It is true that the ideal time to set your child's nose is *immediately* after the fracture occurs. In most cases, however, by the time a physician can examine the child, the degree of swelling makes a conclusive assessment of the nose's condition difficult. The swelling, which starts almost immediately, usually peaks on the second day after the injury, and only as it subsides in the third through the seventh day can an accurate judgment finally be made. But even after a broken nose is definitively diagnosed, most surgeons and ear, nose, and throat specialists will wait five to seven days before setting it.

Despite the necessary delay in setting a broken nose, I still strongly recommend that your child see a physician as soon as possible after the injury occurs. At this time, the doctor can examine the area for a septal hematoma, which is a collection of blood in the midportion of the nose. This bleeding, if present, must be relieved in order to avert serious complications.

MYTH: *Yellow mucus draining from a child's nose must be treated with an antibiotic.*

At the first sign of yellow nasal discharges, some parents reach for the telephone, asking their pediatrician for a prescription for antibiotics. But yellow mucus is usually a normal phenomenon, no more health-threatening than clear mucus.

In the early stages of a cold, or even an allergic reaction, the mucus usually appears clear. But as time passes, and the mucus has resided in the nasal passages for several days, a secondary bacterial growth occurs, which turns the mucus yellow. It's all part of the normal process, and when caused by a cold, the mucus cannot be eradicated more quickly with an antibiotic.

In adults, a persistent, thick, yellow nasal discharge may not indicate a cold or an allergy but rather sinusitis (an inflammation of the air-filled cavities of the skull adjacent to the nose). This condition is best treated with antibiotics, which has fueled the confusion about the appropriate times to use drugs to combat mucus. Sinusitis, though, *rarely* occurs in young children, even when their parents have frequent sinus infections. In fact, until the age of six years, the sinuses are still developing and are so immature that parts of them barely show up on an x-ray. Once they fully develop, sinus infections are still infrequent, but when they do occur, they often last longer than the common cold.

Yellow mucus, then, is an expected part of the common-cold process, and unless it persists for an inordinately long time, no special treatment is necessary—particularly no antibiotics.

MYTH: *You can stop your child's nosebleeds by pressing an ice pack or key to the back of the neck or applying pressure to the upper lip.*

Nosebleeds in children are usually induced by either a drying of the nasal passages caused by an arid environment or frequent picking. About 99 percent of all nosebleeds will eventually cease by themselves without any active intervention (which may explain why various ineffective treatments have sometimes been credited with success). Even so, using reasonable and effective measures to stop a bleeding nose is obviously sensible.

There is no evidence, however, that a key applied to the back of the neck can end a nosebleed. Some parents insist, though, that it calms their child down, and as the youngster's crying and tension subside, the flow of blood stops, too. However, there is no medical basis for the theory that the key itself plays a beneficial role in this process.

Another commonly held belief is that applying pressure to the upper lip can end a nosebleed. True, pressure to the lip can compress the septal branch of the superficial artery located in the upper lip. But this artery does not supply blood to the area most responsible for bloody noses. The most common types of childhood nosebleeds are "anterior nosebleeds," in which the blood flow originates from arteries that lie deep within the face and are not affected by direct pressure to the lip.

The simplest and most effective means of treating most nosebleeds is to pinch the nostrils directly above their openings for a minimum of five to ten minutes. This pressure interrupts the blood flow and allows clot formations to begin. I also suggest exercising patience when using this technique. Sometimes, stubborn bleeding takes twenty minutes to restrain. If the bleeding lasts longer, however, contact your doctor.

MYTH: *Hay fever is an allergic reaction to hay.*

Hay fever is an allergic disorder characterized by nasal secretions, sneezing, itching, and strained breathing. But the term is a total misnomer. It is not caused by hay, nor is there a fever involved.

John Bostock, a British physician, coined the term "hay fever" in 1819, when this reaction was generally believed to be a response to hay. Also, at that time, "fever" was a word commonly applied to various physical woes, including some not associated with elevated temperatures. The clinical thermometer was not in common use in those days.

Because the term "hay fever" is now so much a part of the language, it has become a permanent fixture in the medical literature, despite the inherent discrepancies between the word and the disorder it describes. But it is not the only medical misnomer in common usage. Consider the following terms, which are equally inaccurate:

hypochondria—hypo = under; chondria = diaphram. But the word is used to describe an overexaggeration of symptoms.

hysteria—this term is derived from the Latin word *hyster*, meaning "uterus," although it is commonly applied to a psychoneurotic condition characterized by a lack of control over actions and emotions.

vitamin—vita = life; amin = a brief form of "amino acid." When this word was created, vitamins were inaccurately thought to be life-giving substances derived from amino acids.

Today, some medical etymologists believe that a more accurate term for "hay fever" would be "pollenosis," defined as a symptom resulting from contact with pollen. But custom and tradition are more powerful than the soundest reasoning, and "hay fever" will probably be with us for generations to come.

MYTH: *Yawning helps your child fall asleep.*

Numerous theories have been offered to explain yawning in almost all animal species, but its precise function remains a mystery. Surely, the yawn would not have survived the evolutionary process unless it performed a specific and important function. But while it's true that yawning frequently precedes sleep, no evidence exists that it induces the sleeping state.

Maybe the most acceptable explanation for yawning is based on the heightened sense of awareness that accompanies it. Some researchers speculate that the yawn may have once been an important survival mechanism. The yawn's muscle contractions enhance circulation in the entire body, shunting more blood to the brain in the process. Also, at the moment of yawning, a large, inhaled breath of air heightens the sensitivity of the nasal pharynx, and the sense of smell, in turn, becomes extremely keen. Perhaps many centuries ago, whenever primitive people's vulnerability increased during times of fatigue and drowsiness, the yawn served as a protective device, making them more responsive to signs of danger.

So although the yawn appears to be an attractive invitation to sleep, it may instead be an ancient survival instinct, as basic to human beings and lower animals as eating.

No one, however, knows why yawns are so contagious.

7

TEETH, TEETHING, TONGUE, TONSILS, AND THROAT

Oral hygiene, including brushing and flossing, of the primary, or baby, teeth is just as important as caring for the permanent teeth, but this aspect of child care is often neglected. Many mothers and fathers are surprised when their pediatrician or dentist informs them that their preschool youngster has cavities.

The earlier children begin regular visits to a dentist, the better chance they will have of preventing dental problems later in life. About half of all children have at least one cavity by their second birthday, and consequently, that first trip to the dentist's office ideally should be between two and three years of age. Yet 50 percent of all children in the United States under fifteen years have never been cared for by a dentist. Because dental problems can be both financially and emotionally costly to treat, the earlier a particular problem is detected and cared for, the better.

As well as dealing with myths about primary and permanent teeth, tooth decay, and fluoridation, this chapter will also discuss issues related to both teething and tonsils.

The Teeth and the Mouth

MYTH: *Some children will have three sets of teeth rather than the usual two.*

There are many historical references to some individuals having not only primary (baby) and permanent teeth, but also a full third set of teeth. Most dental authorities, however, doubt that this has ever occurred.

The source of this myth undoubtedly rests in the fact that a few babies are actually born with a tooth or two. These so-called *natal* teeth are imbedded in a pad of soft tissue lining the gum, usually in the lower jaw region. As well as being inadequately developed (small size, poor texture, yellow-brownish color), these teeth usually are loosely attached because of undeveloped roots. In about 90 percent of all cases, these natal teeth are merely primary teeth that appear early rather than being true extra teeth.

In a few children, some teeth break through the gum shortly *after* birth. They, too, are usually primary teeth, and are referred to as *neonatal* teeth.

Because both natal and neonatal teeth are rarely attached securely to the gums, they may easily become dislodged, whereupon the baby can either swallow them or choke on them. They can also contribute to sores on the infant's lips, tongue, and gums, as well as on the mother's nipples during nursing. For these reasons, most dentists and pediatricians recommend that they be removed. True, because these teeth are usually primary teeth, and not true supernumerary, or extra, teeth, they will not be replaced for several years, not until the permanent teeth appear. Still, a missing baby tooth is preferable to the risk of a newborn choking on a dislodged natal or neonatal tooth. In some cases, at about two to three years of age, the child is fitted with a space maintainer to preserve room for the eventual permanent tooth and to prevent possible speech problems or tongue thrusting, which can occasionally be the consequence of this early loss.

Incidentally, throughout history, many famous individuals have been born with teeth. Louis XIV, for example, was born with two teeth, as was Richard III. In earlier times, this early appearance of teeth was considered a sign of vigor. Today, however, dentists know of no relationship between vigor and natal teeth.

MYTH: *Later teeth are stronger; early teeth are softer and thus more cavity-prone.*

Some parents believe that early-erupting baby teeth are more prone to develop cavities. But that is not the case. The first primary tooth is usually one of the lower front teeth, or incisors, and it usually appears between six and ten months of age, although it occasionally surfaces as early as age three months or as late as one year. But no matter when the primary teeth initially begin breaking through, they are extremely hard and strong. In fact, the enamel that covers the teeth is the hardest tissue in the body, even harder than iron or gold.

Enamel consists of tiny calcium crystals. The calcification of the teeth begins before birth, and is approximately 20 percent complete when the child is born. The entire calcification process of the primary teeth is complete by the age of one year, with all twenty primary teeth usually erupting by 2½ years. Although dietary inadequacies can cause deficiencies in enamel production, this phenomenon is extremely rare in developed countries. Metabolic disturbances, certain infectious diseases, and drug ingestion can affect enamel production as well, but these, too, occur infrequently. Tetracycline is the most notorious of the drugs that can cause enamel defects, and thus is rarely prescribed for children and pregnant women.

In general, the susceptibility of your children's teeth to decay is primarily dependent on the youngsters' inherent genetic propensity and overall well-being, as well as the fluoride intake and the degree of exposure to cavity-forming sweets. No correlation exists between decay and the age when tooth eruption occurs. However, if a child is consuming fluoride, the later teeth will probably be less cavity-prone because of the positive effects of this decay-fighting substance.

MYTH: *Cavities in your child's baby teeth do not need to be treated.*

Some parents believe that cavities in their child's baby teeth can be ignored. After all, they say, these teeth are simply going to fall out anyway, replaced by permanent teeth. So why treat them?

For that reason, baby teeth are frequently left unbrushed and cavities dismissed. However, tooth decay, when untreated, can result in abscess formation which, spreading into the gums themselves, ultimately can lead to irreversible damage to the underlying permanent teeth. Cavities can also cause considerable pain, particularly when the decay envelops the pulp (the soft tissue in the center of the tooth that contains nerves).

The primary teeth lay the foundation for the permanent teeth to follow. A set of healthy, well-positioned baby teeth will promote normal, postnatal development of the jaw, which, in turn, will encourage normally positioned permanent teeth.

MYTH: *The more candy or other sugary foods your children consume, the more cavities they will develop.*

Although sugar combined with bacteria in the mouth leads to enamel-destroying acid formation on the teeth, the quantity of the sugar consumed is not nearly as important as the amount of time the sugar spends in contact with the teeth. The teeth of a child who brushes immediately after eating ten chocolate bars are at less risk for decay than those of a child sucking for a long period of time on a single piece of hard candy who doesn't follow this with brushing. If your youngster has a sweet tooth and is prone to cavities, it's best to limit consumption of candy or other sugary foods to a single time of the day, after which you should encourage your child to brush without delay. Bedtime is too late.

Many foods besides candy can contribute to the creation of cavities. Sticky or gooey foods like peanut butter, jellies, jams, and dried fruits tend to prolong cavity-causing contact between sugar and the teeth. So especially when a toothbrush isn't handy, try to emphasize crispy and crunchy foods that have minimal contact with the teeth.

Good brushing habits are particularly important from the time the first teeth erupt. Children under the age of eight often do not have the proper coordination to brush their teeth adequately; they particularly lack the ability to clean their back teeth. Until this age, then, parents must assume the responsibility for supervising or directly brushing their youngsters' teeth. A helpful hint: Small children will be more willing to let you brush their teeth if you let them brush yours.

MYTH: *Refined sugar causes more cavities than honey or raw sugar.*

In terms of the amount of sucrose in each, the variance among honey, raw sugar, and refined sugar is negligible. For instance, raw sugar contains 98 percent sucrose, whereas refined sugar contains 99.9 percent, a difference so minimal that it is hardly worth the effort to give your children raw sugar rather than refined sugar for tooth-saving purposes alone. Honey isn't a better alternative either, since its sticky properties prolong contact with the teeth, promoting decay. Instead, you should be trying to *eliminate completely* as many of the unnecessary sources of sugar in your youngsters' diet as possible.

For a discussion of the dangers of honey to infants, see page 25.

MYTH: *Nothing is wrong with allowing babies to fall asleep with a bottle of juice, sweetened liquid, or milk in their mouths.*

Many parents notice that their baby can be soothed to sleep quickly while sucking on a bottle. This practice seems particularly appealing on nights when mother and dad are extremely tired, and thus neither can really tolerate a prolonged struggle to get baby to bed.

As common as this practice is, it must be discouraged once the primary teeth have appeared. In recent years, pediatricians have become particularly sensitive to the potentially destructive nature of this "nursing-bottle syndrome." Decay can flourish in teeth with prolonged, direct contact with fruit juices, milk, or sweetened water. Some children between the ages of one and three years have lost all of their affected teeth and have developed serious problems with their permanent teeth as well.

Here is what typically occurs: the bottle is given to the baby as a pacifier, and as the infant dozes off, the nipple is still in the mouth, and milk or juice settles there. The lactose in the milk, or the sugar in the juice, coats the teeth, and after it interacts with the normal bacteria in the mouth, the resulting acid begins eating away at the enamel. The upper front teeth are usually the most severely affected, because of their direct contact with the nipple. By contrast, the bottom teeth are protected by the tongue. Children who usually sleep on their sides will often develop cavities on only one side of the mouth.

I often suggest that parents never give their baby anything but milk from a bottle. Juices need not be started prior to eight months of age, at which time children can learn to drink from a cup. This both simplifies the weaning process and prevents the child from becoming accustomed to sucking on sweetened juices from the bottle and not wanting to stop.

MYTH: *Fluoride causes cancer and heart disease.*

Fluoride, a mineral that occurs naturally in most water supplies, makes tooth enamel more resistant to cavity-causing acid. Even so, there has been scattered but constant opposition to the use of fluoride by a number of outspoken groups. Some claim that fluoride is poisoning the population, promoting everything from cancer to heart disease to kidney dysfunction. Others view it as "forced medication," while some insist that adding fluoride to a municipal water system conflicts with freedom of choice. A few political extremists have even claimed that it is a Communist plot, intended to weaken our brains and make mass brainwashing possible.

Yet, the evidence in favor of fluoridation is conclusive. Studies clearly show that fluoridation reduces the rate of tooth decay by as much as 60 to 80 percent, with an accompanying decrease in the frequency and expense of necessary dental treatment. When consumed in proper quantities between birth and eight to sixteen years of age, fluoride can produce a lifetime decline in dental disease.

None of the serious side effects claimed by fluoride's opponents has ever been found by rigorous academic researchers. Public health records show no difference in mortality rates—or in the fequency of heart disease, kidney disease, or cancer—between fluoridated and nonfluoridated communities. The only health problem that is affected by fluoride is tooth decay; in areas with fluoridated water, dental disease is significantly less.

True, some recent publicity has been given to a condition called fluorosis, which is a faint staining of the teeth noticed in some children taking fluoride supplements. However, it occurs only in children consuming dosages larger than those currently recommended. If you follow your own doctor's advice, your children will avoid this problem.

It's not surprising, then, that fluoride has such widespread support among professional medical groups. Its advocates include the American Medical Association, the American Dental Association, the American Heart Association, the Surgeon General, the American Public Health Association, the American Society for Pharmacology in Experimental Therapeutics, and the Food and Drug Administration.

MYTH: *Babies don't need fluoride.*

The most important time for a child to consume fluoride is when tooth enamel is being formed. During this period, the fluoride is incorporated into the so-called hydroxyapatite component of the enamel, and once there, it remains for the life of the tooth. The primary (baby) teeth begin calcification in utero; the first permanent teeth don't erupt until age six, but their crowns start calcifying just after birth. This calcification process of the permanent teeth isn't completed until age eight to twelve years, so it is particularly essential that every youngster be supplied with the recommended doses of fluoride starting soon after birth and continuing throughout the calcification period.

Consult your doctor or dentist about the fluoride needs of your own children. Specific recommendations will be based, in part, on the amount of fluoride in your municipal water supply. If the fluoride level is low, most experts recommend dietary supplementation, no matter what the child's age is. Also, because human milk contains only trace amounts of fluoride, doctors usually suggest that fluoride drops be given to nursing babies who are not also drinking water with fluoride in it.

As general guidelines, the American Academy of Pediatricians provides these recommendations for fluoride dosages:

In communities with less than 0.3 parts per million (ppm) of fluoride, 0.25 mg is suggested for children between two weeks and two years old, 0.5 mg between ages two and three years, and 1 mg between ages three and sixteen.

In areas with between 0.3 and 0.7 ppm of fluoride, no fluoride
supplement is recommended for the first two years of life,
0.25 mg between ages two and three, and 0.5 mg between
three and sixteen years.
In areas with greater than 0.7 ppm of fluoride, no fluoride
supplementation is recommended.

MYTH: *Chewing gum can clean your child's teeth, helping to
avoid cavities.*

As convincing as those chewing gum commercials on
TV may seem, gum does *not* clean teeth. Only regular and
thorough brushing and flossing does. So while gum may provide
good exercise for your child's jaw, it cannot do much more.

Most chewing gum increases the amount of time the teeth
are exposed to sugar. Thus, if your youngster is a gum chewer,
buy only the sugarless variety.

MYTH: *A permanent tooth that has been knocked out is gone
forever.*

Not too many years ago, when a tooth was completely
dislodged, usually in an accident, nothing was done to replant
it. That is still the case with baby teeth. But recent advances
in replantation surgery have made this procedure a workable
reality for permanent teeth, with an amazingly high success
rate if done shortly after the injury. When the process is carried
out within thirty minutes of the accident, the tooth has a 90
percent chance of being saved. By contrast, if replantation is
not done until two hours or more after the tooth has been
displaced, the success rate is only 5 percent.

If your child has an accident in which a permanent tooth
is knocked out, here is the process to follow:

After finding the tooth, wash it in cold water, without scrubbing or touching the root. Then, while holding the tooth by
its crown, gently insert it back into its socket, and proceed
to the dentist's office. However, if you or the child are too

nervous to try planting the tooth yourself, then place it under the child's tongue (but only if the youngster is old enough to be able to hold it there without swallowing it), where it can be bathed in saliva, which is the best transplant medium. If your child is particularly anxious, place the tooth instead under *your* tongue, in order to maintain contact with saliva. Be careful during your trip to the dentist's office to avoid quick stops that could catapult the tooth into the back of the mouth, causing choking or swallowing.

MYTH: *Children should not be allowed to suck their thumb beyond the age of two.*

Various studies have shown from that 61 to 87 percent of all infants and young children suck either pacifiers, thumbs, or fingers. Thumb suckers are often born, not created, with numerous photographs documenting the beginning of sucking in utero among seven-month-old fetuses.

Most children will stop thumb sucking on their own by the age of three to four years, and there is usually no need for parental concern until that time. However, from the age of four through the early teenage years, when the teeth, gums and jaw structure are progressing through their most dramatic growth phases, parents should actively discourage their children from continuing this habit. Persistence after 3½ to four years can contribute to overbites and other developmental problems. Various methods can be used to deter sucking, from behavior modification to dental appliances to bandaging the thumb.

Incidentally, the "experts" disagree on the reasons behind a child continuing the thumb-sucking habit beyond the age of five. While some say it indicates delayed emotional growth, others insist that it is nothing more than a learned behavior. Unless there are signs of psychological problems in your child, however, don't worry about thumb sucking having deep emotional significance.

MYTH: *A pacifier is worse for your baby than thumb sucking.*

All babies have, to some degree, a sucking instinct. Were it not for thumbs, fingers, pacifiers, and bottles, they would probably find some other means of satisfying this apparent need.

A couple generations ago, before the creation of pacifiers as we know them, parents gave "sugarteats" to their babies, which were nothing more than a rag or a section of diaper that was tied into a nipple-like shape and dipped into a sweetened solution. When sucked upon, this had the same calming effect that thumb sucking or the modern pacifier has.

Parents often have mixed feelings about pacifiers. Before their child is born, some mothers and fathers insist that their child will never use a pacifier, which they consider a psychological crutch and a possible detriment to normal tooth development. However, once the baby has arrived, and the parents can't seem to calm the cranky newborn, a pacifier is often turned to as the solution. All the while, though, parents may still be convinced that the pacifier is worse for tooth development than thumb sucking.

In fact, both pacifiers and thumb sucking may cause some dental problems, especially if the habit persists while the permanent teeth are erupting. The severity of any disorder hinges on the force of the sucking, and how often and for how long it continues. But the object being sucked—whether pacifier or thumb—does not seem to influence the problem at all.

Many pediatricians believe that, in some ways, pacifiers are preferable to thumb sucking. Between the ages of one to two years, parents frequently take the pacifier permanently away from the youngster, and after several unhappy days, the child adjusts to its absence. Most often these children do not revert to their hands for an alternative. By contrast, a child who has been thumb sucking from birth cannot have the thumb permanently removed when mom or dad decides that it's time to stop.

Pacifiers are much safer than they once were, particularly since mouth guards have been added to prevent babies from choking on or swallowing the devices. According to U.S. Consumer Product Safety Commission regulations that went into effect in 1978, all pacifiers must now have this safety guard, as well as: an easily grasped handle, an inseparable nipple and mouthguard, and two holes in the shield to prevent choking if the pacifier is swallowed. There also cannot be a cord or a ribbon attached, which a parent could tie around the baby's neck. The most popular pacifier is now the Nuk, orthodontically designed to prevent tongue thrusting, which some dentists believe contributes to an overbite. Also, the unique shape of this pacifier prevents any abnormal forward pressure on the front teeth, a pressure that can occur with thumb sucking.

MYTH: *Children who are tongue-tied at birth need to have their tongues clipped.*

If you stand before a mirror, open your mouth wide, and raise your tongue, you will notice a piece of flesh that attaches the lower portion of the tongue to the base of the mouth. This anatomical structure, called the frenulum, can appear prominent or look small while still falling within the range of normal. The term "tongue-tied" refers to a condition in which the frenulum appears abnormally short, thick, or taut, restraining the tongue so that it cannot easily move forward. This condition is extremely uncommon.

In earlier generations, parents often blamed any speech disorder in their child on the frenulum and rushed to their doctor to have this small part of the anatomy clipped to improve the tongue's maneuverability. In fact, this surgical procedure was once quite in vogue. However, the relationship between tongue tie and any type of speech disorder is, at best, now questionable. Several recent reports indicate that about 7 percent of the childhood population has some kind of speech disorder. Most are articulatory problems and afflict primarily younger children. Research shows, however, that tongue-tie is rarely to blame for these articulatory defects. In a study of 1000 youngsters brought to ear, nose, and throat surgeons because of "short frenulums," only 4 percent actually had speech irregularities.

Today, specialists generally suggest that frenulums *not* be clipped because of the potential for hemorrhaging, infection, and residual scar tissue. Most children who do have a short frenulum and also have an associated speech disorder can be taught to speak properly without resorting to any surgical procedures. When surgery is performed, it usually does not remedy the speech problem, except in cases where the tip of the tongue had been almost totally immobilized. This surgery is rarely performed today, and in fact, most ear, nose, and throat surgeons have never even seen a case of a tongue truly bound down.

MYTH: *A baby tooth, placed under the pillow, will prompt a visit by the Tooth Fairy, who will replace the tooth with money.*

No one has ever seen the Tooth Fairy, so we must consider him/her part of our folklore. Even so, Stephen J. Moss, in his book *Your Child's Teeth*, defends the Tooth Fairy and the widely publicized, late-night depositing of coins: "This has happened in experiment after experiment, in generations of families. Dentists are at a loss to explain this scientifically, but reassure their patients that anything that makes losing primary teeth a little more fun is dentally okay."

Teething

MYTH: *Teething can cause fever.*

Not long ago, a mother told me that her baby had recently had a 104°F (40°C) temperature, but she wasn't particularly concerned because the infant was teething. Numerous studies, however, reveal *no* connection between high fevers and teething. A low-grade temperature of *under* 100.4°F (38°C) is frequently seen in teething children, but such minimal elevations of temperature can also be experienced by healthy youngsters of all ages (see pages 39–40). No medical evidence exists to substantiate a correlation between teething and fevers greater than 100.4°F (38°C).

Interestingly, in a 1975 survey of Philadelphia pediatricians, more than 25 percent of them believed that a temperature above 100.4°F (38°C) could be explained by teething. Apparently, they had not read the recent convincing studies such as the one conducted by Arvi Tasanen of Finland, who made daily observations of 126 teething babies. Although he noted a relationship between teething and gum rubbing, thumb sucking and some increase in salivation, he found no connection between fevers and the eruption of teeth.

Then how can we explain the origin of this commonly held belief? The level of a child's antibodies decreases to its lowest point at four to six months of age, as the antibodies transferred to the newborn through the placenta lose their potency. Consequently, various common viral infections develop during this time of increased susceptibility, with fever as one of their symptoms. This occurs simultaneously with the onset of teeth eruption, and thus parents and some doctors connect these two phenomena. However, if your baby has a fever exceeding 100.4°F (38°C), do not attribute it to teething.

MYTH: *Teething causes seizures.*

Hippocrates thought that teething children suffered from seizures. Even as recently as the early 1900s, some pediatric textbooks still promoted this belief. But studies by Dr. Tasanen (see preceding myth) and others have found no such link.

Seizures, however, do sometimes occur when high fevers are present, and if the child happens to be teething at the same time, parents may find it less anxiety-producing to blame the seizure on the eruption of new teeth. This may be comforting, but is untrue.

MYTH: *Teething causes severe diarrhea.*

There is some evidence that teething may be accompanied by loose stools, which can persist for weeks, but cause no significant decrease in weight. However, this phenomenon is quite different from the severe diarrhea associated with gastroenteritis (inflammation of the stomach and intestines), which may involve vomiting, five to twenty watery stools a day, and loss of weight. If your child is experiencing severe diarrhea like this, teething is almost certainly not the cause, and your doctor should be contacted.

MYTH: *Teething causes crying, irritability, and restlessness.*

There is some truth to this belief. But I find that parents are much too eager to blame their baby's unruly behavior on teething. In fact, there are many other reasons why a baby may cry or exhibit irritability, and mothers and fathers should be sensitive to them as well.

Writing on the subject of teething in *Clinical Pediatrics* (1973), Ronald L. Van der Horst noted that while physical factors can play a role in phenomena like sleep disturbances:

Emotional factors such as being spoiled, overexcited, fatigued, or overstimulated are other reasons why a baby may wake up and cry. Few parents will accept these reasons as valid—in particular, between five months to a year of age.

An infant is able to recognize his own individuality and personality even at a young age. Fussiness in infancy is a problem which requires careful consideration and understanding; the true reason is often obscured by parental misinterpretations. Mothers who cannot quiet their ailing infant often feel inadequate. Conflicting advice from well-meaning friends and relations adds confusion. When the truth is thus obscured, the easy solution is to ascribe the problems to "teething."

MYTH: *Teething causes facial rashes.*

In a definitive study on teething, Arvi Tasanen discovered no relationship between the eruption of new teeth and facial rashes. Even so, some people still insist that such rashes are a symptom of teething, presumably provoked when babies rub their face against the sheets of their crib, which are wet with saliva from their drooling. This initation is not a rash and is a relatively infrequent and insignificant phenomenon. There is no need for parents to worry about it. Ointment or lotion need not be applied.

MYTH: *Drooling indicates that your infant is teething.*

When babies are about four months old, their parents frequently ask, "Is my child teething? He is drooling so much." Although it is true that babies begin drooling noticeably at about the same time that their first teeth appear, there is little direct relationship between these phenomena. After birth, the salivary glands become very active on their own, and in fact, the production of saliva reaches its peak at around four to six months old. Because the newborn has not yet learned to swallow the saliva completely, much of it drools from the mouth. The first tooth usually emerges between six and eight months of age, and some research indicates that as new teeth come through, there may be small increases in drooling. Even so, this additional drooling is minimal compared to the normal saliva production and overflow already present at that age.

Drooling, then, does not necessarily indicate that a child is cutting a tooth, and in most cases it is simply part of the normal developmental process.

MYTH: *Children who place objects in their mouth are teething.*

Beginning at approximately four months of age, children have usually developed sufficient hand-eye motor coordination to grasp an object and bring it up to their mouth. This becomes their primary means of exploring their immediate environment. Babies will chew, suck, and bite on objects as a way of becoming acquainted with the world.

True, the discomfort of cutting a tooth may be soothed by some form of oral stimulation. But generally, placing objects in the mouth is more indicative of a developmental phase than a sign of teething.

MYTH: *A teething child needs pain medication to relieve the discomfort.*

The pain typically associated with teething is probably widely exaggerated. That is the conclusion of several investigators who believe that, as I discussed above, childhood restlessness and irritability can have many causes other than teething discomfort. They wonder why youngsters describe only minor discomfort when their permanent teeth are coming in. Could it really be that the emergence of permanent teeth is so much less painful than the eruption of primary teeth?

Some pediatricians suggest that parents give their teething babies one of the topical, over-the-counter medications that are designed to anesthetize the gums. However, there is a potential problem with these agents. Infants may become sensitized to this substance, and consequently later in life, if they require local anesthesia (perhaps to have a tooth extracted), they may be susceptible to an allergic reaction. Also, even if you accept the premise that teething causes prolonged discomfort, a medication like these that provide only ten to fifteen minutes of relief would hardly be effective.

Equally valuable, and probably safer, is a standard teething ring. In some cases, it may provide a slight numbing effect, but primarily it can serve as an effective distraction.

MYTH: *Cutting the gum with a spoon will ease any discomfort associated with the eruption of a new tooth.*

A new tooth, whether primary or permanent, does not really *cut* through the gum, but rather pushes out by gradual movement. The outdated practice of piercing the gums with a knife or spoon edge undoubtedly caused more pain than the natural process and is totally unnecessary.

Tonsils and the Throat

MYTH: *Most children need tonsillectomies.*

As recently as the mid-1950s, few children reached their sixth birthday with their tonsils intact. However, many physicians have come full circle on this issue. Modern medicine now feels that the tonsils have an important role to play in the body's defense system, and thus they should not be removed routinely.

Tonsils are lymphoid tissues, and are the throat's initial defense against infection. When a child has a throat infection, it is no surprise that tonsillitis is diagnosed, as the tonsils have become swollen and inflamed while fighting the infection. If the tonsils have been removed, the next line of defense—the lymph nodes in the neck—must then assume the burden of battling any invading bacteria or virus.

Most pediatricians now believe that the removal of the tonsils is indicated unequivocally only in cases of malignancy, obstruction of the airway, or a peritonsillar abscess (a severe infection that involves the tonsils and the surrounding tissue). Under some circumstances, a tonsillectomy may also be appropriate when severe tonsillitis occurs repeatedly, particularly in cases of streptococcal infections.

But there is not yet enough evidence to indicate whether removal of the tonsils is actually justified when a child has recurring sore throats, repeated enlargement of the lymph nodes, recurrent upper respiratory tract infections, large tonsils covered with debris, difficulty in swallowing, or snoring. In these instances, your child's doctor must decide on the most appropriate course of action.

Despite the reversal of thinking about tonsillectomies by physicians, this surgery is still among the most common and is a major medical expenditure. In 1976, when W. Shaikh reviewed twenty-nine studies of tonsillectomies covering a fifty-year period, he found that every study written by an otolaryngologist (ear, nose, and throat surgeon) approved of this operation. These specialists, of course, are those who most benefit financially from this procedure. He concluded that the studies did not convincingly show that a tonsillectomy is advantageous to the patient in most of the cases in which it is performed, and he recommended, because of the enormous financial and human costs associated with this operation, that very strict criteria be used in deciding when the surgery is proper.

MYTH: *Removing the tonsils will eliminate your child's sore throats.*

Some studies have actually substantiated the belief that a tonsillectomy will prevent sore throats. However, these researchers generally overlooked the fact that children often outgrow the tendency to have sore throats and thus would have had less frequent infections anyway, with or without tonsils.

The general consensus within the medical community now is that streptococcal sore throats are more common in children *with* their tonsils. But at least 80 to 90 percent of all sore throats are viral, not streptococcal, and their incidence is essentially unaffected by the presence or absence of the tonsils.

Tonsillectomies can prevent any chance of contracting tonsillitis (because the tonsils are gone), but children will still get sore throats and run fevers when infections are present.

MYTH: *Your doctor can determine if your child has a strep throat simply by looking.*

Occasionally, a streptococcal epidemic sweeps through a community. In these instances, a high percentage of patients complaining of sore throats have strep infections. But except for these rare epidemic circumstances, a doctor needs more than just a visual examination to diagnose this condition properly.

Two major studies have examined this question, one in 1954, the other in 1977. The earlier study found that certain symptoms (severe sore throat, extreme swelling, vomiting, chills, headache, and abdominal pain) were related primarily to strep throat; others (cough and hoarseness) more probably indicated a viral infection. Still, both studies came to the identical conclusion: even under ideal circumstances, physicians performing only a visual examination properly diagnose viral sore throats only about 70 percent of the time; with strep throat, their accuracy rate drops to about 50 percent. The researchers agreed that a throat culture is the only way to tell with certainty if a strep throat is actually present. Since this determination would also influence the course of treatment, including whether an antibiotic should be prescribed, the studies recommended that a throat culture be performed on all children over the age of two suffering from a sore throat.

MYTH: *Younger children are just as susceptible to strep throat as older children.*

Statistics show that streptococcal tonsillitis is much less common in children under two years of age than in older children. In a study of forty-seven children under three years old who had tonsils covered with pus, only 14 percent had a streptococcal infection. When streptococcus does infect a child this young, the primary symptom is usually a runny nose that may persist for four to six weeks, rather than the sore throat usually seen in older youngsters.

MYTH: *Penicillin will make strep throat feel better faster.*

Several studies indicate that children will probably recover from a strep throat just as rapidly whether they receive penicillin or not. When penicillin is prescribed for a streptococcal infection, its primary function is not to alleviate the immediate symptoms, but to prevent complications like rheumatic fever.

In a 1953 study conducted by Floyd Denny, several different antibiotics, including penicillin, were used to treat patients with streptococcal tonsillitis and pharyngitis. A separate group of patients did not receive any antibiotics. Dr. Denny found that penicillin only mildly affected the natural course of the disease, reducing the normal five-to-six-day duration of symptoms by only one to 1½ days.

In my own practice, unless a child is seriously ill with high fever, severe sore throat, headache, and abdominal pains, I refrain from prescribing penicillin until I receive the results of a throat culture, which normally takes twenty-four to forty-eight hours. When a child has only a mild to moderate throat infection, research shows, penicillin treatment can begin within ten days of its onset and still protect against rheumatic fever and other complications. Because an individual who is repeatedly exposed to a particular antibiotic, including penicillin, risks developing sensitivity to that drug, I advise waiting for the culture results rather than routinely starting treatment.

8

HEAD

A certain mystique has always surrounded the human head, primarily because the brain—the center of consciousness and intellect—and all the primary sense organs are located there. Parents treat injuries to the head with much greater concern and importance than injuries elsewhere, and normal, temporary variations in infant head shape can cause anxiety in even the most unexcitable parent. This chapter may serve to alleviate some of the anxiety caused by myths about the head.

MYTH: *All head injuries should be x-rayed.*

A blow to a child's head can be more emotionally distressing to mother and father than an injury to any other part of the body. Parents immediately imagine the worst, fearing a skull fracture and even brain damage. They often insist that an x-ray of the head be taken and are relieved if their pediatrician orders one, assuming that this would determine *for certain* the extent of the injury.

But although many physicians and hospital emergency rooms order skull x-rays almost routinely, several recent investigations question this policy. Contrary to popular belief, the presence of a skull fracture alone does not necessarily indicate that the prognosis is worse than if the fracture did not exist. In fact, some research shows that a skull fracture may actually *decrease* the chances of serious problems, because part of the blow has been absorbed by the skull itself instead of being transmitted to the underlying brain tissue. Your physician's treatment plan, then, will be dependent primarily on your child's appearance and a neurological examination (checking reflexes, balance, etc.) and should not be significantly influenced by the presence or absence of a skull fracture as indicated by an x-ray.

Numerous studies have concluded that skull x-rays should be taken only under certain high-risk circumstances, including coma, unconsciousness, unusual drowsiness, a foreign body in the head, a depressed fracture, and certain other specific neurological findings. If these guidelines were followed, the number of skull x-rays could be reduced dramatically, without subjecting the patient to unnecessary danger or reducing the quality of medical care. One study showed that most skull x-rays of children are taken because parents demand them or because doctors order them to protect themselves in this era of obsession with lawsuits. These researchers observed that at least 20 to 30 percent of the 8 million x-rays of the head and neck in the United States each year could be eliminated, at a net savings to patients, insurance companies, and the government of $15 to $20 million annually.

So if your child suffers a blow to the head, the decision about taking a skull x-ray should be based on the circumstances of the accident and the condition of your youngster as determined by your physician rather than on the preconceived (and inaccurate) notion that an x-ray is always necessary.

MYTH: *All children who fall out of bed or from a crib or*
a sofa must be examined by a physician
for head injuries.

At some time almost all youngsters fall out of bed, off a swing, or from some other elevation. When this happens, parents usually feel both guilty and frightened, and they run for the telephone to call their pediatrician.

Fortunately, however, rarely do these children incur an injury serious enough to warrant a pediatrician's attention. A

1977 study at Michigan State University by Ray E. Helfer and Thomas L. Slovis sought to determine the nature and likelihood of injuries resulting when children aged five and under fell from a bed or a sofa. In 80 percent of the cases examined, there were no observable injuries, and in 17 percent, there were only minor bumps, bruises, and scratches. Just 3 percent of the children suffered more severe injuries—fractured clavicles, skull fractures, fractured arms—that warranted medical attention. *None* of the youngsters experienced any injury in which life was threatened or permanent damage resulted.

Thus, serious head injuries are extremely rare in falls from beds, cribs, or sofas. But if you have any question as to the seriousness of a bump or blow to your child, you should certainly contact your pediatrician.

MYTH: *Never let a child who has suffered a head injury fall asleep.*

Remember the nursery rhyme about the old man who "bumped his head and went to bed and couldn't get up in the morning"? Childhood stories like this taught most of us to fear going to sleep after a blow to the head. But this concern needs to be explored.

Head injuries are more common than you might imagine. They usually occur late in the day when youngsters are tired and more accident-prone. After the blow to the head, and after the crying spell that usually follows, it's not surprising that the child is exhausted and might want to sleep. If a child cannot be kept awake after a head injury (day or night), the child should be checked. But I often receive late-evening calls from parents exclaiming, "Billy hit his head a couple of hours ago. He wants to go to sleep now, but I think I should keep him awake, don't you?" In fact, there's no increased risk in permitting sleep at this time. If a head injury is going to worsen, it will do so whether your child is sleeping or awake.

What is the basis of this myth? Parents are concerned that their child will lapse into a coma as a result of a head injury. Obviously, if their youngster is awake and talking, this apprehension will be eased, at least for the moment. Thus, I'm not surprised that so many parents feel most comfortable when their child is awake and talking to them. But if the youngster is coherent and lucid, and is ready for bed and wants to sleep, I usually suggest that the tired child be allowed to sleep, with the stipulation that the child be awakened every two hours throughout the night. If the youngster is alert and responds coherently to your questions ("How are you feeling?," "Does your head hurt at all?") after being awakened, then he or she is fine and can be allowed to return to sleep. In itself, sleep is not bad for the child; while asleep, however, the youngster can't be observed as well. Consequently, following a significant blow to the head, check your child approximately every two hours, whether he or she is awake or asleep.

A doctor should definitely be contacted if your youngster demonstrates any of the following symptoms after receiving a head injury:

- Unconsciousness or any loss of consciousness, no matter how brief.
- Stiffness of the neck, weakness or inability to move the limbs, or loss of coordination.
- Drainage of blood or clear fluid from the ear or nose (but note that children with colds at the time of the accident will already have runny noses).
- A blank stare, crossed eyes, or pupils unequal in size.
- A complaint of a persistent or increasingly severe headache.
- Persistent dizziness beyond 45 minutes after the injury.
- The inability to become aroused to a fully alert state, no matter what time of day or night.

- Repeated vomiting. Although one or two vomiting episodes are not unusual after a head injury, persistent vomiting may indicate a serious problem.

MYTH: *If amnesia occurs after a blow to the head, a second blow will bring the memory back.*

Following a significant head injury, usually accompanied by a concussion, a condition called retrograde amnesia may occur, in which past events cannot be recalled. The forgotten events may represent a block of time dating back minutes or years from the time of the accident.

No one really understands exactly why and how this memory loss develops, but fortunately, memory almost always returns gradually, although it may occasionally take months to years to do so. As the memory comes back, older events that had been forgotten return first, and with time the period of memory loss eventually disappears completely, although the actual incident that caused the amnesia is usually never remembered.

A second blow should not intentionally be struck in an attempt to return a child's memory. Although this procedure is often seen in cartoons and slapstick comedies, it is never effective in real life and can cause even more serious damage.

MYTH: *Head banging is a sign that your child is retarded.*

Intentional and repeated banging of the head against the crib by your baby does not mean that your infant is or will become retarded or hyperactive. As unusual as the behavior may appear, it is relatively common among children. While some severely retarded people persistently display various exaggerated, rhythmic behaviors, periodic head banging or body rocking is quite normal in young children and even in a small number of older ones.

Head banging, like body rocking, is one of those rhythmic behaviors that seem to have no real purpose other than self-stimulation. Head banging occurs in as many as 15 percent of all children and typically begins at about eight months of age, usually stopping before the fourth year. It is three times more prevalent in boys than girls and usually occurs at bedtime, when the child is tired, upset, or irritable. By contrast, body rocking affects 21 percent of all children, with onset at six to ten months of age, usually stopping by 2½ to three years. Many head bangers were body rockers first.

Studies have shown that most children who exhibit these rhythmic behaviors have excellent motor coordination. Except in the severely retarded, this behavior does not deter growth and other normal development. Head banging and body rocking disappear in adults, but interestingly, many people still have some remnants of body rocking well into adulthood. Did you ever notice a person sway from side to side while talking or lecturing? It is interesting to note that such people usually sway or rock at a rate similar to the heartbeat (about sixty beats per minute).

MYTH: *If you touch the "soft spot" on your baby's head, you can poke a hole in it; Never pull a nipple or pacifier too quickly out of a baby's mouth, or it will "pop" the soft spot.*

See pages 26–27.

9

HAIR

Human hair is composed primarily of a dense form of keratin, the same substance that constitutes the outer layer of the skin. But parents are typically interested in more than the physical makeup of their child's hair. These are some of the questions I am frequently asked: Is it normal for a newborn to be bald? Will the cutting of hair affect its growth? Can frequent shampooing cause hair loss? Will hair color affect a youngster's disposition? This section will answer these questions and clarify some misconceptions about the hair of children.

MYTH: *Children cannot suffer from baldness.*

Certainly there are more bald men than women or children, but they do not have a monopoly on hair loss. Women and even children may also develop varying degrees of baldness.

In youngsters, hair loss is usually reversible. The most common type is called alopecia areata, in which hair unexplainably falls out in patches. This phenomenon may cease and then reappear again and again throughout childhood, and some researchers believe it could be stress-related.

Children who consistently wear their hair pulled tightly into pigtails or braids also sometimes experience temporary baldness, always limited to the area where the greatest stress has been placed upon the hair roots. A phenomenon called trichotelomania can also occur in children, in which youngsters pull out their own hair, usually in the very front or back of the head. This tends to be a nervous habit carried to an extreme.

There are other rarer causes of childhood baldness, which are the result of various medications (including anticancer drugs) and autoimmune diseases. If your youngster is exhibiting any type of excessive hair loss, consult your pediatrician.

MYTH: *All babies become bald after birth.*

Several weeks after birth, a baby completely sheds the fine downy hair on the head and other parts of the body; even so, many babies *never* become totally bald. In all babies a new layer of hairs begins growing at around the sixth week of age. If this process begins before the original hair has all fallen out your child will never appear bald. There is no way to predict what will happen with a particular infant.

MYTH: *A baby with thick hair will have thin hair later in life; conversely, a baby with thin hair will develop thick hair.*

Although this myth is frequently raised by parents in my office, there is no scientific evidence to support it. The texture and consistency of a baby's hair does not automatically reverse later in life, but typically remains the same as the child matures.

MYTH: *Cutting a baby's hair weakens the infant.*

This myth is probably (pardon the pun) "rooted" in the biblical story of Samson and Delilah. But there is no medical substantiation for the belief that cutting the hair affects a child's (or an adult's) strength.

MYTH: *Singeing your child's hair can invigorate it.*

In the 1930s beauticians often treated their customers to a faddish process called singeing, thought to be an effective

method of invigorating hair. According to its advocates, singeing sealed the ends of the hair strands and prevented nutrient
juices from flowing out of them. The individuals subjected to
this process, however, were only wasting their time and money.
In fact, all hair cells are *dead* cells. There are no living processes
occurring in the hair itself that singeing may have encouraged.
Thus, this process was only another fad that benefited primarily
the provider (the beautician), not the customer.

MYTH: *Cutting or shaving your child's hair will make it grow
faster or thicker.*

Some women hesitate to shave their legs, convinced
that shaved hair will grow back thicker and faster. Likewise,
some teenage boys, in an attempt to make their facial hair
grow as quickly as possible, shave their chins and mustaches
several times a day, convinced that a hairier appearance will
be the eventual result. Although I'm certain that razor blade
companies are delighted with this teenage behavior, the dedi-
cated efforts of these boys in front of bathroom mirrors are
in vain, just as the concerns of the women about shaving are
unwarranted.

The issue of shaving hair has been long discussed and argued
by dermatologists, but today the nearly universal belief among
physicians is that repeated shaving will *not* make hair grow
back either faster or thicker. The hair visible above the skin
is essentially dead tissue, and the care it receives can in no
way influence future growth. Consider the 1970 study by Yelva
Lynfield and Peter MacWilliams, who examined the change
and growth of hair on healthy young men who shaved one
leg weekly for several months, leaving the other leg unshaven
as a source for comparison. At the end of the study, no differences were found, either in the weight or growth rate of the
hair on the two legs. A similar study involving male chest hair
provided identical results.

MYTH: *Never shave your child's eyebrows because they won't grow back.*

This is one of those myths that is as prevalent among physicians as it is among the rest of the population. True, many surgeons avoid shaving eyebrows because the fringe of hair above the eye can serve as an important landmark to ensure that lacerated skin is joined together as perfectly as possible. But some surgeons avoid shaving the eyebrows because they believe that eyebrows will never grow back and consequently that shaving them can be even more cosmetically unattractive for the patient than the laceration or other injury that made surgery necessary.

But in fact eyebrows—on both adults and children—will return just as certainly as hair on the scalp. The myth to the contrary probably evolved because of the slower and more erratic growth rate of eyebrows. All human hair—whether on the head, face, or elsewhere—proceeds through regular growing phases, but the duration of these periods varies, depending on the site of the hair. For example, each strand of hair on your scalp will grow steadily for several years, enter a three-month rest period, and then fall out. At any particular time, about 10 to 20 percent of your scalp hairs are in this resting and falling-out stage.

By contrast, eyebrow hairs grow for only thirty to sixty days, and then pass into a resting period that typically lasts for more than a hundred days. Thus, at any one time, most eyebrow hairs are not growing. When the eyebrows are shaved, only a minority of the hairs will begin regrowing immediately, with several months needed for the growth process to affect them all.

Eyebrows also grow at a slower rate than other bodily hair. Whereas scalp hair sprouts at 0.014 inches (0.35 mm) per day, eyebrows grow only at 0.006 inches (0.16 mm) per day. Under

normal circumstances, then, taking into consideration both
growth rate and long periods of nongrowth, a shaved eyebrow
can take six to eight months to return to a normal appearance.
If you don't have to shave off the eyebrow, don't do it. But if
you do, the eyebrow will grow back.

MYTH: *Frequent shampooing is bad for your child's hair and
could cause it to fall out.*

A fully developed head of hair has about 100,000
strands. Under normal circumstances, the scalp will routinely
lose a relatively small number each day—from 50 to 300—
with a new strand waiting to replace each lost one.

This process will continue no matter how rarely or frequently
your child's hair is washed. Although the texture of the hair
can be affected by shampooing—as oils are removed or traces
of minerals are deposited—this will have no lasting or dangerous effect and pose no risk of hair loss.

In fact, frequent shampooing can have a *positive* influence
upon hair health, simply because repetitive washing is usually
accompanied by routine brushing and combing as well. These
processes are almost always beneficial to the hair, unless the
comb has ragged edges or the brush has squared nylon bristles.

MYTH: *Hand soap is just as effective as shampoo in washing
hair.*

Occasionally, I am asked by a mother or father whether
a mild hand soap would be just as effective in cleaning the
hair as a shampoo. I suggest that shampoos be used, simply
because the detergents in them provide better lather than a
bar of soap, even in hard water, and leave few dull deposits
as they wash away dirt. Incidentally, there is no harm in shampooing a child's hair with shampoos containing conditioners.
They may replace some of the natural oils lost during shampooing, and make it shinier and easier to comb. But they cannot

permanently repair a child's hair structurally damaged by permanents, hair straighteners, or hot combs.

MYTH: *Baby shampoos are better for children's hair.*

Thanks to the incessant indoctrination of TV and magazine advertising, most of us believe that baby shampoos are the best choice for a child's hair. Actually, in order to minimize irritation to the eyes, manufacturers of baby shampoos have forsaken some features that would make their products better cleaning agents. For example, the detergents in baby shampoos usually generate lower amounts of lather, which reduces their cleaning effectiveness. Although they may not be better as cleansing agents, they are better for a child's *eyes*. Baby shampoos include detergents that are less irritating to the eyes than normal shampoos. Also, they usually do not contain perfume, which may also cause discomfort in some youngsters.

Thus, for children with particularly sensitive skin, or difficulty keeping their eyes closed, a baby shampoo is probably the most logical choice; for other youngsters, it is not necessarily a "better" choice.

MYTH: *Your child should not use someone else's comb or brush.*

"I never let my kids use other people's combs," a mother told me recently. "That's the quickest way I know of for them to catch dandruff."

As well-intentioned as her efforts may be, this parent is not going to prevent dandruff in her children by eliminating their use of other people's combs, for in fact most dandruff is neither contagious nor symptomatic of a disease process. It is really nothing more than an excess shedding of the surface layer of the skin, and it can't be "caught" from a comb or a brush.

Some dermatologists say that dandruff is present in 99 percent of the population and that no one is immune to it. Even so, Americans spend $20 million each year on products that promise to eliminate it.

Here is what normally happens on our heads: The scalp is covered and protected by a tough surface layer of skin, composed of millions of dead cells that safeguard the tissue beneath. As these dead cells become worn or rubbed off with normal brushing, a new layer of cells replaces them. When this process of discarding cells occurs in excess, the phenomenon we call dandruff occurs. Dermatologists theorize that everything from heredity to microorganisms may share some of the blame for dandruff, but no one knows for certain. Several studies, however, have conclusively ruled out diet and vitamin deficiency as factors.

While dandruff has become an all-encompassing term referring to every type of excess shedding, only rarely does it involve an actual disease. True scalp ailments—like seborrhea and psoriasis—do exist but are much less common and are not contagious.

The belief that people should not exchange combs, then, is for the most part unfounded. It is true that medical historians have told us about anthrax, a malignant disease of cattle and other mammals, being transferred in an earlier era by animal bristles. But today anthrax is almost unheard of.

Therefore, the use of another person's comb is permissible, except in the rare cases when the comb is being borrowed from someone with certain scalp diseases, especially fungal infections, impetigo, and head lice.

MYTH: *A single hair whorl on your child's head is a sign of a calm personality; a double whorl indicates that your child will be mischievous or even retarded.*

Naturally unruly hair is *not* necessarily a sign of abnormality. However, this myth about aberrant hair patterns has persisted in the Western world for more than seventy years, since German researchers first noted an association between extremely disorderly hair and a condition in infants called neuralpathic dysfunction. The Japanese apparently noted this phenomenon thousands of years ago, using the term *tsumugi majari* to mean not only "whorl to the side," but also "idiot" or "someone difficult to get along with."

Scalp hair patterns are established between the tenth and sixteenth week of fetal life. The hair starts growing straight out. As the brain and skull grow underneath, the skin is pulled in one direction or the other over the surface of the skull, influencing the number and location of the hair whorls. Imagine what happens when you blow up a balloon. There is one point on the surface of the balloon that does not move as the balloon expands. Compare this to the scalp as the brain grows and expands—this point on the scalp becomes a whorl.

A majority (56 percent) of people have a single hair whorl, located to the left of the midline, apparently because the left side of the brain is slightly larger than the right. Approximately 30 percent of hair whorls are on the right side, and about 14 percent are on the midline itself. About 5 percent of all *normal* individuals have two hair whorls, one on each side of the scalp.

In otherwise healthy children, unusual hair patterns are of no concern. Extremely unruly hair exists in about 2 percent of all normal individuals. But in certain children who have severe neurological abnormalities, there may be a variation in the hair whorl pattern, caused possibly by abnormal brain growth. So though there may be a grain of truth to the origin of this myth, variations in hair pattern are so common that no accurate predictions can be made on their basis alone.

Interestingly, horse trainers often select their race horses by hair patterns; a horse with a hair whorl at the midline of the horse's nose could be a great runner, they say; by contrast, an animal with a whorl to the side is considered more difficult to train.

MYTH: *Hair color determines a child's disposition or a child's health.*

Some people believe that redheaded children are more hotheaded and impetuous than other youngsters, but there is no evidence to substantiate this. Even so, you may find a study by Brigid Peer, a University of Western Ontario (Canada) registered nurse, interesting. She compared the health of thirty redheaded children and thirty youngsters with less striking hair colors. She found that the redheaded children were ill more frequently, for greater lengths of time, and with more complications. Her statistics showed that during sickness, the redheaded children had temperatures ranging from 103° to 106° F (39.4 to 41.1° C), compared with a 101° F (38.3° C) average for the other youngsters.

As intriguing as this study may seem, don't consider it gospel. Her research was poorly documented and would probably not stand up to rigorous scientific scrutiny. In my own practice, I have seen no evidence that redheadedness can be hazardous to your health.

MYTH: *The only way to remove chewing gum from your child's hair is to cut away the hair itself.*

There is hardly a youngster who escapes childhood without getting a piece of bubblegum stuck in the hair. Usually parents resort to a scissors to remove it, cutting away not only the gum but the hair, too.

But there is another, lesser-known remedy—rubbing some peanut butter into the hair to get the gum out. As untantalizing as this approach may sound, the oil from a small lump of peanut butter will allow you to slip the gum off the hair fibers relatively easily. And with the price of haircuts these days, peanut butter may seem like a welcome alternative to chopping away at a "hairstyling" your child received just the day before.

10
SKIN

The skin is the body's largest and most visible organ. As a multifunctional covering for the body, the skin offers a shield against infection, protects the inner organs and tissues, provides for the partial excretion of waste material, and regulates body temperature. But many of the skin's infections and other abnormal conditions—from acne to eczema to warts—are poorly understood. As much as possible, let's clarify these misconceptions now.

MYTH: *Frequent bathing is always good for the skin.*

The skin must be regularly cleaned. But for some people, particularly those with dry skin, frequent washing with soap and water can be damaging to the skin. Water acts as a drying agent, draining out the natural protective oils from pores. Although the water temporarily replaces these oils, the water eventually evaporates, leaving the skin drier than before.

A child with unusually dry skin should bathe only once or twice a week. Between baths, a cleansing oil can be used to remove uncomfortable or unsightly dirt. Frequent washing, however, is not a problem for the average child.

MYTH: *Babies must have a daily bath.*

See page 29.

MYTH: *Acne is caused by poor hygiene.*

Acne is *not* a disease provoked by dirt and poor hygiene. Most dermatologists find that acne patients have better hygiene habits than the general population. Rather, acne is caused by the improper functioning of the pilosebaceous (sweat) units that are concentrated on the face, chest, back, and upper arms. (Because these sebaceous units do not exist in animals, acne is unique to human beings.)

Acne develops when certain hormones, particularly those that flourish in adolescence, cause the canals of the pilosebaceous glands to become blocked. Consequently, an oily substance called sebum, which is normally secreted through these glands to the skin's surface, is prevented from being expelled. The sebum accumulates in the skin, eventually resulting in blemishes and pimples.

Blackheads, the classical lesions that often precede the formation of a pimple, are frequently seen as accumulations of dirt, probably because of their dark appearance. Possibly for this reason acne is often attributed to improper washing. But in reality, their black tint is caused by melanin, a dark pigment in the sebaceous glands.

MYTH: *Acne is a disease only of adolescence.*

Acne, the most common human skin disease, is a normal part of almost everyone's adolescence, but it is certainly not limited to teenagers. Most babies experience a form of acne, called acneneonatorum, in the initial weeks of life (see page 34), and acne appears in some people for the first time when they are in their twenties or thirties. Even for those people in whom acne first emerged in their teens, the condition can continue (although usually to a lesser degree) into their thirties and even forties.

As a general rule, adolescent acne runs about a ten-year course, but there are wide variations in duration and severity among individuals. There is no cure for acne; however, recent advances in therapy can greatly improve the skin's appearance by controlling the process during the susceptible years.

MYTH: *Acne is worsened by chocolate and greasy foods.*

Most people, it seems, grow up believing that certain foods—particularly chocolate and other sweets—cause or aggravate acne. But as yet there is not a single, well-documented study to support this widely held viewpoint. A 1978 article in the *Journal of the American Medical Association* concluded, "Diet plays no role in acne treatment in most patients. . . . Even large amounts of chocolate have not clinically exacerbated acne."

In a recent study examining the controversy over acne and diet, patients who claimed to be sensitive to chocolate were given candy in large quantities. No change was observed in either the number or severity of blemishes. Additional research indicates that other sweet foods, like cola drinks and ice cream, as well as greasy foods, do not incite or worsen acne either.

MYTH: *Iodine can cause acne.*

Some people contend that eating foods like fish, kelp, and shellfish that are high in iodine can cause eruptions of acne. But a study of more than 1000 North Carolina high school students showed that iodine in the diet has absolutely no effect upon blemishes.

So all the dietary restrictions usually imposed on acne patients may be worthless. Even so, for patients who strongly believe that their acne worsens following the consumption of certain foods, there is no harm in eliminating the suspicious agents from the diet until their influence can be sufficiently evaluated.

MYTH: *Acne is more common among girls.*

Acne plays no favorites between the sexes. It is just as prevalent in boys as girls. But because girls generally tend to be more concerned about their appearance and thus more frequently consult dermatologists for treatment, some physicians think that girls experience the disease more often. That's not the case. In fact, severe cystic acne of the back tends to occur more frequently in boys, not girls.

MYTH: *Eczema is contagious.*

Eczema is an allergic condition characterized by red, itching skin that may be crusty and ooze fluid. This rash may be a reaction to a particular food or material (wool, silk) to which the child is allergic, and it can persist for months and sometimes years. In babies, the rash often occurs on the cheeks, and in older children it tends to develop in the creases of the neck, elbows, and knees.

At no time is eczema contagious. If you touch a child with eczema, even directly on the rash itself, you will not "catch" this disorder.

MYTH: *All birthmarks are permanent.*

See pages 34–35.

MYTH: *Never intentionally burst a blood blister.*

A blood blister is a collection of blood under the skin, caused by an abrasion or other local injury. In earlier generations, there were many stories of deaths caused by burst blood blisters. But it's doubtful that anyone has ever died from a burst blood blister. If and when such fatalities did occur, they were almost certainly caused by the *infection* that accompanied the broken blister, infections that could not be effectively controlled in the pre-antibiotic era. Today infections can still occur when a blister bursts under unsanitary circumstances. But fortunately, we have antibiotics that can bring them under immediate control.

As a general rule, a blood blister heals with less risk of infection if left closed; it need not be opened unless it is causing considerable discomfort. In such cases, many doctors recommend puncturing the blister with a sterilized instrument in order to relieve both pressure and pain. Although antibiotics can control an infection if one should occur, infection can usually be avoided if the blister is opened under sterile conditions.

MYTH: *Sunbathing is good for the skin.*

Moderate exposure to sunlight can have some healing effect on blemishes, but there is little else about sunbathing that is beneficial to the skin, particularly when it is done in excess.

Although your child may tell you that a deep suntan promotes an image of youth and good health, prolonged sun exposure actually accelerates the skin's aging process, promoting premature wrinkles, sagging, and irregular pigmentation. It is also a major cause of skin cancer.

MYTH: *Touching a frog or a toad causes warts to develop on the hands.*

Before the medical profession understood the cause of warts, frogs and toads seemed as easy to blame for them as anything else, particularly since toads looked as though they had a few warts themselves.

But there's no need for your children to stay away from the lily pads in order to avoid a wart or two. We now know that frogs and toads are innocent of all charges. A virus is the actual culprit. This slightly contagious wart virus—called the human papilloma virus—stimulates the reproduction of skin cells, causing the familiar small swellings or (noncancerous) tumors to appear almost overnight.

MYTH: *If a wart is not surgically removed, it will stay forever.*

If left untreated, almost all warts will disappear on their own, usually within two years time. But dermatologists—with their bag of amazing tools—are often invited in for some immediate attention, often because a parent can't bear the sight of the protuberance "for even one more day." Although warts can be burned (electrocauterization) or frozen off (cyrosurgery), hypnosis may work just as well. No one knows exactly why hypnosis or autosuggestion is effective, but in 50 percent of the cases of warts, *any* treatment works if the patient has faith in it. So if your child is a believer in rabbit's feet or four-leaf clovers, they may be just what the doctor ordered.

11

LEGS, FEET, HANDS, BONES, AND JOINTS

Fortunately, as in some other areas of medicine, the primary childhood orthopedic problems that cause parental concern are self-correcting. As abnormal as disorders like knock-knees or bowlegs may seem to mothers and fathers, most cases rectify themselves without therapy.

Controversy still exists, however, even among orthopedists themselves, about the nature and the most appropriate management of some of these problems. Corrective shoes, for example, constitute a $40 million a year industry, yet their effectiveness in remedying the more common orthopedic disorders is debatable. Conditions like "toeing-in" (pigeon-toe) and "toeing-out" are generally considered less serious than they once were and are now treated less aggressively by pediatricians and orthopedists. More than 600 million pairs of shoes are purchased in the United States each year, yet there are many misconceptions about when shoes are appropriate and the best types for children's feet. Misconceptions and myths about these and other orthopedic problems will be considered in this chapter.

Standing, Walking, Growing, and Other Orthopedic Concerns

MYTH: *Helping a baby stand too early can lead to bowlegs.*

Usually between the ages of four to six months, most babies enjoy being upright and placing weight on their legs. Although most parents respond by supporting their child in this standing position, they believe there are risks in doing so. Some say they've heard that it causes bowlegs, weakens the legs, or even stunts growth.

This parental concern is groundless. Your child won't be harmed in any way, and in fact, while in the standing position, the budding toddler will develop a sense of balance that will eventually be needed in order to stand unassisted and to walk.

MYTH: *Bowlegs are abnormal in babies.*

Bowlegs in babies are more the rule than the exception, present in almost all normal children up to the age of eighteen months. It is often caused by the position of the baby's legs in the mother's uterus and may appear worse because of a mild turning in of the baby's foot.

In earlier generations, rickets, a vitamin D deficiency, was sometimes linked to bowlegs, and vitamin supplements were prescribed. But in the modern American diet, this vitamin deficiency is rare. Some pediatricians treat bowlegs with sleeping splints or daily exercises, but there is little evidence that these methods are either necessary or helpful in correcting this phenomenon.

For almost all children, bowlegs are self-correcting. When the leg muscles strengthen as youngsters become proficient walkers, the legs will straighten on their own, without treatment, usually by the age of two. A pediatrician should be consulted, however, if

- the condition persists beyond the age of two;
- one leg appears much more involved than the other; or
- the condition is extremely exaggerated.

As a general rule, if greater than two inches separates your toddler's inner knees when the ankles are touching, a pediatrician's analysis should be sought. Some treatment—perhaps casts below the knee or a specially designed night splint—is sometimes prescribed in the most severe cases.

MYTH: *Bulky diapers on a baby can cause bowlegs.*

The origin of this myth is unknown, but it may simply be the result of anxious parents' need to explain their child's bowlegs. Diapering is not related to bowlegs in any way.

Ironically, though, bulky diapers are often used to *treat* another orthopedic disorder, called congenital hip dysplasia. This condition, which exists at birth, occurs when the femur (thighbone) is not properly attached to the pelvis. During your baby's routine checkups, your pediatrician has probably examined your child's hips closely for this condition. You may have noticed your doctor's grasping of your infant's lower legs, and bending them outward into the position of frog's legs. If a dislocation existed, your pediatrician would have felt some resistance or even a click when attempting this maneuver.

Hip dysplasia occus in one of every 600 births, with a higher incidence in breech deliveries, and is eight times more prevalent in girls than boys. Although the precise cause of this disorder is not known, pediatricians agree that it should usually be treated early by a cast or a splint. In very mild or questionable cases, until the presence or the severity of the problem is verified, often an attempt is made to keep the infant's thighs wide apart, thus forcing the end of the femur firmly into the hip socket. This may be accomplished by using several diapers instead of one when diapering the infant. Appropriate management of this condition can prevent lifelong, crippling complications.

MYTH: *Knock-knees always require treatment.*

Knock-knees, or an inward deviation at the knee, is as normal a phenomenon in the two-to-five-year-old as bowlegs is in the child under two. According to one study, 22 percent of children between three and 3½ years had knock-knees, while at age seven and over, only 1 to 2 percent had it.

You may notice that the insides of your own youngster's knees almost seem to touch while he or she is walking or standing straight, but keep in mind that this condition exists almost universally in this age group, it is self-limiting, and your child will outgrow it. Treatment is rarely necessary, except in extreme cases.

Frequently, as a child normally progresses out of the bowlegged period at about age two, knock-knees will develop. This is the normal course of the physiological development of the lower extremities. However, knock-knees may be in need of treatment if:

- with knees touching, the distance between ankles exceeds 3½ inches;
- the condition is more exaggerated in one leg than the other;
- the child is short for his or her age (which occasionally indicates an endocrine problem or other disorder); or
- a family history of severe knock-knees or other bone deformity exists (which suggests that a metabolic disorder might be present).

Your pediatrician should be consulted for the best possible advice on your own child's particular condition.

MYTH: *All flat feet should be treated with corrective shoes.*

If your baby's feet look flat, that's because *all* babies' feet do. In your newborn's foot, fat accumulates in the so-called "fat pads" in the hollows of the feet, concealing the arch. But as your infant grows, these pads slowly disappear, and the arch becomes clearly visible. By the time walking is well established, flat feet have most often resolved themselves. One study showed that when babies (birth to eighteen months) were examined and their footprints analyzed, 97 percent of them had flat feet (using a fallen arch as the criterion of that condition). But by age ten, only 4 percent of that original 97 percent still exhibited this characteristic.

If your youngster's flat feet persist into later childhood, the condition will still probably *not* require any special treatment. Most likely, your child has flexible, or "hypermobile," flat feet, which tend to be hereditary and rarely cause problems in day-to-day functioning. Despite widespread prescribing of stiff shoes with arch supports for these children, there is *no* evidence that this treatment can effectively correct this condition.

A growing number of physicians now agree with orthopedic surgeon Lynn T. Staheli, director of Seattle's Children's Orthopedic Hospital's department of orthopedics, who at a recent American Academy of Pediatrics meeting stated that corrective shoes haven't been shown to change the course of *any* orthopedic "variation of normal," suggesting that their use be reserved for only the most serious, fixed, structural deformities. (A "variation of normal" is a condition that some people might consider unsightly—like a big nose—but is not a physiological abnormality.) Dr. Staheli observed that the wearing of corrective shoes is "not necessarily innocuous," since they alter the child's appearance, impairing both self-image and socialization, and are expensive for the parents. He concluded that for the most common minor childhood foot problems "allowing the child to be corrected by nature is really in the best interest of the child, parents and physician."

A much rarer form of flat feet, more commonly seen in black children, is caused by a rigid Achilles tendon, the tissue joining the calf muscles to the heel bone, which prevents the foot from bending properly. In such cases, your pediatrician or orthopedist may suggest that your child wear special shoes that can provide extra support, or your doctor may prescribe stretching exercises to create flexibility in the tendon.

As general guidelines, consult your doctor if your child's feet exhibit rigidity, pain, loss of side-to-side motion, or an inability to bend upward toward the leg (dorsiflex). You can examine the wear on your youngster's shoes, too; if the inner edges of the shoe are wearing out more quickly than the outer edges, then extreme flat feet may be present.

To further complicate the phenomenon of flat feet, there is some research indicating that feet with high arches may not necessarily be preferable to those with low arches. In fact, in children over age twelve observed in one study, the only youngsters with foot pain were those with high arches. Perhaps, then, a high arch is not necessarily the most desirable foot condition.

MYTH: *Walking on the toes is always abnormal.*

When children learn to walk, many begin by walking on their tiptoes. This is expected and normal in the first six months of walking.

But if your child's toe walking continues beyond this normal six-month period, consult your doctor. Though often a normal variation, long-term toe walking may also be an indication of a structural foot problem, and further evaluation and treatment may be suggested to counteract this tendency.

MYTH: *Children who begin walking early will be more intelligent than those who start walking later.*

The normal onset of walking can begin as early as eight months old, or as late as eighteen months. There is absolutely no correlation between the onset of what we call gross motor skills (like walking, sitting, and crawling) and either the child's future intelligence as measured by IQ tests or his or her future athletic prowess—as long as these basic motor skills begin within the normal ranges.

One of the most comprehensive studies of this subject was conducted by Nancy Bayley of the University of California, as part of the Berkeley Growth Study in the 1940s. After many years of observation and research, Bayley concluded that no correlation existed between a child's intelligence and the early or late onset of rolling over, sitting, crawling, and walking, as long as they fell within the range of normal.

When Bayley's research findings were substantiated by many later studies, a popular theory surfaced in the 1960s, purporting that future intelligence could not be accurately predicted early in life. However, psychologists have now developed sophisticated techniques that are much more complex than simply observing gross motor skill development and can more accurately estimate future intelligence.

MYTH: *Children who are late walkers or crawlers have a higher incidence of stuttering.*

Stuttering, characterized by interruptions in the rhythms of speech, afflicts about 1 to 2 percent of the adult population, primarily men. Many children pass through a normal stuttering period at about age three, but they outgrow it in a few months. This childhood stuttering typically occurs because a child's language ability is inadequate to keep up with his or her thought processes. No evidence exists to connect stuttering with late crawling or walking.

Perhaps you've also heard the belief that stuttering is more common in left-handed children, or children who have changed handedness. Though earlier reports seemed to support this assumption, more recent studies show no significant difference in the frequency of stuttering between the general population and individuals who are left-handed, or who have shifted handedness.

In older children, stuttering seems primarily a stress- or pressure-related phenomenon, rather than one based on social or economic level or intelligence. Interestingly, among cultures in which childrearing occurs in a relaxed atmosphere, stuttering is nonexistent. In the languages of American Indians, there is not even a word for stuttering.

MYTH: *Feet that toe in always require immediate treatment.*

Do your baby's feet seem out of alignment, with one or both turning inward rather than pointing straight out? Not only is this condition relatively common, but it rarely requires treatment, usually correcting itself over time.

There are three general causes for toeing-in, or pigeon-toe. The most common is tibial torsion, in which the feet are structurally normal but the tibia (the leg bone between the knee and the ankle) is rotated inward, causing the foot to point that way as well. Observed most often during the first year of life, it is considered a normal physiological variant by most pediatricians, mimicking the position of the baby while still in the uterus, in which the lower legs are turned inward.

Considerable controversy exists about the nature and preferred management of this condition. I find that tibial torsion rarely requires treatment, because the lower leg almost always "unwinds" by itself during the first year of life. If, however, this malalignment does not gradually disappear on its own, particularly by the time your child begins walking, keep in mind that some pediatricians suggest therapy, often a special shoe and brace. Other pediatricians simply recommend that the child's feet be placed in an old pair of regular shoes before going to bed, in which the heels are tied together with a shoelace, or that the pajama heels be sewn together; with the youngster sleeping in the stomach-down position, the feet will point in the desired toes-out position, promoting gradual and permanent correction. Although these maneuvers may hasten the straightening process, the rarity of toeing-in among adults indicates that almost all childhood cases of this disorder normalize on their own.

In addition to tibial torsion, there are two other, less common causes of toeing-in. One is metatarsus adductus, in which the foot itself, rather than the tibia, curves inward from heel to toe, in the shape of a modified letter C. If the curved foot can be straightened and deviated outward with simple hand pressure, usually simple stretching exercises are the only treatment prescribed. In the more severe, nonflexible cases, where the foot is *fixed* in the curved position, a cast or special shoes may be necessary. G. F. Rushforth, in the *British Journal of Bone and Joint Surgery (1978)*, reported that in an eleven-year study of 130 youngsters with flexible metatarsus adductus, "nine of ten children had normal feet by age three years" without treatment. But since it is impossible to identify at a young age which children will or will not respond to treatment, most doctors choose to treat.

Toeing-in is also occasionally caused by femoral antiversion, in which the thighbone (femur) is turned farther inward than normal at the point of attachment to the hip joint, creating a rotation that causes the pointing-in of the knee and foot while walking or running. Children with this malalignment, which usually affects both legs, often sit on their knees, with their legs tucked under them or to the sides; they usually find it difficult to sit cross-legged. Most orthopedists agree that this condition peaks at ages five to six, after which it usually resolves itself without treatment. Children who have this condition should be encouraged to sit in chairs with their feet dangling over the edge of the seat, rather than in the tucked position described above. Corrective appliances are rarely prescribed. In isolated cases of severe deformity, surgery is sometimes recommended in the teenage years.

MYTH: *Feet that toe out always require immediate treatment.*

A mother will often tell me that when her baby was standing upright in a pre-walker, she noticed that the child's feet turned out, sometimes to a nearly 90-degree angle. An examination almost always shows that this is due to an external rotation at both hips, which is neither unusual nor abnormal in babies. Such children often sleep with their knees drawn up to their chest, with their feet pointed outward—a sleeping position, incidentally, also exhibited by some children *without* this malalignment. The toeing-out position usually persists into the first month of walking and then self-corrects. Rarely is treatment necessary. Ask yourself how many adults you see who walk with their feet dramatically pointed outward.

Interestingly, when parents complain to me that one of their child's feet is pointing out, their concern is often directed toward the wrong foot. The "toeing-out" foot may only appear that way because the other foot is toeing-in. Typically, the toeing-in foot is the one that warrants the closest observation.

MYTH: *Growing pains are caused by growing.*

The scenario is a familiar one to many parents. Their child awakens in the middle of the night, complaining of leg pains, often localized deep inside the calf or thigh. No other symptoms of illness, like fever, are present. The discomfort can frequently be relieved with a massage, a warm bath, or aspirin.

This phenomenon afflicts about 15 to 20 percent of five-to-seven-year-olds, although it can occur at any age through early adolescence. The pains have no medical significance and are no cause for alarm.

Physicians have traditionally referred to these intermittent leg pains as "growing pains," although there is *no* evidence that they are associated with the growing process. Although millions of children suffer from them, the cause is generally unknown. In some cases, they may be an excuse for children to encourage their parents to sit up with them during the night. But if you yourself experienced these pains as a child, you know there is usually more involved here than a psychological component. Various doctors have speculated that the discomfort may be caused by muscle fatigue, poor posture, knock-knees, or food allergies. If the problem persists in your child, mention it to your pediatrician, although rarely is this symptom connected to a serious disorder.

MYTH: *A second toe longer than the big toe is abnormal.*

Not only is there nothing abnormal about a second toe that extends out farther than the big one, but it is common to millions of people, especially those with Mediterranean ancestry. The feet of all ancient Egyptian statues exhibit this common variation, and some people believe a longer second toe is the sign of an aristocrat.

The longer second toe, however, is also a component of a condition called Morton's foot, which is characterized by susceptibility to various foot injuries, particularly while running.

MYTH: *Never lift a child by the arms.*

Many parents tell me how they avoid picking up their child by the arms, afraid that such lifting might cause physical damage in the youngster. However, the human body, whether an infant's or an adult's, can withstand considerable force on all its limbs without any significant risk of damage.

True, there are some rare cases of nerve damage (brachial plexus palsy) that have occurred during difficult vaginal deliveries, when enormous force is placed on the upper arms and shoulders of the infant to complete the birth. But after birth, the relatively gentle force needed to pick up your child—either under the arms or by pulling on them—cannot cause damage.

However, a sudden, fierce jerking of a young child's arm can be harmful. A dislocation of the elbow's radial bone may occur in children from eighteen months to three years old, whose arms, forearms, or hands are suddenly pulled on, perhaps by a parent or a nursemaid who may yank the arm of a misbehaving youngster. This is why their condition is frequently called "nurse-maid's elbow" or "temper-tantrum elbow." Or this dislocation might arise when a child stumbles off a curb while being held by the arm by an adult. But even in these cases, although the child will experience pain and temporarily will be unable to move the arm, the elbow can be quickly and easily maneuvered back into place by a physician, without any permanent damage to the area.

MYTH: *Chronic knuckle cracking in children can cause arthritis or enlarged knuckles.*

Knuckle cracking can be an annoying habit; it often begins in childhood and persists into adult life. Neither knuckle cracking or the loud popping noise that accompanies it is dangerous or leads to joint disorders or particularly arthritis.

The cracking sound itself is produced when traction on the joint space converts thin, fluid films to vapors. This gas seemingly acts like an air cushion, which may explain why knuckle crackers often report that their joint feels more comfortable after it has been cracked. Approximately twenty minutes is required for the gas to be converted back to liquid form, which is the reason why some people find that their joint cannot be immediately cracked a second time. Even in people who can repeat the popping sound, it is usually not caused by actually cracking the joint but by a ligament passing over an anatomical protuberance, mimicking the cracking sound.

As you might imagine, there have not been many studies of knuckle cracking and its long-term effects. After all, it's not exactly a pressing concern. But in 1974 twenty-eight residents of a Jewish home for the aged were examined and x-rayed for arthritis. All of them could recall whether or not they had cracked their knuckles as children. As part of the same study, a group of twenty-eight schoolchildren with an average age of eleven years were surveyed as to their knuckle-cracking habits. The study discovered that the frequency of knuckle cracking in the elderly group was identical to that in the children—that is, about 15 to 20 percent of the individuals in each sampling cracked their knuckles. But more significantly, among the elderly (average age 78.5 years) there was no higher incidence of osteoarthritis, the most common degenerative form of arthritis in the elderly, in the individuals who had cracked their knuckles than in those who hadn't. In fact, there was *less* arthritic disease among the knuckle crackers.

Thus, the most negative aspect of knuckle cracking is probably its ability to annoy everyone within hearing range. There are no documented, physiological ill effects.

MYTH: *A single crease across the palm of the hand means your child has Down's syndrome (Mongolism).*

A solitary crease across the palm, although existing in 40 percent of all Down's children, is not unique to people with this genetic abnormality. In fact, it occurs in 5 percent of the normal population, with 2 percent having a single crease on both palms.

The technical term for this single line or wrinkle is the "simian crease," so named because it is an anatomical trait of all monkeys. In human beings, two or more deep creases that do not completely cross the palm develop during the tenth through the fourteenth week of fetal life. At this stage of development, the fetus is first able to bend its fingers downward, touching the thumb to the fifth finger (which monkeys are incapable of doing). If only a single crease is visible on the hand after birth, it may be because of the fetus's failure to develop the full, more complex hand movement during the short, critical time of skin-crease development. Occasionally, this is due to a disorder like Down's syndrome. Keep in mind, however, that in otherwise normal individuals, the single crease may merely be an indication of a slight, normal variation in development.

In medical school, one of my professors related the story of how he used to be proud of the long "intelligence" lines on his hands. But when he showed them to a group of doctors, one of the physicians pointed out to him the relationship between Down's syndrome and the single crease on the hand.

From that day forward, my professor stopped bragging about his "intelligence" lines.

MYTH: *Infant jumpers and umbrella strollers may be injurious to a baby's back.*

Since they were introduced a few years ago, controversy has surrounded infant jumpers, the canvas seats or swings that can be hung from doorways. Articles appearing in lay periodicals have suggested that the baby's growing bones might be injured as the infant moves about in the apparatus. Concern has also been expressed about the risk of injury in umbrella-type collapsible strollers.

However, there is no medical evidence to substantiate these suspected dangers. I tell parents that until their babies have adequate control of their head and upper extremities and until their back muscles are strong, the infants may be uncomfortable and thus may not enjoy the experience of these devices. But discomfort is the only potential problem here, not risk of injury, no matter how young the child is.

When using these devices for a one- or two-month-old baby, I suggest that parents roll up some blankets or towels and put them at the sides of their child's head for comfort and extra support.

Shoes

MYTH: *A child's first shoes should be high-topped.*

Millions of dollars are spent each year on expensive, high-top shoes for babies, shoes usually equipped with a medial wedge for arch support.

In most cases, however, the extra dollars that these shoes cost can be saved, despite the insistence by grandma that they're "absolutely essential" to provide ankle support for the young walker. There is only one advantage to fitting your child with high-top shoes—they sometimes stay on the foot easier.

Ironically, the high-top leather not only doesn't provide reinforcement for the ankle but it could actually contribute to a weakening rather than a strengthening of the foot. Some research indicates that with high-top shoes, your child's feet could become "lazy"—that is, they may rely on the shoe for strength and support, rather than relying on the ankle muscles that already exist and are capable of that support.

A well-fitted tennis shoe is all that your baby needs for initial footwear. Its sole is flexible enough to allow an infant to walk naturally in the normal heel-to-toe gait. A baby's foot is usually not strong enough to bend the stiff sole of some children's shoes, forcing the child to step flatly and awkwardly rather than naturally.

When parents ask me how to determine whether a shoe fits properly, I suggest that they check that the new shoe extends about one-half inch beyond the longest toe and that it fits firmly but not too snugly in the heel, to prevent blistering that often occurs with a shoe that is either too tight or too loose.

MYTH: *Always put shoes on an infant.*

Despite what your neighborhood shoestore salesman may tell you, babies do *not* require shoes for proper foot development. Except for shoes specifically designed to correct serious foot problems, the only reason shoes are needed—by children or adults—is for protection. In cold weather, a loose-fitting shoe to keep your baby's feet warm may be appropriate; however, in warm weather, shoes are not necessary, particularly for a child who has not yet begun to walk. Once your child begins walking, shoes are needed only for protection from rough or hard surfaces.

Studies in Hong Kong have revealed that various foot disorders, like bunions and corns, occur much less frequently in the non-shoe-wearing populations than among regular shoe wearers. There was also no evidence in these studies that walking barefoot caused fallen arches or flat feet.

MYTH: *Tennis shoes often cause flat feet.*

Despite studies that clearly refute it, the myth persists among pediatricians, parents, and shoe salesmen that regular wearing of tennis shoes will almost inevitably produce flat feet. It's simply not true. In a study by E. E. Bleck, reported in his classic paper "The Shoeing of Children: Sham or Science?," forty children, who were determined to have "normal feet," were asked to wear tennis shoes about 85 percent of the time. They were observed annually over a ten-year period, and *none* of them showed any evidence of flattening or falling of the arch. Tennis shoes are not only safe to wear but, as I mentioned earlier, are often the best choice.

MYTH: *Tennis shoes cause athlete's foot.*

Athlete's foot (tinea pedis) is usually a fungus-induced disorder characterized by dry, itchy, and scaly skin. When caused by bacteria, it is wet and painful. The most likely area for this infection to occur is between the fourth and fifth toes, which are usually closer together than any of the other toes.

But the fungus or bacterium that causes athlete's foot is *not* contracted from tennis shoes, but rather from walking barefoot at poolside or in the locker or shower rooms.

The myth linking tennis shoes with athlete's foot emerged during the days when these shoes were nonporous, making it difficult for perspiration on the feet to evaporate. Damp feet ultimately become scaly, making them more susceptible to athlete's foot.

Fortunately, most of today's tennis shoes are fitted with ventilation holes, allowing air to reach the feet. To guard against athlete's foot, the feet can be kept dry by dusting them with powder, as well as by encouraging your child to change socks after his or her feet have perspired.

Athlete's foot is much more common in adults than children, and in fact, most dermatologists report that they rarely see a case of it in youngsters until adolescence.

12

EXERCISE AND SPORTS

America is currently experiencing a surge of interest in physical activity among both young and old. Soccer and jogging have become popular in recent years, and the opportunities for girls to participate in organized sports have increased dramatically. About 10 million children in the United States now participate in organized sports programs, of which about 5.5 million are teenagers engaged in high school athletics.

Children's sports injuries are on the increase, too, despite sophisticated training programs and safety equipment. In a recent two-year period, more than 500,000 sports-related injuries occurred among high school students. A study conducted by the Division of Sports Medicine at the University of Washington revealed that injuries in girls' high school sports occur at a rate of 22 per 100 participants; among boys, the rate jumps to 39 per 100. Football and wrestling caused the most injuries, while tennis and swimming were responsible for the least. Many of your own beliefs—not only about athletic injuries but also about controversies like high-energy drinks and vitamins—may be dispelled in the following pages.

MYTH: *Don't drink water during exercise or while participating in an athletic event.*

For many years, physicians, coaches, and parents alike discouraged the consumption of water during not only strenuous but even mild exercise. Drinking water was believed to bloat the body (a condition called "waterlogging") or to cause stomach cramps, which, in turn, made the athlete's performance less efficient.

However, this longstanding belief has been refuted by a solid, growing body of evidence. We now know, for instance, just how vital water is, whether the body is active or immobile. It transports life-supporting minerals, gases, electrolytes, and organic compounds; it is essential for thousands of biochemical processes; and it is a vital part of the body's heat-regulation mechanism.

There is a greater percentage of body water content in children than in adults, and thus children are more vulnerable to the risks of water loss. And these risks are significant: severe water dehydration during exercise can actually be life-threatening, because water is essential to allow body heat to be released through perspiration, in order to avoid heat stroke.

We obtain our body water from many sources—not only from directly drinking many types of liquids but also from eating food, especially fruits and vegetables. Water loss occurs constantly through breathing, urination, and evaporation from the skin and is influenced by many factors, including exercise level, air temperature, and even jet travel. While flying in a jet airplane, water loss is increased by the low humidity (leading to increased evaporation), as well as by the continual consumption of coffee or alcohol (thus increasing the frequency of urination). If your son or daughter is a high school or college athlete who flies to competitions, particularly on transcontinental trips, make your child aware of this dehydration process in the skies.

While athletes may experience up to a four-pound water loss during vigorous exercise, they may not even be aware of it. They can't depend on the thirst mechanism alone to let them know how dehydrated they are; in studies where thirst alone was relied on as an indicator of dehydration, only one-half to two-thirds of the water loss was replaced.

Before strenuous exercise, children should consume from one to two glasses of water. During the activity itself, additional water should be made available. Throughout a strenuous event like a basketball game, drinking should actually be scheduled periodically. There is no evidence that either cramps or "waterlogging" will occur, but maintaining a proper body water level will *enhance,* not harm, performance.

Fortunately, most Little League, high school, and college coaches are gradually becoming aware of this change in thinking and of the dangers of dehydration. It is not uncommon for children to lose more than 2 percent of their body weight during vigorous activity, and thus water should immediately be replaced or the child should stop exercising. Warn your child that one of the most important rules to abide by on the practice field or the playground is "Drink up!"

MYTH: *High-energy drinks consumed during strenuous exercise are the ideal way to compensate for water loss.*

A child's best approach for offsetting water loss is to drink *water,* not the heavily advertised quick-energy liquids now on the market. These glucose-electrolyte preparations are widely recommended and used by coaches, but their advantage over water or other drinks is questionable. If you think that by consuming these preparations, you'll receive a boost of energy because of their high sugar content, consider the study showing that while these drinks' caloric content is about 5 calories per ounce, orange juice supplies 12½ calories per ounce, and apple juice 15 calories.

But water may be even better for the athlete. Sports medicine experts have told me that drinks consumed during exercise should have a sugar content of under 2.5 percent. Greater sugar concentrations inhibit the liquid's absorption in the intestinal tract, and it remains in the stomach for a relatively long period of time, producing a bloated feeling and perhaps contributing to a decreased performance level. Also, sugar can't be relied on to provide the bursts of energy it promises. One study found that sugar consumed immediately before an athletic event had no measurable effect on performance.

The best drink during activity, then, is simply water. The other mixtures, however popular or exotic they may be, are not nearly as efficient.

MYTH: *Salt tablets should be consumed during exercise.*

The advice on salt tablets is simple and straightforward: Your children should *not* be taking them. They will not improve physical well-being or athletic performance and could actually be harmful.

The average person consumes more salt than is needed in the diet. Too much salt can cause disorders ranging from heat exhaustion to elevated blood pressure.

Here's why salt tablets are particularly dangerous when your children are exercising: when one perspires, one loses proportionately less salt than water, resulting in an even higher-than-normal salt level in the bloodstream. Swallowing salt tablets further enhances this imbalance, increasing the risk of heat exhaustion.

If coaches at your child's school routinely pass out salt tablets to athletes, ask them why. There is no justification for doing so.

MYTH: *Vitamins can provide extra energy for the young athlete.*

Although vitamins are necessary for many body processes to occur, they do not have any specific energy-producing functions. Energy is provided by carbohydrates, fats, and proteins. So don't count on vitamin supplements to provide extra energy or enhance your child's athletic performance, because they won't.

You've probably heard some professional athletes publicly claim that they could not play as well as they do without vitamin supplements. In fact, no evidence exists to support their belief. To make matters worse, excessive amounts of fat-soluble vitamins, A and D, can be toxic, and these two vitamins must be avoided in large dosages.

MYTH: *Muscle mass can be increased by eating steak.*

Two-pound steaks are the traditional food items on the pre-game meal table. Because of their high protein level, steaks are assumed to enhance muscle mass and strength.

True, a large slab of red steak is the muscle of the animal, but there's no basis for the belief that by eating animal muscle, you will build up human muscle. Muscle production is totally dependent on exercise; supplementing the diet with muscle protein has no effect.

I tell high school and college athletes to pursue a balanced diet and a well-designed exercise program to build up their strength and muscle mass. To create a pre-game or pre-exercise storehouse of energy sources, carbohydrates (bread, crackers) are much preferred over steak, since they are easily digested and absorbed from the gastrointestinal tract and they are a readily available source of glucose during exercise.

MYTH: *Children frequently sprain their ankles.*

A sprain is a partly torn, painful, and swollen ligament; by contrast, a fracture is a break of the bone itself.

I seldom see actual ankle sprains among very young children in my practice, and in fact some orthopedists insist that they rarely occur among preschoolers. After all, they argue, sprains involve injury to the ligament where it attaches to the bone, but in young children, injuries tend to occur instead in the weaker rubber-like epiphysis (the end portion of the bone where childhood growth occurs). Since damage will usually take place in the weakest tissue, the force of any injury in youngsters is transmitted through the stronger ligament to the

more vulnerable epiphysis, resulting in a separation there
called a Salter 1 fracture, which requires casting. In an adult,
the epiphysis is fused and thus stronger, and so the force of
the injury results in the characteristic adult ligament sprain
or pulled ligament. No matter what the specific injury, however, consult your pediatrician if your child is limping and
has pain in the ankle area.

Childhood bone structures differ from those in adults in other
ways. For instance, while the periosteum (the bone's outer lining) is paper-thin in adults, it is thick in children, thus reducing
the severity of a fracture when it occurs. A child's bones are
also more porous and pliable, permitting more bending and
buckling and often resulting in "green-stick fractures" (small,
multiple cracks at the fracture site—as with a broken fresh
branch—rather than a single, major break). Bone injuries also
heal more quickly in a child—for example, a fractured femur
can heal in three weeks in a baby, compared with twenty weeks
in a twenty-one-year-old.

MYTH: *Common athletic injuries should be "played off."*

Influenced by the "macho" image dictated by our culture, many boys ignore the injuries (sprains, strains, aches) that
they sustain during exercise or sports competition. Coaches
sometimes even tell a child with a twisted ankle to "run it
off," to ignore the injury and play on it.

But injuries and the accompanying pain are messages from
the nervous system, telling your child that something is wrong.
The most common sites of childhood sports injuries are the
joint, the bone, the ligament, the cartilage, the tendon, and
the muscle. Damage to any of these areas can be *worsened*
by further activity and can become permanent if not properly
treated. Encourage your child *not* to continue exercising or
playing with severe pain, limited mobility in the injured area,
significant swelling (particularly around a joint), or loss of sensa-
tion.

As general guidelines, see a physician for:

- All injuries to joints and ligaments.
- An injury accompanied by serious pain, or even mild pain that persists in a joint or a bone in excess of two weeks.
- Any injury that doesn't heal within three weeks.
- An infection characterized by pus, red streaks, or fever.
- Any injury you believe needs to be seen by a physician.

For an injury that has just occurred and is accompanied by pain, swelling, and limitation of movement, I suggest immediate treatment that can be abbreviated RICE (rest, ice, compression, elevation):

Rest: Immobilize the injured areas as much as possible. If an ankle or knee is involved, crutches should be used to keep weight off the injured region.

Ice: Apply an ice pack to the area. This causes the blood vessels to constrict and decreases the blood supply to the region, thus minimizing the swelling. Apply the ice for twenty minutes, three times a day on the first day. After twelve to eighteen hours, however, coldness will probably no longer be effective in reducing swelling; thus, once the acute phase is over, apply heat to increase circulation and possibly to hasten both comfort and the healing process.

Compression: Place an elastic wrap over the area. I often suggest wrapping the bandage around the injury once, then applying the ice bag to the area, and continuing wrapping to hold the ice in place. After treatment with ice, rewrap the bandage snugly but not so tight as to cause numbness or blueness.

Elevation: Raise the injured area above the level of the heart, if possible. This will reduce the blood supply to the region and diminish the swelling.

MYTH: *Swimming should be avoided when training for other sports because it lengthens or softens muscles.*

Contrary to popular belief, swimming is an excellent athletic endeavor that can help prepare your child for any sport. Swimming will *not* cause overdevelopment or softening of muscles and will not detract from the ability of your child to participate in any other sport. Swimming is, incidentally, excellent for the cardiorespiratory system and is among the most effective rehabilitative regimes for an injured arm or leg.

MYTH: *Steroid injections can prevent an injury from worsening.*

Your son, a high school football player, has a badly inflamed tendon, and the team doctor suggests that steroids (cortisone) be injected into the area. Should you agree to the treatment?

I advise against young athletes receiving steroid shots. Yes, cortisone is an anti-inflammatory agent that can reduce pain, increase mobility, and allow an athlete to perform almost as if an injury had never occurred. Though shots may be acceptable in professional athletics, the potential long-term risks in children are hardly worth the short-term benefits. Animal studies show that steroid injections weaken the strength of a tendon or ligament by 35 to 40 percent, for up to three weeks. Because of the stress that an athlete may place on the injured area, this mechanical weakening could result in an even more serious impairment than the primary injury.

As with all areas of medicine, the advantages of steroids must be weighed against the potential risks. I believe that in young athletes, the danger of long-term, serious injury should rule out this drug, if it is used primarily to allow the child to continue playing.

MYTH: *Asthmatics should not participate in school sports.*

Asthma is an allergic, respiratory disorder; the most prominent symptom is a wheezing or whistling noise evident while exhaling. Many parents tell me that they have restricted the activities of their asthmatic child, so as not to worsen this condition. However well-intentioned these imposed restrictions are, they are based on inaccuracies and are potentially detrimental.

In fact, asthmatics under appropriate medical therapy should be encouraged to participate in regular physical activity. Exercise will improve not only their *physical* well-being by increasing their lung capacity but also their *emotional* condition by fostering a positive self-image and normal peer relationships.

Although running and bicycling are notorious for initiating wheezing in children susceptible to "exercise-induced bronchospasms," your pediatrician can often provide medications to prevent these sports-related asthmatic attacks. Swimming rarely provokes these attacks, although physicians do not know exactly why. There is speculation, though, that the swimming pool provides the high humidity and the warm temperatures that may decrease irritation of the asthmatic's hyperexcitable airways. It is interesting to note that several Olympic medal winners have been asthmatics.

Don't overprotect your asthmatic child from physical exercise once appropriate medical care has been initiated. Let your child enjoy life to the fullest.

MYTH: *Throwing a Frisbee is a harmless outdoor sport.*

Who said the Frisbee was all fun and games? Although tossing these circular disks is certainly not the most dangerous activity your youngster could participate in, it is not always hazard-free.

In the journal article "Medical Aspects of Frisbee," a physician maintains that prolonged use of the toy may induce "Frisbee finger," a condition characterized by small cuts on the catching finger caused when the jagged edge of the disk is caught. For children who make the Frisbee a way of life, "Frisbee finger" is not uncommon, but it can be prevented by adhesive bands on the finger tips.

Other Frisbee hazards have been noted in the medical literature, including bruises, eye injuries, and elbow, shoulder, and fingernail injuries.

A contributor to the prestigious *New England Journal of Medicine* (1975) even composed the following ode to the Frisbee:

A frisbee's fun is not as fabled,
In fact, you might become disabled;
With bursting blisters on your finger,
You'll fail in feigning as a flinger.

Yes, frisbee finger now is put
With tennis elbow, athlete's foot,
Abuses of athletic action—
Will someone's tossing thumb need traction?

13
NUTRITION

"You are what you eat."

Although many factors contribute to your child's well-being, this popular slogan certainly carries some degree of truth. The types and quality of food we put into our bodies significantly influence how well our physiological processes function.

Fortunately, most Americans are eating better than earlier generations did. Millions of people have become nutrition-conscious in recent years, and medical school education is placing greater emphasis on understanding the value of nutrition and its relationship to health.

But even as accurate information about nutrition increases, many of the myths surrounding the foods we eat are dying slowly. Questionable healing qualities assigned to various vegetables, herbs, and vitamins are still believed by millions of individuals. Some people even cling to old home remedies based primarily on the color, shape, or smell of the particular food. For example, in earlier eras, squash was often used to treat jaundice because its yellow color was similar to the skin tint present in this disease.

This chapter will not only deal with nutritional myths that have persisted for generations ("Fish is brain food," "Coffee stunts growth," etc.) but will also discuss some of the newer misconceptions emerging out of recent food fads. The health food industry, a multi-billion-dollar enterprise, has caused confusion among consumers about foods and diets. Vitamins, too, are big business today, and are swallowed in massive doses by both children and adults, despite controversy over how worthwhile they really are. In this chapter, I will also discuss issues such as food allergies, obesity, and hyperactivity.

Diet and Foods

MYTH: *"Organic," "natural," or "health" foods are nutritionally superior.*

Although most advocates of "health foods" are well intentioned when they recommend that people eat only "organic" or "natural" food, there is no scientific evidence that these items are necessarily more healthful or that they provide any real advantage over supermarket food.

To health food advocates, health foods are those in their original state, or those that have undergone only minimal processing. "Natural" foods are those that contain no additives, such as preservatives. When foods are called "organic," they have theoretically been grown without artificial chemicals. The premise is that animal manure is a better and more natural source of necessary growth-supporting substances such as ammonia phosphate, nitrogen, and potassium ions, than are commercially produced fertilizers.

But there are some flaws to this reasoning. Since all chemicals must be broken down to their elemental form before plants can utilize them, it really does not matter whether they come from living matter or a laboratory. Food growing in the ground simply can't distinguish nitrogen or trace elements that have originated with organic rather than processed fertilizer; chemically, the substances are the same.

To further complicate the issue, so-called "organic" foods rarely are completely free of pesticides and other artificial chemicals, because of the chemical residues that remain in the ground from past use. A study in Los Angeles revealed that pesticide levels in "organic" vegetables were barely distinguishable from those in conventionally grown foods. In a 1972 investigation in New York State, pesticide residues were discovered in 30 percent of "organic" foods, compared to 20 percent of supermarket foods.

No one can object when health food advocates suggest that we become more attentive to what we eat and how we cook it. But some food faddists base their thinking on the belief that urbanization is a calamitous phenomenon and it's time to return to nature. They forget, however, that meals weren't all that delectable in more "natural" times. In the *Journal of the American Dietetic Association* (1964), S. E. Weigley described food in the era of the American Revolution, when "frontier meals leaned heavily on game, 'hog' and hominy, cornmeal mush, molasses, bear oil for frying, and beans and peas. . . . [M]any foreign visitors rebelled at the amount of grease and pork."

"Organic" and "natural" foods usually cost 50 to 85 percent more than the same regular foods, even when sold in the same store. Since there is no compelling evidence that organic foods are nutritionally superior, they probably aren't worth the extra cost, particularly for families on tight budgets.

If you are going to buy health foods, there are unfortunately no universally accepted guidelines to ensure that they are "organic," and thus you really must depend on the integrity of each grower and storeowner for a guarantee that the food meets the claims made for it. Incidentally, because of the public confusion over terms like "organic," "natural," and "health foods," the Food and Drug Administration is considering banning these words in advertising.

MYTH: *All vegetarian diets are more healthful.*

Certain dietary practices—based on lifestyle, religion, or ecology—have questionable or exaggerated nutritional benefits for both children and adults. Vegetarianism is one of the most popular alternative nutritional programs, particularly among adolescents and young adults. The exact contents of the vegetarian diet can vary, and thus so does its nutritional value. While some vegetarian regimens can meet your child's nutritional needs if foods are selected wisely, others, such as certain types of Zen macrobiotic diet, are often too restricted and can be dangerously inadequate in the nutrients they supply.

If your children are on a vegetarian diet, be sure they're well nourished by having them consume sufficient calories, a balance of necessary amino acids, and enough vitamin A, vitamin B_{12}, vitamin D, calcium, iron, and riboflavin. With adequate vegetarian diets, obesity is rare and cholesterol levels are low.

Vegetarian diets that depend heavily on a single vegetable source or cereal item can be dangerous, causing nutritional disorders such as rickets, scurvy, and anemia. Two British researchers have called these severely restricted food programs a form of child neglect.

MYTH: *Homemade baby foods are nutritionally superior to the storebought variety.*

Many parents are convinced that the jars of baby food sold in supermarkets are hardly an ideal food. But in recent years baby food manufacturers have improved their infant formulations, producing higher-quality items for baby consumption. The leading baby-food manufacturers no longer add salt to their products, particularly meats and vegetables. They have also reduced or eliminated the amounts of refined sugar in their foods.

If you carefully prepare your own baby preparations at home, the quality can equal or surpass the commercially prepared foods while saving you money. A recent study in Pittsburgh, however, noted, "Home prepared foods had a sodium (salt) concentration 1005 percent higher than similar baby food products produced by Heinz and Beechnut." The amount of salt in commercial products, then, may be preferable unless parents take special care to use less salt when preparing their own baby food.

Salt, of course, is not the only concern that parents have. They are also rushing to their refrigerators and blenders to protect their children from MSG (monosodium glutamate), preservatives, artificial colors and flavors, modified food starch, nitrates, and nitrites. But the situation with packaged baby food is not nearly as dire as some parents presume. Nitrates, nitrites, and food cured with them have been banned from all baby foods for several years by order of the U.S. Department of Agriculture. None of the major infant food manufacturers uses MSG, artificial colors, artificial flavors, or flavor enhancers either. So while baby foods were once produced to please the taste buds of parents who would sneak a bite of them, they are now designed to comply with the recommendations of nutritionists.

MYTH: *"Fast foods" are really junk food.*

The eating habits of Americans changed dramatically in the 1950s, when Colonel Harland Sanders introduced the world to Kentucky Fried Chicken and the era of fast-food dining. Since then, McDonald's, Pizza Hut, Taco Bell, Burger King, and dozens of other food chains have become part of our culture and eating patterns.

Many people consider the items served at fast-food restaurants "junk food," empty of all nutritional value. But that isn't the case. Hot dogs and hamburgers are not only the favorite lunch and dinner items of millions of children, they are also good sources of protein and other necessary nutrients. Hamburgers provide vitamins, iron, and other minerals, and if served with cheese, they contain additional protein, calcium, and vitamins A and B. Even french fries offer vitamins B and C, while milkshakes contain calcium and protein.

The major problems with fast foods are their caloric, salt,

and saturated-fat content. For instance, three pieces of Colonel Sanders chicken, plus mashed potatoes, gravy, coleslaw, and a roll, are high in fat and protein, low in vitamins A and B, and total 830 calories. Other fast-food meals often register about 1000 calories. If, however, your child replaces the customary Big Mac or Whopper with a simple hamburger and substitutes milk for a shake, this can reduce the amount of calories to 400. Fast-food restaurants are here to stay, and if you select lower-fat hamburgers, reduce the frequency of french fries, and add a salad now and then, your children won't be harmed by occasional visits to the golden arches.

Incidentally, the McDonald's Corporation will send you a free diabetic food exchange list, describing the exact contents of their foods. Write to McDonald Plaza, Oakbrook, IL 60521. Other chains also may be able to send you similar nutritional breakdown charts.

MYTH: *Begin feeding solids to your baby as early as possible.*

See pages 15–16.

MYTH: *Many children don't eat as much as they should.*

Almost every healthy youngster consumes all the food he or she needs for growth and energy. Nevertheless, many parents become concerned about their child's "inadequate" food intake upon noticing that their youngster is no longer gaining weight regularly and rapidly. But this slowdown in weight gain is quite normal.

The period of most rapid human growth is during the first four weeks of life. This fast weight and height gain continues until age four months, at only a slightly slower pace, with 33 percent of all calories consumed going toward growth. However, after age four months, the rate of human growth decreases significantly, and most of the calories consumed by your children are used instead for energy needs. Between the ages of four months and twelve months, only 7 percent of the calories taken in are utilized for growth, and that figure eventually decreases to 1 percent or less after the second birthday.

So if your child's rate of growth noticeably slows down after the age of two years, don't blame it on poor eating habits. This is a normal phenomenon that occurs with all youngsters.

MYTH: *An apple a day keeps the doctor away.*

Apples, as tasty as they may be, are not likely to keep either doctors or diseases at a distance. Their nourishing properties are limited, with relatively low levels of vitamins and minerals. They have also been described as the fruit equivalent of the potato, because they are quite starchy.

Apples contain a carbohydrate called pectin, which some studies have credited with lowering cholesterol levels. Although this evidence is not yet conclusive, pectin has other positive physiological benefits as well, including its ability to promote normal bowel movement patterns. Often, when a child has diarrhea, apple juice or applesauce is employed as a means of stabilizing stool consistency.

MYTH: *Apples are nature's toothbrushes.*

Although munching on an apple can stimulate the mouth's chewing apparatus and even the gums, it is far from being a hygienic tool for the teeth. Apples contain sugar, and whether sugar originates with apples or candy bars, it can produce cavities. Because some sugar remains on the teeth after apples are chewed and swallowed, the teeth should be cleaned with a conventional toothbrush. Apples will not reduce tooth decay and in fact will promote it without proper brushing. Even so, they are a much better snack than sticky or gooey candy. (For more information on food sugar content and tooth decay, see pages 130–131.)

MYTH: *Apple seeds cause appendicitis.*

The appendix is a wormlike protrusion of the large intestine which, when inflamed, usually requires emergency abdominal surgery. The inflammation often starts when the opening to the appendix becomes blocked by intestinal debris, which is usually a piece of firm feces.

Some people believe that this inflammation is commonly caused by apple seeds. While in some cases small seeds have been found lodged in removed appendices, this is so rare that it is more a medical curiosity than anything else. If your child swallows apple seeds, you need not worry that an attack of appendicitis is imminent.

Because apple seeds contain minute amounts of cyanide, a few people who have eaten several sacks of seeds at one time have actually died doing so. But unless you are consuming extremely large amounts of seeds—many more than you would swallow by eating a reasonable number of apples per day—there is nothing to be concerned about. Even if your child eats a dozen apples in a single sitting, he will not run any risk of cyanide poisoning.

MYTH: *Apples that have had nails hammered into them can prevent anemia.*

In earlier generations, pregnant farm women in Poland ate apples that had been pierced with nails, which were left in the apple for a day and then removed. According to the old wives' tale, when iron nails had been marinated in the apple this way, the fruit would be filled with usable iron that the body could absorb.

A study by a nutritionist at the University of California at Berkeley did, in fact, recently reveal that this procedure can result in increases in the blood level of iron. When the nails are hammered into apples, their iron content is converted into an ionic form that the body can utilize.

Even so, I don't recommend this technique as a form of mineral supplementation. The amount of iron that the body can absorb this way is hard to measure and may not be enough to normalize a true iron deficiency anemia. Follow your physician's advice about your own child's particular circumstances.

MYTH: *Fish is a brain food.*

So many people believe in this myth that it is generally accepted among most segments of the populace. But no matter how plentiful the supply of trout, sole, and salmon is in a child's diet, I.Q. will not rise because of it.

This myth dates back to the mid-1800's, when researchers discovered that the brain's nerve cells contained phosphorus as well as several other elements. Buchner, a German philosopher, declared, "Without phosphorus, there is no thought," although he could have also included several other chemical compounds in that statement as well. It didn't take much stretching of logic, then, to conclude that fish, because of its high phosphorus content, could promote human thought processes. Louis Agassiz, the famous Harvard zoologist, strongly argued that fish really was brain food.

Today, we know much more about the complex workings of the brain. Its most rapid growth occurs in the years immediately after birth, and by age six the brain is nearly adult size. During this period of brain development, children consume relatively little fish, and still their brains grow quite well. In fact, the best "brain food" seems to be *any* nutritious food that can contribute to the well-being of not only the brain but the rest of the body as well.

MYTH: *Muscle mass can be increased by eating steak.*

See page 189.

MYTH: *Everybody needs milk.*

No, not everybody needs milk. Over 30 million Americans cannot tolerate milk, because they lack or have low levels of an enzyme in their intestines called lactase. This enzyme must be present in sufficient amounts for the body to properly digest lactose, the nutritious milk sugar.

Although almost all healthy babies are born with lactase,

its quantity gradually reduces as the child gets older, starting at about age five. By adulthood, many people have permanently lost the ability to produce adequate lactase. According to recent studies in the United States, this includes up to 70 percent of blacks, 95 percent of Orientals, and about 65 percent of Jews and other individuals whose heritage can be traced to central and eastern Europe and the Mediterranean countries. No wonder, then, that babies tolerate milk well, but as they move through childhood and into adulthood, their tolerance may progressively decrease and eventually vanish. This same phenomenon apparently occurs in other animal species as well; in fact, human beings are the only species that consumes milk after the suckling period, leading some scientists to conclude that since other mammals do not drink milk beyond infancy, there is probably no need for us to either.

Children having a lactase deficiency usually respond to milk and milk products with severe gasiness, cramping, bloating, and diarrhea. The severity of these symptoms depends not only on the level of lactase enzyme present but also on how much lactose is consumed. In my practice, when schoolage children complain of frequent and severe stomachaches, their discomfort can often be permanently alleviated by taking them off milk. Avid milk lovers with the problem who don't want to give up this drink can obtain the deficient enzyme in commercially prepared powdered form, called LactAid.

MYTH: *Whole milk is healther for infants than formula.*

For generations, milk has been considered a critically important nutrient by most parents. For that reason, they are often eager to remove their newborns from formula feedings, placing them on whole milk as early as six months of age. However, whole cow's milk contains a protein that can irritate the intestinal lining of a baby, even causing microscopic bleeding that can lead to iron deficiency anemia. Some babies also experience a colicky reaction to whole cow's milk, which has a large curd formation, making it more difficult to digest than human milk.

The American Academy of Pediatrics currently recommends that babies remain on breast milk or infant formulas or both until ten to twelve months of age. These formulas are specially prepared to meet an infant's unique nutritional needs.

MYTH: *When babies begin drinking cow's milk, nonfat is preferable to whole milk.*

Skim milk is usually not the best alternative, because it does not sufficiently provide for the child's energy needs, its fat content is inadequate for the growing baby, and its levels of vitamin C and various minerals (including iron) are too small. Furthermore in reducing the fat level of the milk the protein and sodium salt content is increased. This places a strain on the young kidneys and it has been hypothesized that this may increase the risk of developing hypertension later in life. Low-fat milk is an acceptable drink for children over age 1½ years, but generally not for those younger.

MYTH: *Goat's milk is just as nutritious as human breast milk.*

Goat's milk may be fine for goats—and adults—but it's certainly not the best choice for your own baby. Not only does goat's milk present the same problems discussed above with cow's milk, but it also contains inadequate levels of folic acid, one of the B-complex vitamins. A chronic deficiency of folic acid can cause a severe form of anemia.

MYTH: *Spinach will give your child added strength.*

Although no one can deny that spinach provided Popeye with boundless vigor, its special mystical properties work only in the comic pages. While it's true that spinach contains large amounts of iron and calcium, they exist in a form that is difficult for the human body to digest. Because spinach is extremely low in calories, it is a poor energy source, and even though it is rich in vitamins A, B, and C, these chemicals are present in many other foods as well.

So while spinach is a fine food for your children to eat, it is not indispensable, as many parents believe, and is probably not worth the family battles that often occur when the kids refuse to eat it. If your child does not like this particular green vegetable, the same nutrients are available in other food items that children usually consider more palatable.

MYTH: *Grapefruit will melt away body fat.*

The amount of human fat is determined by the number of calories consumed, the amount of energy expended, and hormonal influences. In general, if your diet includes more calories than your body burns up, you will gain weight; if you eat fewer calories than your body uses, you will lose weight. That's the formula, and there's not a gimmick in existence that can change it. Any diet that claims that grapefruits—or any other food—will "melt away" excess pounds is only kidding you.

Even so, grapefruits may have a role to play in helping the overweight child reduce. This citrus fruit contains only about 50 calories per half, and if eaten slowly, it represents a relatively small caloric intake while helping to satisfy the youngster's hunger. Grapefruit is also rich in vitamin C, as well as providing calcium, thiamin, iron, niacin, vitamin A, and protein.

MYTH: *Yogurt is an excellent diet food.*

Plain yogurt is a fine food for children trying to lose weight. The low-fat type contains only about 120 calories per half-pint container. But some of the fruit-flavored yogurts have enough sweeteners, syrups, and sugars to double the calories per serving, making them not much more helpful to a weight-reduction program than cookies.

In whatever form, yogurt does have other undeniable benefits. It is a good source of calcium, having higher levels of this mineral than either cottage cheese or ice cream. Some recent evidence also points to a possible role in the prevention of vascular disease. In a study reported in the *American Journal of Clinical Nutrition* (1979), volunteers were fed various yogurt preparations, and after only seven days their serum cholesterol levels decreased 5 to 10 percent. The exact cause for this drop is not yet precisely known, and further investigations are now in progress. But even these early findings have attracted many joggers to yogurt, since they seem particularly interested in minimizing the level of cholesterol in their blood.

MYTH: *Yogurt can prolong life.*

In recent years, various health-enhancing properties have been attributed to yogurt. Probably the most publicized "benefit" centers around an intestinal bacterium called lactobacilli, which is present in all milk products, including yogurt. Earlier in this century, scientists speculated that the consumption of large amounts of lactobacilli promoted the unusually long life spans of people in the Balkan countries. We now know, however, that the primary strain of lactobacilli in yogurt is *Lactobacillus bulgaricus,* which is not able to survive for long in the gastrointestinal tract and thus has a doubtful effect upon human longevity.

MYTH: *Yogurt can shorten bouts of diarrhea.*

The limited survival of yogurt lactobacilli within the human intestinal tract, which is discussed above, also casts doubt on another widely proclaimed "advantage" of yogurt— namely, that when an individual has a bout with diarrhea caused by prolonged antibiotic treatment, the lactobacilli can replace the intestinal bacteria destroyed during the illness.

By contrast, a similar bacterium called *Lactobacillus acidophilus* does proliferate for a longer time in the intestines and thus may have some real benefits. This explains the current popularity of Sweet Acidophilus milk among health food devotees, although the actual advantages of this bacterial strain are still being debated by scientists. *Lactobacillus acidophilus,* incidentally, is *not* present in yogurt.

MYTH: *Chocolate causes allergies and headaches.*

Pity the poor chocolate bar. Not only is it blamed for obesity but also for everything from allergies to migraine headaches to acne and tooth decay.

In a comprehensive review of the alleged negative effects of chocolate, which was published in the *Annals of Allergy* (1978), Joseph H. Fries indicated that although chocolate appears frequently among the food people say they are allergic to, an actual allergy to this popular snack food is found in relatively few individuals and is often overdiagnosed by physicians. Although chocolate may induce migraines in some children, it apparently does so relatively rarely, and only in particularly susceptible individuals.

Chocolate, then, receives more blame for allergies, headaches—and almost everything else—than it deserves. There is no evidence to support the almost universal belief that chocolate is a prime cause of acne (see page 164), and while sugar in chocolate *can* cause cavities, decay is primarily due to prolonged contact of the sugar in the chocolate with the teeth. If children brush their teeth immediately after eating chocolate, the risk of tooth decay will be significantly reduced.

MYTH: *Eating too much sugar causes diabetes.*

There are essentially two types of the metabolic disorder called diabetes: juvenile diabetes, resulting from insufficient insulin production by the pancreas, and maturity-onset diabetes, which begins in adulthood and in which there is adequate or even excessive insulin but the body tissues have developed an inability to utilize it. To treat childhood diabetes, insulin injections are necessary; by contrast, maturity-onset diabetes rarely requires injections except in the most severe cases.

Although some researchers think that a link may exist between sugar consumption and the onset of diabetes, there is no conclusive evidence that such a connection exists. Diabetics are advised to eat less sugar, since it converts quickly to glucose and produces an immediate need for insulin. But in a nondiabetic person, there is no evidence that eating sugar places stress on the pancreas or triggers diabetes.

The exact cause of diabetes is unknown, although there seems to be a strong genetic influence at play. Many endocrinologists believe that a viral infection may sometimes trigger the onset of the disorder in a person genetically prone to diabetes. The adult type is aggravated by excessive weight gain and can often be controlled by losing weight.

MYTH: *Food additives cause hyperactivity.*

There are many hypotheses on the cause of hyperactivity in children. One of the most publicized theories was proposed in 1974 by Ben Feingold, a California pediatric allergist, who stated that various food substances—including artificial colors, artificial flavors, and salicylates—were factors in hyperactivity. Diets free of these substances, he claimed, could significantly reduce hyperactive behavior in 40 to 70 percent of all cases.

However, several recent investigations have failed to substantiate Feingold's hypothesis. Using Feingold's dietary guidelines, most hyperactive children in these studies showed *no* changes in their behavior. In one study, for example, only one of twenty-two hyperactive children exhibited some behavioral improvements when the additives were carefully controlled—a far smaller percentage than Feingold purports. Most researchers have concluded that if there is any relationship between diet and behavior, it is either barely significant or it exists in only an extremely small number of children.

MYTH: *Coffee stunts your growth.*

Caffeine, most commonly associated with coffee, has long been blamed for limiting height. But there is absolutely no evidence to substantiate this belief. While caffeine may promote insomnia and a rapid heart rate, it has no effect on normal growth.

Children and adolescents do not have to drink coffee to get caffeine; this substance is present in large amounts in cola drinks. Coca-Cola contains 36.8 mg per eight-ounce bottle (140 mg per liter) and Pepsi-Cola contains 24 mg (91 mg per liter). As a comparison, decaffeinated coffee contains 3 mg caffeine per cup, instant coffee, 60 mg per cup, and roasted or ground coffee, 85 mg per cup.

There are some important facts about caffeine to keep in mind. Although there is not yet any conclusive evidence that excessive caffeine consumption during pregnancy can harm the human fetus, some preliminary research shows that caffeine may have some harmful druglike side effects, and thus women should use it in moderation during the childbearing years.

While the side effects of excessive caffeine consumption can vary from heartburn to diarrhea, perhaps the most troublesome was recently uncovered by a study at Vanderbilt Medical School. When healthy people who did not drink coffee consumed the equivalent of two to three cups of coffee, their blood pressure rose an average of fourteen points. While more studies are necessary in this area, the Vanderbilt findings should be taken into account by individuals who already have elevated blood pressure.

Caffeine, by the way, is also being used experimentally as a treatment for hyperactivity. Because some researchers now consider hyperactivity a depressive, not an excitatory, phenomenon, they are using stimulants like coffee to control it. In some studies, caffeine has proved as effective as other commonly used drugs in managing this disorder.

MYTH: *Pickles are poisonous.*

This is one of those myths that persists among some people, with little known about its origin. For those intent on believing in it, however, a little imagination can provide all the "proof" that is necessary. For example, in *Dietetic Currents* (1979), Fergus M. Clydesdale fantasized about a make-believe study of the eating habits of people born in the late nineteenth century. Most of those who had eaten pickles in their lifetimes were now dead, he noted, "substantiating" the toxic effect of pickles. Of those pickle-eating individuals still alive who were born before 1900, all had wrinkled skin, had lost most of their teeth, and had weakening eyesight—once again "proving" the "terrible" effects of pickles. Can anyone conscientiously deny evidence as convincing as this?

Vitamins

MYTH: *All children need vitamin supplements.*

Nearly half a billion dollars is spent every year on supplemental vitamins in the United States. The advocates of these products insist that this country is brimming with people deficient in vitamins because of imbalanced meals and too much junk food, and unless they are consuming vitamin supplements, they may be prone to disease.

Despite these claims, most nutritionists concur that a child or an adult on a normal, varied diet is already consuming all the vitamins necessary and that for children over the age of eighteen months, *no* vitamin supplements are needed. Under that age, there is still some controversy about the advisability of supplements, but most pediatricians agree that even then, supplements of vitamins are not necessary if the recommended infant-formula, breast-milk, or dietary regimens are followed. However, some doctors do believe that extra supplements of the following vitamins are needed for babies, as described:

Vitamin K: Breast milk has inadequate amounts of vitamin K, and consequently most babies receive a vitamin K shot shortly after birth, eliminating this shortage.

Vitamin E: Although the vitamin E content of breast milk is variable, a routine diet usually provides enough of it. The sole exception is in the case of premature infants, for whom most pediatricians recommend vitamin E supplements.

Vitamin D: Some physicians suggest that breastfed babies receive vitamin D supplements. However, the most recent research suggests that *no* such supplementation is needed (see pages 11–12).

Vitamin B₁: A nerve disease called beriberi is caused by a vitamin B_1 deficiency. This disease is almost nonexistent in the United States, but when a mother has this ailment, her breast milk may be toxic to the infant. Vitamin B_1 supplements for the mother can alleviate this condition.

In general, multi- or polyvitamins are not needed by children. Some pediatricians, however, prescribe them when they include recommended amounts of fluoride, simply as a means of giving the child this important, decay-fighting compound.

If you are a strong believer in vitamins, you won't be harming your youngster by giving him or her the suggested dosages of commercial vitamin preparations. But in most cases, these tablets are nutritionally unnecessary and are an added expense.

MYTH: *Vitamin C can prevent colds.*

    See pages 82–84.

MYTH: *Vitamin A deficiencies can cause eye problems.*

    See pages 100–101.

MYTH: *Vitamins are natural compounds that are safe, even in large doses.*

    If you were to believe everything printed in newspapers and popular magazines, large doses of vitamins are the ultimate cure-all for almost every conceivable disease and condition. Advocates of vitamins often insist that if a little bit is good, then a lot must be better. Large doses of vitamins have been credited with aiding everything from mental disease to alcoholism to the problems of aging.

The megavitamin theory began more than two decades ago when large amounts of vitamin B were first used in an attempt to treat schizophrenia. Then, in 1968, Linus Pauling blamed some forms of mental illness on nutritional or biochemical imbalances, claiming that vitamins could play a role in alleviating these psychological disorders. Supporters of Pauling eventually developed a treatment system they called "orthomolecular psychiatry," which employs large vitamin doses as part of its therapy.

However, the dangers of high doses of vitamins are well documented. Large amounts of vitamin A may cause a syndrome called pseudotumor cerebri, with symptoms similar to a brain tumor. High doses of vitamin C have been linked with abnormal childhood bone growth, diarrhea, and kidney stones. Large amounts of vitamin D can cause excessive absorption of calcium, which can trigger various physiological problems.

So although taking the recommended daily allowances of supplemental vitamins is harmless, check with your physician before placing your child on high doses.

MYTH: *Vitamins will give your child added energy.*

Energy is obtained from three nutritional sources—fat, protein, and carbohydrate—none of which is present in vitamins. Unless youngsters are victims of a *severe* vitamin deficiency, the consumption of additional vitamin supplements will not elevate their activity level.

Vitamin deficiencies are actually very rare, usually caused by either severe malnutrition or a specific medical disorder that prevents the body from properly utilizing the vitamins it is consuming. It is much more important to determine the reason for a true deficiency than to try to immediately counter-act it with vitamin preparations.

MYTH: *"Natural" vitamins are nutritionally superior to synthetic ones.*

The "natural" vitamins sold at your local health food stores are absolutely identical in their molecular structure to synthetic vitamins. Neither is any more healthy than the other, and they act the same within the body, whether they come from the ground, a plant, or a chemical laboratory.

So a vitamin is a vitamin is a vitamin. And although your body can't tell synthetic and natural vitamins apart, once you see the inflated prices of the natural variety, your pocketbook will certainly notice the difference.

Obesity

MYTH: *The fatter the baby, the healthier the baby.*

No one is going to become overly concerned with a layer of baby fat on an infant. But even so, excess fat is not a healthy sign and could be an indicator of problems to come. Obesity is now a common nutritional problem in the Western world, and about one-third of overweight adults were over-weight children.

In earlier generations, most babies doubled their birth weight by the age of six months. Today, studies indicate that the birth weight of many infants doubles by three to four months. Al-though this phenomenon is most likely a reflection of improved nutrition, it concerns those physicians who believe that if an overweight problem occurs in childhood, there may be a higher risk of adult obesity.

According to an interesting but still unproven fat-cell theory, there are two major periods in life—infancy and adolescence—when the body's fat cells (adipocytes) increase in number in response to a child's eating habits. Once these fat cells are formed, they remain for the rest of the youngster's life, waiting to be filled with excess body fat. Proponents of this theory argue that if eating habits can be controlled during childhood, there will be a diminished chance of weight problems in the adult years, since fewer fat cells will be present.

Incidentally, a recent study revealed that obesity tends to run in families—that is, children exhibit a high risk for obesity if one of their parents is obese, and an even higher one if both parents are overweight. Social and emotional factors play a role in obesity, too, with an increasing frequency of overweight problems seen in urban environments, lower socioeconomic groups, broken homes, and when maternal-infant separations exist.

MYTH: *Overweight children do not develop any obesity-related health problems until adulthood.*

Many medical problems have been linked with adult obesity, including cardiovascular disease and diabetes. Some research, however, now indicates that when obesity begins in childhood, the risks of developing serious cardiovascular problems later in life are even greater.

In addition, several less severe disorders directly related to childhood obesity can surface early in life. Overweight babies, for example, have more frequent and more serious respiratory tract infections. They also have more orthopedic problems, particularly affecting the legs.

While it is popular to blame obesity on glandular disorders, such metabolic causes of obesity are extremely rare. Less than 1 percent of childhood overweight conditions are caused by such underlying medical problems.

MYTH: *Breastfed babies are never obese.*

Some parents believe that breastfeeding babies can eat as often as they like, without any risk of becoming overweight.

Several studies have examined this issue, and while they found that bottle-fed infants tended to be more obese than breastfeeders between birth and six weeks of age, there were an equal percentage of breastfed and bottlefed obese babies by six months of age. None of the available evidence supports breastfeeding as a hindrance to obesity.

When bottlefeeding babies become overweight, it is often because parents fill the bottle with a specific number of ounces, feeling they know best just how much the infant needs. However, as with breastfeeding babies it is better to let bottlefeeding newborns stop feeding when they want to and not encourage them to "squeeze the last ounce out."

14

INFECTIOUS DISEASES

Many of the feared and potentially harmful infectious childhood diseases—such as polio, diphtheria, measles, and tetanus—can now be controlled with proper immunizations and preventive care.

However, there are still many myths and misconceptions that persist about infectious diseases—their origin, transmission, and treatment. This chapter will discuss and dispel many of these and provide you with information to guarantee that your child has the best possible protection from major infectious illnesses.

MYTH: *Your child is better off being exposed to the "common childhood diseases" at a young age, since they are usually less severe then than if caught later in life.*

There is considerable confusion over diseases like measles and chicken pox, which are typically associated with childhood. Although some parents believe that these illnesses will be less severe when contracted early in life, there is no evidence to support this hypothesis. In fact, some illnesses tend to be *more* troublesome at a young age. For example, whooping cough (pertussis) is an infection that can be fatal when it occurs during infancy. When contracted in later childhood or the adult years, it is still serious but rarely life-threatening.

MYTH: *"Common childhood diseases" are so rare that immunizations are no longer necessary.*

Some childhood illnesses have become almost an academic issue, thanks to immunizations that can virtually prevent mumps, measles, rubella (German measles), diphtheria, whooping cough, and tetanus. In 1954, before the polio vaccine, there were 18,000 new cases of polio reported in the United States; by 1967, only 30 cases were reported. Ironically, the effectiveness of these immunizations has caused another problem: the parental belief that these illnesses are no longer a threat, and thus inoculations are really not essential. As one mother recently said to me, "Nobody ever gets polio any more. Why should my child be vaccinated when there's a risk of getting polio from the immunization itself?"

While it's true that one out of every 3 million children immunized with polio develops a serious, paralytic reaction to the vaccine, this risk is minimal compared with the consequences of contracting the actual disease. An adverse response to the polio inoculation occurs primarily in children with abnormal immune systems.

Similar situations have occurred with other childhood illnesses. While one in every million people receiving the measles vaccine may develop a brain disorder, the risks of the disease itself are much more ominous. In addition to the high fever and rash commonly associated with measles, one of every 1000 children with the disease develops deafness, blindness, convulsions, and brain disorders. All parents *must* take advantage of the immunizations available to their children. Only continuous protection will keep the epidemics of the past from returning.

MYTH: *If a child catches a "common childhood disease"*
from a youngster with only minor symptoms, his or
her own illness will also be mild.

Contrary to popular belief, the severity of a disease
in a particular child is not influenced by the condition of the
youngster from whom the illness was contracted. Thus, exposure to a mild case of, say, the measles will not ensure that
your child's ailment will be mild; conversely, exposure to a
serious case will not increase the chances of a serious illness.
So your own child's measles or mumps may be either mild
or severe, without being affected by the particular condition
of the youngster who transmitted the disease.

MYTH: *Tetanus is caused by rusty nails.*

Tetanus, or lockjaw, is a serious infection that involves
the central nervous system and causes painful muscular spasms
and stiffness. Rusty nails have long been blamed for this disease,
but neither nails nor the rust on them is directly to blame.
Tetanus, in fact, is caused by a bacterium called *Clostridium*
tetani, which is present in the intestines of horses, cattle, and
other plant-eating animals, and even in some people. A nail
or other object in a farm field would be a likely source of
tetanus germs, since the soil that the object came in contact
with (not the rust), when contaminated with animal excrement,
is the environment in which the bacteria thrive. However, a
nail—whether rusty or not—located inside a house is unlikely
to carry any tetanus-causing bacteria.

Tetanus can now be prevented by immunization, but before
such vaccines were developed and the cause of tetanus fully
understood, this infection frequently was contracted by newborns, particularly in country areas where, as part of a folk
treatment, animal excrement was placed over the unhealed
umbilical cord, on the assumption that there were anti-infective
properties within the excrement. It is now understood that

any opening or any wound, ranging from burns to crush injuries to punctures, can serve as the entry point for the tetanus germs, so preventive immunizations are extremely important.

MYTH: *Every puncture wound requires a tetanus shot.*

I am repeatedly contacted by anxious parents, reporting that their child has just stepped on a nail or a tack and thus requires a tetanus shot. However, if the youngster has already received a full series of immunizations, an additional tetanus shot usually is not necessary.

Typically, a child receives four DPT (diphtheria, pertussis, tetanus) shots in the early stages of life—at ages two, four, and six months, with a booster at age eighteen months. This series will provide the youngster with at least five years of protection. Once a repeat booster is administered between the ages of four and six years, a child is considered well protected until at least the age of ten. Boosters are then routinely suggested between ages twelve and sixteen and then every ten years thereafter.

When a wound occurs in a child who has already received at least the four original DPT shots, physicians usually decide upon the advisability of an added injection of tetanus toxoid (the "T" of DPT) by using the following criteria: no booster is necessary in the case of a clean cut or accident where there is little risk of exposure to the tetanus bacterium; however, a booster *is* necessary with wounds caused by machinery or instruments that may be contaminated with animal or human feces—but *only if more than five years have passed since the last booster.* For a youngster who has had less than the full series, a booster is usually suggested for even a low-risk injury.

When a child or adult receives a high-risk wound and has never had *any* tetanus shots, then the shot alone is usually not considered enough protection. An additional safeguard is provided with the injection of an extract of serum, called tetanus immunoglobulin, from a previously immunized individual.

MYTH: *Children who have the mumps on only one side of the face can still catch it on the other side.*

Mumps is an acute, contagious viral infection, characterized primarily by a swelling and tenderness of the salivary gland, called the parotid gland, located behind the jaw. The illness is usually relatively mild but sometimes involves the pancreas, the central nervous system, and, in males, the testicles.

Like many other viral illnesses, the mumps provides its own immunity against a second occurrence. This natural protection is usually lifelong with the mumps, even if only one side of the face was originally involved. Second attacks of the mumps are extremely rare.

Even so, some people report that they've known someone who had the mumps on one side of the face, and then caught it later on the other side. In almost all these cases, the mumps was probably not to blame in the second instance, or possibly even the first. Instead, this inflammation of the parotid glands could have been caused by an allergy, another type of viral infection, a bacterial infection, or a stone in the duct that's attached to the gland. Since these inflammations look the same as mumps, they are often confused with it.

A newly identified syndrome that also causes recurring parotid swelling is called wind parotitis, which occurs primarily in musicians who play instruments like the clarinet or the trumpet. It even afflicts people like glass blowers or balloon blowers. Perhaps you've had the experience of blowing up a particularly stubborn balloon and feeling shooting pains in your upper jaw. This, in fact, is air being driven from the mouth into the parotid duct. Interestingly, a 1915 textbook on communicable diseases cited a recurring phenomenon among French Foreign Legionnaires, who would blow forcefully into bottles, propelling air into their parotids, which invariably resulted in hospitalization for mumps and thus an escape from the desert sun. This condition was "epidemic" during the hottest times of the year.

MYTH: *Children can catch polio from swimming pools.*

This myth was nurtured by the epidemics of polio that often occurred near the end of summer, when children were plunging into pools to escape the heat of August and September. As outbreaks of polio would occur in a particular community, hysteria would often reign, and the municipal swimming pools were frequently closed down, blamed as the cause of the epidemic.

There are, in fact, some viral infections that can be transmitted by water, like the hepatitis virus. Also, recent outbreaks of a throat and eye infection called pharyngoconjunctival fever have been attributed to swimming pools that were inadequately chlorinated. But studies clearly indicate that the polio virus is transmitted not in water but in the fecal or oral secretions of infected individuals. The worse the sanitary conditions, from inadequate plumbing to poor handwashing habits to overcrowded living conditions, the greater the chance of infection.

Paul Wehrle, director of pediatrics at the Los Angeles County–University of Southern California Medical Center, thoroughly investigated this issue in the early 1950s, during the mass epidemics of that era. Dr. Wehrle identified two and possibly three individuals who seemed to have acquired polio at a swimming pool. But closer scrutiny of these cases indicated that these individuals had experienced extensive physical contact with each other and with a lifeguard who was infected with polio. According to Dr. Wehrle, "Since the contact was outside the water as well as in the water, and represented wrestling and other close physical contact, there was no way to incriminate the swimming pool per se in facilitating transmission."

Thus, there is no medical support for the belief that polio

can be caught or is transmitted in swimming pools. Instead, it is facilitated by close, intimate contact, particularly among individuals with poor hygienic techniques. The closing of swimming pools and even theaters in the past at least prevented the crowding together of susceptible children.

Interestingly, when polio is depicted in books and movies, a child often comes down with the disease the night after swimming against parental wishes. But in fact, the paralytic symptoms of polio do not appear until ten to fifteen days after exposure to the virus. Before then, usually two to three days after exposure, a minor coldlike illness surfaces. Of the individuals exposed to the polio virus and who have not been vaccinated against it, only about 1 percent ever experience any paralysis; the other 99 percent simply have what seems to be a minor cold and never know they caught a mild case of polio and for a short time ran the risk of developing the more severe paralytic symptoms.

MYTH: *Tuberculosis is inherited.*

Tuberculosis is a bacterial infection usually affecting the lungs, eventually causing the destruction of the infected tissue. Although it still causes some deaths in the United States each year, its incidence has generally declined over the years. Pediatricians typically test children annually for TB through a simple skin test that can detect prior exposure and contact with the tuberculin bacterium, called the mycobacterium.

For many years, the cause of TB was unknown, but because several members of the same family often suffered from it, heredity was erroneously blamed. Also, in earlier generations this illness was usually called consumption, since the disease seemed to consume the entire body.

Today, we know that the TB bacterium is typically transferred when an infected individual, usually an adult with open infected cavities in the lungs, coughs minute droplets of mycobacteria into the air. The chance of infection usually depends on the degree or frequency of a person's contact with the TB victim. Repeated and close contact increases the risk, and thus it is more often caught in the home, rather than at schools, churches, or other public places.

Children with tuberculosis, incidentally, rarely transmit the illness because they almost never develop the cavity lesions in the chest responsible for the communicable secretions.

MYTH: *People with tuberculosis must be placed in sanitariums.*

After physicians recognized that bacteria and not heredity were responsible for the transmission of tuberculosis, sanitariums provided isolation to control the communicability of the disease. As soon as individuals were diagnosed as having TB, they were separated from the rest of society in these institutions. But with the emergence of antibiotics, it was possible to bring the infection rapidly under control and thus significantly decrease the period during which the infected individuals were contagious. So although a few TB sanitariums still exist, they are very rare; most patients are treated with drugs in their own homes.

MYTH: *Scarlet fever is a much more serious illness than strep throat.*

Scarlet fever is a bacterial disease characterized by a red rash over the entire body, which may be accompanied by a sore throat, vomiting, and a fever. Its real danger is from the same complications that can ensue from an untreated strep throat—rheumatic fever and kidney problems.

Although scarlet fever was little heard of until the mid-1800s, there were epidemics of it in England in the latter part of the nineteenth century, resulting in many deaths. The illness spread through the United States in a more severe form in the 1920s and 1930s, understandably causing enormous anxiety among millions of parents. As mysteriously as this serious form of scarlet fever flourished in the mid-1800s and the first part of this century, it has unexplainably decreased in both frequency and severity in recent decades. Today, it is considered nothing more than a subcategory of streptococcal disease. Because of antibiotics, it need not be any more alarming than a strep throat infection itself.

No one clearly understands why the prevalence and gravity of scarlet fever have diminished. One hypothesis is that antibiotics have minimized the number of organisms that lead to the illness. But this is only a theory.

MYTHS: *Your doctor can determine if your child has a strep throat simply by looking; Younger children are just as susceptible to strep throat as older children; Penicillin will make a strep throat feel better faster.*

See pages 146–147.

MYTH: *Blood poisoning that goes to the heart can cause death.*

The term "blood poisoning" is commonly used to describe a bacterial infection in the bloodstream. This type of infection is serious and requires medical attention and antibiotic treatment. But despite beliefs to the contrary, the infection does not move into the heart, causing instant death.

The following events may contribute to this misconception. An individual will incur an injury to a particular part of the body, and a local infection will develop there, distinguished by redness, swelling, tenderness, and pus. If not controlled by the body in the original site, the infection begins spreading, and as it does, red streaks often appear on the involved bodily areas. These streaks are infections moving along lymphatic tracks, which are part of the body's natural defense system. As the streaks appear to approach the heart, individuals become fearful of impending disaster, as if the heart will suddenly stop beating as soon as the red lines reach it.

In fact, these lymphatic streaks are not directed into the heart; they are moving toward so-called "regional lymph nodes" that are located throughout the body. However, even though sudden death will not occur as these lines seemingly converge toward the heart, they are a sign of a significant infection and should be treated by a physician immediately.

MYTH: *Botulism is found only in bulging food cans.*

Botulism is a serious, often fatal type of food poisoning, caused when the poisons (toxins) produced by the bacterium *Clostridium botulinum* are consumed. This bacterium needs an oxygen-free environment in which to multiply, which is why food cans are a conducive setting for this process to occur. As the bacteria grow in number, they emit a gas that causes the cans to bulge.

However, botulism can survive in many other kinds of containers. On page 25 I discuss the small but still very real risk of botulism occurring in commercial honey preparations, whether packaged in bottles, cans, or other containers. Studies have shown that about 10 percent of the honey preparations found in supermarkets contained a culture in which the botulism bacteria could survive and multiply. While the toxin produced there cannot harm adults, it could provoke problems in infants, although this is an extremely uncommon occurrence. Children six months of age and under are those at risk, so just to be safe, I suggest that children do not consume honey during the first year of life.

MYTH: *Boiled skim milk is good for diarrhea.*

For generations, some families have given boiled skim milk to children with diarrhea. Although the origin of this treatment is unclear, it has absolutely no beneficial effect and in fact could cause some serious problems.

When milk is boiled, water evaporates and the concentrated liquid that remains behind contains excessively high levels of salt. When consumed by an infant, this can worsen the complications of the diarrhea by aggravating the dehydration from fluid loss and increasing the blood salt levels. To make matters even more complex, when gastroenteritis (inflammation of the stomach and intestines) is present—and it is the most common cause of diarrhea—there may be a short-term scarcity of the enzyme called lactase, which breaks down milk sugar. When this happens, any milk sugar present in the intestines—whether from whole milk, skim milk, or a cow's-milk formula—can prolong the diarrhea.

Consequently, when your child has diarrhea, all milk products should be eliminated, to allow the intestines to rest. In place of milk, special electrolyte formulations made for children, such as Pedialyte or Lytren, can be given to your ill youngster. If these are not available, you can safely substitute a Jell-o–water preparation (two parts Jell-o, one part water) or a soft drink that has been stirred or left standing until it has lost its carbonation. When your child has improved sufficiently to resume the intake of solid foods, many pediatricians recommend a BRAT diet—ripe *b*ananas, *r*ice, *a*pplesauce, and *t*oast, which should be continued until the stool is clearly solidifying.

MYTH: *Yogurt can shorten bouts of diarrhea.*

See pages 207–208.

MYTH: *Medicine should be given to childen with diarrhea.*

While adults are often given narcotic-derivative drug medications such as Lomotil to arrest their diarrhea, most pediatricians now avoid prescribing this type of drug for children because of the serious side effects. Although studies show that the drugs can curtail the observable symptoms of diarrhea in children, they may also sometimes mask the onset of dehydration, cause increasing lethargy, and possibly complicate certain bacterial diarrheal states. So although Lomotil is a convenient and helpful treatment for adults, research shows that it has no place in the care of children.

Diarrhea, of course, is a problem often associated with foreign travel. It is sometimes caused by dangerous bacteria (like salmonella and shigella), but most often it can be blamed on a bacterial strain called *Escherichia coli.* Although a form of *E. coli* is found in the intestinal tract of all human beings, its subtypes differ from one geographic region to another. When a tourist is exposed to an unfamiliar subtype, diarrhea is a common although not life-threatening reaction.

Numerous therapies have been attempted to care for this type of diarrhea. The latest vogue is bismuth subsalicylate, sold over the counter as Pepto-Bismol. Recent studies indicate that when consumed daily, Pepto-Bismol can often prevent and relieve traveler's diarrhea in adults. The efficacy of this treatment for children, however, is not yet well researched. Check with your doctor before attempting any type of therapy for diarrhea.

MYTH: *You can't get gonorrhea from a toilet seat.*

No, I'm not about to proclaim here that toilet seats are hazardous to your child's health. But I would like to present an interesting report which suggests that perhaps— just perhaps—the gonococcal germ can be transmitted this way.

A study in the *New England Journal of Medicine* (1979) discovered that gonorrhea contained in pus can survive on toilet paper or on a toilet seat for up to three hours. The researchers emphasized that merely sitting on a contaminated seat during this three-hour period could not transmit gonorrheal organisms to the urethra or genital tract. However, they noted that transmission might occur via the individual's hands.

Let me add that these and other researchers have never found conclusive evidence that gonorrhea can definitely be spread this way. In fact, as part of the study cited above, there was an examination of toilet seats in seventy-two public rest rooms, including those in hotels, hospitals, department stores, depots, and a high school. Not a single trace of gonorrhea was found on any toilet seat.

So even though it's *possible* that gonorrhea could be transmitted via a toilet seat, door knob, or any other object on which the gonococcal germ existed, it is still quite unlikely.

15

ACCIDENTS AND
ENVIRONMENTAL HAZARDS

Parents are justifiably concerned about the five primary life-threatening illnesses of childhood—pneumonia, meningitis, congenital malformations, heart disease, and cancer. But they are usually much less anxious about accidents, which cause more childhood deaths than these five diseases combined.

Over 14,000 youngsters under the age of fifteen die in accidents each year in the United States. While the number of illness-related fatalities among children has steadily decreased in recent decades, the incidence of accidental deaths has remained unchanged. Fortunately, most childhood accidents do not result in death. But accidents can be disabling, sometimes permanently, and cause 10 million school days to be missed each year. They certainly deserve more attention than they typically receive.

This chapter will delve into this leading cause of childhood injuries and deaths. Misunderstandings related to accidental poisonings, burns, choking, drownings, and automobile seat restraints will be discussed. You'll also learn about the effects of other environmental hazards that children commonly encounter, from cigarette smoke to dog bites. By the end of this chapter you may come to understand that the dangers in your child's environment are to be taken as seriously as illnesses your child may contract.

MYTH: *All poisons have an antidote.*

Many parents believe that if a poisoned child is treated soon enough, a specific antidote can be administered for the toxin, which can eliminate any possible dangers. However, there are less than a handful of poisons for which particular antidotes are available. In almost all cases of poisoning, other approaches are necessary, usually beginning with the removal of as much of the toxin as possible.

Because rapid removal from the body of most poisons is very important, I tell every parent to have syrup of ipecac in the home. This substance can be purchased without a prescription in a one-ounce container, and when swallowed in the recommended dosage (one tablespoon), it causes vomiting. However, before administering it, call your physician, an emergency room, or a poison control center, since there are certain situations (as when corrosives have been swallowed) when vomiting is not recommended. If vomiting is suggested, you can save precious minutes by having ipecac on hand. More than 2 million cases of poisoning are reported annually in the United States, but since most are successfully managed before worrisome symptoms develop, few ever require emergency room care. A study at Childrens Hospital of Los Angeles revealed that of 117 poisoning cases seen in the emergency room over two months, more than 75 percent required no treatment at all or were successfully cared for by using ipecac alone.

Even so, accidental poisoning is such a serious problem that Congress passed the Poison Prevention Packaging Act in 1970, which baby-proofed many hazardous products by requiring them to be sold in containers with safety caps. Since then, research shows that the number of childhood aspirin ingestions has been cut in half. However, one study indicated that while some adults, particularly arthritis sufferers, could only remove the safety caps with a pair of pliers, many retarded children opened the bottles within thirty seconds by prying them open with their teeth. To worsen matters, because of the difficulty some adults have in removing these caps, they leave them off, defeating the entire purpose of having child-resistant closures.

The majority of poisonings occur in children under five years of age, with 78 percent involving household products and non-prescription drugs. As general guidelines, Eugene L. Keller, director of Emergency Services at Cedars-Sinai Medical Center in Los Angeles, has made the following suggestions to prevent accidental poisonings:

- Presume that all drugs and household products are potentially harmful if swallowed.
- Lock up all dangerous substances—don't just put them out of reach.
- Place childproof catches on all doors under the sink.
- Store medications for internal use separately from those for external use so as not to confuse them.
- Keep all substances in their original containers. Too often, children have unsuspectingly drunk gasoline that had been stored in soft drink bottles or made some similar mixup.
- If you're interrupted by the phone or doorbell while working with household products or containers, take all unopened bottles with you, or seal them securely before you leave them.
- If a label is detached or blurred, replace it with a new label securely taped to the container.
- Administer medication in proper lighting to eliminate any confusion.
- Avoid taking medications yourself in front of children, who often like to imitate their parents.
- Never refer to medicine as "candy."
- Dispose of all empty containers and unused medication.

• Keep the purses of grandmothers and other visitors out of a child's reach.

MYTH: *Place butter on burns.*

About one of every seventeen American homes experiences a fire each year. Although most of these are minor kitchen fires, they can nevertheless cause serious burns in both children and adults.

People used to place butter on a burn to soothe the pain, and in fact some people still do. But burn experts now recognize that butter has no antibacterial and antidisinfectant properties, and can actually place an undesired layer of debris-collecting material on burns.

They now recommend that the affected area be immersed in cool water as soon as possible. Even after the burned part of the body is pulled away from the fire, thermal damage may continue to progress until the burned area has thoroughly cooled to a normal temperature. So although pain may subside immediately upon submerging the burned area in water, thirty minutes or more may be required to cool down the burned area completely. Make certain that the water you use for your child's burn is *cool,* not ice cold, because extremely cold temperatures can further damage the injured tissue. With deep burns, continue to apply the water by immersions or cool compresses until medical attention can be obtained. As a general rule, any burn covering an area larger than a square inch, or involving the face, hands, or genitals should be seen by a physician.

Fortunately, most burns in the home can be prevented from ever happening. A common source of burns among both children and the elderly is tap water scalding, which usually occurs because the thermostat of the household water heater is set far in excess of safe levels. The ideal setting is 125° (52°C), but a study in Seattle showed that 80 percent of the homes there had their temperature setting at over 130° (54°C), which is hot enough to cause severe skin burns within thirty seconds. Some thermostats were set at 160°, high enough to produce severe third-degree burns almost instantaneously. There is absolutely no evidence that certain appliances, like automatic dishwashers, require hot water in excess of 125° (52°C).

Some burns accidentally occur when a child is being bathed in a bathtub or sink and unsuspectingly turns off the cold water knob or turns on the hot water knob. A young child should never be allowed to be within reach of the hot and cold knobs.

MYTH: *Frostbitten areas of your child's body should be rubbed with snow.*

Frostbite is an inflammation caused by exposure to extreme cold. The areas of the body with the poorest circulation—fingers, toes, ears, and nose—are the most vulnerable.

Because tissue loss or infection can set in when the afflicted region becomes completely white and loses all feeling, immediate measures must be taken. But rubbing the area with snow is *never* the proper treatment and could actually worsen the cold damage. The frostbitten parts of the body must be *warmed*, preferably by submerging them in water at about body temperature. Be sure the water is not hotter than that, since the numb, frostbitten extremities will not be capable of sensing the water temperature, and the entire area could be severely burned if the water is too hot. You should be trying to thaw out the area gradually, not so quickly that it could cause even more harm.

When very large areas of the body are frostbitten, particularly when they are thoroughly white and numb, a physician should be contacted to guide you toward the most appropriate treatment.

MYTH: *All head injuries should be x-rayed.*

See pages 148–149.

MYTH: *Broken noses must be set as soon as possible.*

See page 122.

MYTH: *Cigarette smoking is hazardous only to the person who is smoking.*

The evidence is overwhelming and widely publicized that smoking really is hazardous to your health. I'm sure you've read dozens of articles about this subject, and there's no need to cite studies here to convince you.

In this book, I'm much more interested in making you aware of the potential dangers to your youngsters—including the unborn fetus—if you smoke. Research shows that cigarette smoke causes a higher frequency of allergy problems and irritation to people in close proximity to it. In their first year of life, children of smoking parents experience an above-average incidence of bronchitis and pneumonia. Several studies demonstrate that they also have an increased number of various respiratory illnesses throughout their entire childhood and early teens. The elevated carbon monoxide levels caused by the release of this gas in cigarette smoke may also decrease a child's exercise threshold.

A breastfeeding mother who smokes only ten cigarettes a day can significantly reduce the amount and quality of her breast milk and thus contribute to poor weight gain in her baby. There is also evidence that when nicotine passes through the mother's body directly into her milk, her infant can experience anxiousness and irritability.

Similar difficulties can afflict the fetus of a smoking mother. Birth weight averages about one-half pound less when a mother smokes, although the discontinuation of smoking by the fourth month of pregnancy can avoid this weight problem. Researchers theorize that carbon monoxide in cigarette smoke reduces oxygen delivery to the unborn child, producing these weight-gain difficulties. Pregnant women who smoke also experience more complicated pregnancies and an increased risk of premature delivery.

MYTH: *Cigarette smoking stunts your growth.*

In an attempt to discourage their teenage, and sometimes younger, children from smoking, many parents tell their offspring that cigarette smoking will stunt their growth. But aside from the evidence cited above that a smoking, pregnant woman can impede the growth of an unborn child, there is no evidence that people who themselves smoke actually inhibit their own height.

Related research shows, however, that when children smoke they experience other serious problems similar to those of adult smokers, from respiratory tract infections to allergies.

MYTH: *Alcohol can safely be consumed by a pregnant woman.*

For many centuries, alcohol has been suspected of causing malformations in the unborn fetus. In the Old Testament, an angel warned Samson's mother: "Behold, thou shalt conceive, and bear a son; and now drink no wine or strong drink. . . ." An ancient Carthaginian law prohibited married couples from drinking on their wedding night.

In recent years, these concerns have been scientifically validated, and the so-called "fetal alcohol syndrome" has been thoroughly described in medical literature. David W. Smith and Kenneth L. Jones reviewed tens of thousands of pregnancies and concluded that there is a clear connection between a mother's consumption of alcohol and fetal malformations of the eyes, nose, mouth, heart, height, weight, and intellectual function. While the chronic alcoholic woman clearly runs the highest risk, the precise dangers of moderate drinking during the first weeks of pregnancy are not known, but it may have a detrimental effect on the fetus.

Until even more studies are conducted, I suggest that pregnant women refrain from drinking. Although a single glass of wine on a special occasion is probably acceptable, most obstetricians now discourage any alcohol intake in excess of this minimal amount.

MYTH: *A child who is choking should be slapped firmly on the back.*

When a healthy child suddenly begins choking or has problems breathing, there may be an object stuck in the upper airway. Under these circumstances, if the youngster is still able to breathe or talk, proceed to the hospital emergency room as quickly as possible. The air tube probably is only partially blocked, and consequently, you should *not* slap the back, shake the child, or carry out any other maneuver that might jar the object into a more dangerous position in which the breathing tube becomes completely blocked.

If your youngster is choking and cannot breathe, the air tube is probably totally obstructed, and you must take some immediate action yourself. If you can see or feel the object, try to extract it with your finger, being careful not to push it even farther in. If this fails, then back slapping is an appropriate measure. Place the child stomach down, resting over your knees, with his (or her) head down. With the heel of the hand slap him sharply four times between the shoulder blades, which hopefully will cause him to cough and eject the object.

Another technique to try is the Heimlich maneuver, which has proved successful with both children and adults. Stand behind and wrap your arms around the child, grasping your fists together between the youngster's navel and lower rib cage. With the thumb side of one of your fists resting directly on his or her abdomen, quickly press up and in. This will rapidly increase the air pressure in the child's lungs and perhaps force the object outward, like popping a cork. In infants where the abdominal thrust can cause injury to the abdominal organs, especially the liver, a modification of this technique is used. External chest compressions are performed by the rescuer in an attempt to expel the object without putting pressure on the abdomen. Repeat this and the preceding back slap procedure several times if necessary. After breathing has resumed, you should then seek immediate medical attention. All parents are encouraged to take cardio-pulmonary resuscitation courses to master these techniques.

A young child, of course, cannot be expected to know what objects are safe. All food should be cut into small pieces, and youngsters should be taught to chew thoroughly. And for very young children who tend to place everything in their mouth, there should never be any small objects within their reach.

MYTH: *Small children can safely eat peanuts.*

Peanuts, because of their small size and firm consistency, are a common cause of choking in children. If a child chokes on a peanut, there is the additional risk of provoking a "chemical pneumonia." This phenomenon results when the peanut is sucked into the lungs and its oil irritates the lung linings. Although the initial symptoms may be nothing more than a mild cough, the irritation can develop into pneumonia, which could require hospitalization and surgical removal of the peanut.

I warn parents that young children should never be allowed to eat peanuts, and even older youngsters should only be permitted to have them while calmly seated, rather than eating them while they are playing or actively moving about. Tripping or falling can quickly cause choking and aspiration of the peanut into the lungs.

MYTH: *Babies don't require car seats after the first year of life.*

Automobile accidents are the number-one killer of children, causing more deaths (about 5000 fatalities each year under age fifteen years) than all other types of accidents combined. Below the age of five, for example, there are five times more deaths due to car accidents than to poisoning. As

I mentioned in the newborn chapter (page 36), it is essential for infants to be placed in car seats from the day they are brought home from the hospital. Some parents, however, believe that these safety restraints are only necessary during the first year of life, after which normal seat belts can be used.

But research shows that until children weigh forty or more pounds, they should continue riding in upright car seats. Standard seat belts rest too high on a small child's abdomen, and in an accident, the force of any injury will concentrate on the abdomen, often causing crushing damage to the vulnerable organs in that area. By contrast, a car seat usually lifts the child higher, placing most of the belt pressure across the more rigid and bony pelvis. It also provides the child with restraint for the head and chest.

Many parents are still not convinced that *any* type of car restraint is necessary. But the facts thoroughly refute this notion. In a 30 mph crash, a baby weighing ten pounds who is unrestrained can hit the instrument panel with a force equal to a fall from a three-story building. A mother weighing 100 pounds, who is also unrestrained and holding her baby in her lap, becomes a 3000-pound force in a 30 mph accident, capable of crushing the child against whatever they hit, whether dashboard or seat.

It is tragic that currently only approximately 15 percent of American children are properly protected while travelling in moving vehicles. Dr. Donald Shifrin, pediatric safety adviser, explains the problems associated with establishing consistent automobile safety habits compared with general accident prevention: "Each time a child is placed into a vehicle parents are required to take a definite physical action to secure their child in a safety apparatus. This is in contrast to prevention of other child-related accidents, as burns, poisoning or drownings, where precautions consist of mere parental vigilance or a one time parental action as fencing a pool, or locking up medications and poisons. The necessity of deliberate repeated

attention to automobile safety devices is what makes compli-
ance more difficult." Yet, if all youngsters would use an appropriate safety device—car seats for young children, seat belts
for older ones—over 90 percent of all auto deaths could be
prevented, with disabling injuries reduced by as much as 78
percent.

MYTH: *Playgrounds are safe places for children to play.*

Children are certainly safer playing in playgrounds than
in the street. But playground equipment like swings and slides
poses risks as well and in fact ranks fifth in the U.S. Consumer
Product Hazard Index, according to a study in *Pediatrics* (1979).
In 1978 alone, 167,000 persons were administered hospital
treatment across the country for injuries related to public
(75,000), home (41,000), and unspecified (51,000) playground
apparatus. Most of the injuries occurred in children in the five-
to-ten-year-old range, with falls, particularly from slides and
climbing apparatus, ranking as the most common accident.
Other children were injured when struck by moving equipment, or when they collided with protruding bolts or rough
edges. Deaths on playground equipment were attributed primarily to falls and to hangings on ropes and chains.

The Consumer Product Safety Commission has recently recommended that playground equipment be installed over grass
or sand and not over hard surfaces like concrete, brick, or
blacktop. According to the CPSC, all apparatus must also be
well anchored and separated from walls and sidewalks by at
least six feet. All protrusions must be covered, and nuts and
bolts checked about every two weeks.

Before your own children play at any playground, examine
the equipment there and make certain that it meets basic safety
requirements.

MYTH: *You can teach a child under three to be "pool-safe."*

About 150,000 people drown in all parts of the world
each year, with about 6000 to 7000 of those deaths occurring

in the United States. Next to auto accidents, drowning is the leading cause of accidental death in children between the ages of one and fourteen years. The average age for swimming pool drownings is three, and the accident occurs usually in the victim's own family pool.

With ominous statistics like these, I am not surprised that some parents begin their children on swimming lessons before the youngsters are even one year old. But a false sense of security can often result when a child that young is taught to swim. While youngsters can learn the physical act of swimming, and can be taught to be "pool-safe" (to float to the surface and roll onto their back to breathe until help comes), these skills are usually very short-lived in young children. Unless swimming techniques are practiced almost daily, youngsters can forget them. And if a parent becomes complacent, believing the child is pool-safe, he or she may not feel it necessary to keep a constant eye on the youngster at poolside.

Another danger sometimes arises because of parents' natural tendency to brag about their little swimmer. The parent may know the child's actual limitations and inexperience, but a neighbor, babysitter or friend may be misled. This overconfidence on the part of the poolside observer could result in tragedy, no matter how many swimming lessons a child has had.

So although I think that water safety courses are invaluable for children, no matter what their age, *nothing* should replace the constant vigilance of an adult's watchful eye near the pool or the ocean, or anywhere a young child is swimming.

MYTH: *Little dogs bite more frequently than big dogs.*

Small dogs have been accused of being more temperamental and jealous of the arrival of a baby in the house, and thus supposedly bite more frequently than their larger counterparts. But the statistics don't bear this out.

In an evaluation of the emergency room records at the Milton S. Hershey Medical Center in Hershey, Pennsylvania, German shepherds inflicted more bites than any other breed. Smaller dogs accounted for only a small percentage of the bites (6 percent by dachshunds, 5 percent by poodles).

More families are buying dogs today for protection, and consequently the frequency of dog bites is rising across the country. If you are deciding upon the type of dog you want, keep in mind that larger dogs tend to bite more often and with greater force than smaller ones. Writing in *American Family Physician* (1977), the Hershey researchers concluded, "Only under exceptional circumstances should the German shepherd be considered as a pet for a family with small children or in a neighborhood in which a large number of children reside."

MYTH: *Cats can suck the breath out of a newborn.*

A few parents have told me that they really believe that cats can kill an infant by drawing the air out of the baby's mouth. As ridiculous as this myth may sound to most people, it has a long history. Some old medical textbooks recount stories of cats being seen with their mouth open over infants who have been found dead. But not surprisingly, there is no evidence to support such sinister behavior in cats.

Superstitions and a certain evil mystique have always surrounded cats. Black cats are considered "bad luck" by some people, and children's stories are filled with witches who have a cat or two by their side. Blaming a cat for a child's death, however, is probably nothing more than an unenlightened explanation for the Sudden Infant Death Syndrome (SIDS), the unexplained death of a baby under one year of age.

About 8000 infants die in the United States each year without explanation, and these fatalities are typically categorized under the SIDS label. Most of the affected children are between the ages of one month and six months old. Many theories have been offered by pediatricians and pathologists as to the cause of SIDS, but no one really knows for certain. Most researchers now tend to believe that what we call SIDS is really a collection of different phenomena, with most of them somehow related to the suppression of normal breathing at the central nervous system site. A relatively minor cause of SIDS is apparently infant botulism, sometimes related to the consumption of commercial honey. For this reason, honey is not recommended for babies under one year of age (see page 25).

In the 1920s and 1930s, SIDS was erroneously believed to be linked with a large thymus, which is an organ at the base of the neck with no apparent function. During that era, researchers theorized that SIDS victims had larger thymuses than did autopsied children who had died of known causes. A youngster found to have a "large" thymus during a routine x-ray was often subjected to radiation treatment to reduce the size of the thymus on the mistaken assumption that this would minimize the chance of sudden infant death. In the process, however, this radiation therapy caused a higher incidence of cancer later in life.

Subsequent knowledge showed just how erroneous medical thinking was on this subject. We now know that the thymus shrinks in size during times of stress, including illness. So those autopsied bodies of chronically ill children, who were once thought to have "normal-sized" thymuses, actually had small ones because of illness; by contrast, the "abnormally large" organs of the previously healthy SIDS victims were really quite normal. Their sudden deaths were not caused by thymus size but by some still-unidentified factors. The practice of irradiating the thymus was stopped once physicians became aware of this terrible but well-intentioned blunder.

So although we still have no clear understanding of the primary causes of SIDS, the thymus and cats are free of all culpability. But while cats have never sucked the breath out of a baby, I still suggest that they be kept away from infants. Cats enjoy cuddling next to people, and though it's extremely unlikely, it's not inconceivable that they could nestle next to a newborn's face and smother the child who is too young to roll over or shove the cat away.

MYTH: *Cats cause leukemia.*

Cats have been involved in many health-related controversies. For example, leukemia is common in cats and is known to be caused by a virus. Human leukemia, however, has never been conclusively shown to be virus-related, and furthermore, no proof exists that this disease has ever been transmitted from a cat to a human being. Even so, some individuals avoid cats for the unwarranted fear of "catching" leukemia.

There is also a direct link between cats and a human illness commonly called "cat scratch fever." When a person is scratched, usually by a kitten, the lymph nodes may swell and the individual may develop a fever as part of this cat-induced disease.

Finally, cats have been implicated in a serious parasitic disease called toxoplasmosis, which afflicts the human central nervous system, lymph nodes, and spleen. It can be carried by cats who typically roam outside, where they can eat infected rats and mice and excrete small parasites in their stool. When these parasites are transmitted to human beings, toxoplasmosis can result. Pregnant women run the risk of contracting this disease, and when they do, their fetus could be damaged. Once infected, a cat can transmit the illness to human beings for approximately three weeks; however, since no one knows when a particular cat may be infected, women should not clean up the litter in a cat box during their pregnancy.

MYTH: *Fluoride causes cancer and heart disease.*

See pages 133–134.

MYTH: *The full moon makes people crazy.*

From the Bible to eighteenth-century medical literature, the full moon has been linked with mental illness. The word "lunacy" is derived from luna, the Latin word for "moon." Even today, some people blame everything—including psychosis, epilepsy, and suicide—on the full moon, and some physiologists have theorized that the gravitational pull of the moon may influence human behavior.

No connection exists between the full moon and human activity. One study showed that the highest rates of admission to psychiatric institutions occurred during the new moon, not the full moon, as many people believe. A separate study revealed that homicides were higher at the time of the new moon, which seems logical because the dark nights of this particular lunar phase are probably conducive to crime.

An evaluation of an emergency room logbook at Symmes Hospital in Arlington, Massachusetts, reported in the *New England Journal of Medicine* (1978), found that emergency hospital visits do not increase during a full moon. One physician at that facility commented that even if there weren't more patients, at least they seemed "loonier" than usual. Actually, once all the evidence is evaluated, the "loony" label will probably more accurately be applied to this myth itself.

REFERENCE NOTES

The Newborn

A baby's normal fussy periods are discussed by T. B. Brazelton in "Crying in Infancy" in *Pediatrics*, April 1962, vol. 29, pp. 579–88.

An explanation of tears in newborns appears in "Newborns Do Secrete Tears" by L. Apt and B. F. Cullen in the *Journal of the American Medical Association*, September 21, 1964, vol. 189, pp. 951–53.

The time required for breastfeeding is addressed by A. Lucas et al. in "Breast Milk Flow" in *Lancet*, July 1979, vol. 2, pp. 57–58.

Research on chocolate consumption while breastfeeding is discussed in "Breast Milk Distribution of Theobromine from Chocolate" by G. H. Resman et al. in the *Journal of Pediatrics*, September 1977, vol. 91, pp. 477–80.

The need for additional water consumption during breastfeeding is described by P. A. Armelini and C. F. Gonzalez in "Breast Feeding and Fluid Intake in a Hot Climate" in *Clinical Pediatrics*, July 1979, vol. 18, pp. 424–25.

Information on colic appears in "Colic in Breast-Fed Infants Related to Maternal Ingestion of Cow's Milk" by I. Jakobsson and T. Lindberg in *Lancet*, August 26, 1978, vol. 2, pp. 437–39. Colic and gas are discussed by R. B. Lasser in "The Role of Intestinal Gas in Functional Abdominal Pain" in the *New England Journal of Medicine*, September 1975, vol. 293, pp. 524–26.

For an overview of the taping of umbilical hernias, see L. J. Halpern's article "Spontaneous Healing of Umbilical Hernias" in the *Journal of the American Medical Association*, November 24, 1962, vol. 182, pp. 851–52.

Sleep positions and the quality of sleep are discussed by Yvonne Brackbill et al. in "Psychophysiological Effects in Neonates of Prone vs. Supine Placement" in the *Journal of Pediatrics*, January 1973, vol. 82, pp. 82–84. Research on sleeping through the night is explored in "Night-Waking in Infants During the First Year of Life" by T. F. Anders in *Pediatrics*, June 1979, vol. 63, pp. 860–64.

For an explanation of the risks of honey consumption in the first year of life, see "Honey and Other Environmental Risk Factors" by S. S. Arnon et al. in the *Journal of Pediatrics*, February 1979, vol. 94, pp. 331–36.

A discussion of early toilet training appears in "Cultural Relativity of Toilet Training Readiness: Perspective from East Africa" by M. W. deVries and M. R. deVries in *Pediatrics*, August 1977, vol. 60, pp. 170–77.

Fevers

Normal temperatures in children are reviewed by T. E. Cone in his article "Diagnosis and Treatment: Children with Fever," in *Pediatrics*, February 1969, vol. 43, pp. 290–93.

Information on using your hand to determine a fever appears in "How Dependable is Palpation as a Screening Method for Fever?" by P. L. Bergeson and H. J. Steinfeld in *Clinical Pediatrics*, April 1974, vol. 13, pp. 350–51. The effectiveness of Clinitemp skin thermometers is evaluated by K. S. Reisinger et al. in the article "Inaccuracy of the Clinitemp Skin Thermometer" in *Pediatrics*, July 19, 1979, vol. 64, pp. 4–6.

Research on the natural course of high fevers in 1500 children appear in "High Fever: Experience in Private Practice" by W. A. Tomlinson in the *American Journal of Diseases of Children*, June 1975, vol. 129, pp. 693–96. High fevers are also discussed by E. F. Dubois in "Why Are Fever Temperatures Over 106 [41.1] Degrees Rare?" in the *American Journal of Medical Science*, April 1949, vol. 217, pp. 361–68.

An explanation of the possible beneficial effects of fever appears in "The Evolution and Adaptive Value of Fever" by M. J. Kluger in *American Scientist*, January–February 1978, vol. 68, pp. 38–43. Also see "Fever" by Elisha Atkins in *The New England Journal of Medicine*, January 6, 1972, vol. 286, pp. 27–34.

A description of the natural course of simple febrile seizures appears in "Prognosis in Children with Febrile Seizures," by Karin B. Nelson and Jonas H. Ellenberg, in *Pediatrics*, May 1978, vol. 61, pp. 720–27.

The use of alcohol versus water in sponging a feverish child is described by R. W. Steele et al. in "Evaluation of Sponging and of Oral Antipyretic Therapy to Reduce Fever" in the *Journal of Pediatrics,* November 1970, vol. 77, pp. 824–29.

Colds

A considerable portion of the material in this section was obtained from studies at the Common Cold Research Unit in Salisbury, England. For further information, see *The Common Cold* by Christopher Andrews (London: Weidenfeld & Nicolson, 1965).

A discussion of the transmission of colds appears in the article "Hand to Hand Transmission of Rhinovirus Colds" by J. M. Gwaltney in *Annals of Internal Medicine,* April 1978, vol. 88, pp. 463–67. Also see "Transmission of Rhinovirus Colds by Self-Inoculation" by J. O. Hendley et al. in the *New England Journal of Medicine,* June 28, 1973, vol. 288, pp. 1361–64.

For a detailed examination of the relationship between cold weather and colds, refer to "Exposure to Cold Environment and the Rhinovirus Common Cold" in the *New England Journal of Medicine,* October 3, 1968, vol. 279, pp. 742–46. Also see *The Common Cold* by Christopher Andrews, cited above.

The effects of cold baths upon colds is examined in "Exposure to Cold Environment and Rhinovirus Common Cold" by R. Gordon Douglas Jr., et al. in *The New England Journal of Medicine,* October 3, 1968, vol. 279, pp. 741–46.

Stress and the common cold are described in "Influence of Life Events and Family Routines on Childhood Respiratory Tract Illness" by W. T. Boyce et al. in *Pediatrics,* October 1977, vol. 60, pp. 609–15.

The effects of antihistamines on colds are examined in "A Review of Antihistamines and the Common Cold" by S. West et al. in *Pediatrics,* July 1975, vol. 56, pp. 100–106. Ear infections and decongestants are discussed by J. E. Randall and J. O. Hendley in their article, "A Decongestant Antihistamine Mixture in the Prevention of Otitis Media in Children with Colds" in *Pediatrics,* March 1979, vol. 63, pp. 483–85.

Additional information on treating colds with antibiotics appears in "Antibiotic and Chemotherapeutic Agents in the Treatment of Uncomplicated Respiratory Infections in Children: A Controlled Study" by L. M. Hardy and H. S. Traismon in the *Journal of Pediatrics,*

February 1956, vol. 48, pp. 146–56. This same subject is discussed by E. H. Townsend and J. F. Radebaugh in "Prevention of Complications of Respiratory Illness in Pediatric Practice" in the *New England Journal of Medicine*, April 5, 1962, vol. 266, pp. 683–89. Also see "Antibiotic Prophylaxis in Acute Viral Respiratory Diseases," by D. Davis Starkey et al. in *American Journal of Diseases of Children*, June 1965, vol. 109, pp. 544–52.

The relationship between chicken soup and colds is explored by M. A. Sackner in "Is Hot Chicken Soup To Be At Long Last Vindicated" in *Pediatric Alert*, July 20, 1978, p. 64.

The possible benefits of bed rest are examined in "The Dangers of Going to Bed" by R. A. Asher in the *British Medical Journal*, December 13, 1947, vol. 2, pp. 967–68. Also see "Effects of Early and Vigorous Exercise on Recovery from Infectious Hepatitis" by N. R. Lawrence and R. K. Freebern in the *New England Journal of Medicine*, December 18, 1969, vol. 281, pp. 1393–96.

Information on gamma globulin and colds appears in K. C. Finkel's article, "Clinical Trial to Assess the Effectiveness of Gamma Globulin in Acute Infections in Young Children" in *Pediatrics*, May 1960, vol. 25, pp. 798–805.

The effects of vitamin C on colds is explored in "Vitamin C Prophylaxis in Marine Recruits" by N. A. Pitt and A. M. Costrini in the *Journal of the American Medical Association*, March 2, 1979, vol. 241, pp. 908–11. Also see "Vitamin C and the Common Cold" by J. L. Coulehan, et al., in the *New England Journal of Medicine*, October 28, 1976, vol. 295, pp. 973–77.

Eyes and Vision

An explanation of visual acuity in infants appears in "Visual Acuity Development in Human Infants: Evoked Potential Measurements" by E. Marg et al. in *Investigative Ophthalmology*, February 1976, vol. 15, p. 150.

The relationship between nearsightedness and intelligence is addressed by P. A. Gardiner and H. Goldstein in "Acquired Myopia in Eleven-Year-Old Children" in the *British Medical Journal*, February 26, 1977, vol. 1, pp. 542–45.

Research on the safety of TV sets is discussed in *What's Being Done About X-Rays from Home TV Sets?* by the U.S. Department of Health, Education and Welfare/Bureau of Radiological Health, Superintendent of Documents, U.S. Government Publication 1715-0012.

Ears

For a discussion of the risks of ear piercing in jewelry stores, see "Another Hole in the Head," by the Massachusetts Department of Public Health in the *New England Journal of Medicine,* July 11, 1974, vol. 291, p. 99.

Teeth, Teething, Tongue, Tonsils, and the Throat

A general review of the care of children's teeth appears in Stephen J. Moss's book *Your Child's Teeth* (Boston: Houghton Mifflin, 1979).

The relationship between teething and fever is explained by H. Kravitz et al. in "Teething in Infancy" in the *Illinois Medical Journal,* April 1977, vol. 151, pp. 261–66. Also see "On Teething in Infancy" by M. B. Van Der Horst in *Clinical Pediatrics,* October 1973, vol. 12, pp. 607–610; "Teething—Are Today's Pediatricians Using Yesterday's Notions?" by P. J. Honig in the *Journal of Pediatrics,* September 1975, vol. 87, pp. 415–17; and "Teething in Children" by A. Tasanen in *Annales Paediatriae Fenniae,* 1968, Supplement 29, p. 14.

Research on the need for tonsillectomies is explained by W. Shaikh et al. in "A Systematic Review of the Literature on Evaluative Studies of Tonsillectomy and Adenoidectomy" in *Pediatrics,* March 1976, vol. 57, pp. 401–7.

The visual diagnosis of strep throat is discussed by B. B. Breese and F. A. Disney in "The Accuracy of Diagnosis of Beta Streptococcal Infections on Clinical Grounds" in *Journal of Pediatrics,* May 1954, vol. 44, pp. 670–73. Also see "Streptococcal Pharyngitis in Children: Difficulties in Diagnosis on Clinical Grounds Alone" by R. T. Rowe and R. T. Stone in *Clinical Pediatrics,* October 1977, vol. 16, pp. 933–35.

For an examination of whether sore throats improve faster with penicillin, see "Comparative Effects of Penicillin, Aureomycin and Terramycin on Streptococcal Tonsillitis and Pharyngitis" by F. W. Denny et al. in *Pediatrics,* January 1953, vol. 11, pp. 7–14.

Head

A discussion of the necessity of x-rays after a head injury appears in "Head Injuries in Children, Aetiology, Symptoms, Physical Findings and X-Ray Wastage" by Z. F. Boulis et al. in the *British Journal of Radiology*, November 1978, vol. 51, pp. 851–54.

For a general overview of the outcome of minor falls, refer to "Injuries Resulting When Small Children Fall Out of Bed" by R. G. Helfer et al. in *Pediatrics*, October 1977, vol. 60, pp. 533–35.

Information on head banging can be found in "Body Rocking, Head-Banging and Head-Rolling in Normal Children" by F. Sallustro and C. W. Atwell in the *Journal of Pediatrics*, October 1978, vol. 93, pp. 704–8.

Hair

A discussion on shaving hair and its subsequent thick return appears in "Shaving and Hair Growth" by Y. L. Lynfield and P. MacWilliams in *Journal of Investigative Dermatology*, September 1970, vol. 55, pp. 170–72.

Research on hair whorls appears in "Scalp Hair Patterning as a Clue to Early Fetal Brain Development" by D. W. Smith and R. T. Gong in the *Journal of Pediatrics*, September 1973, vol. 83, pp. 374–78.

Skin

For an examination of acne, chocolate, and greasy foods, see "Diet and Acne" by J. E. Rasmussen in the *International Journal of Dermatology*, July–August 1977, vol. 16, pp. 488–92.

Legs, Feet, Hands, Bones and Joints

Bowlegs and knock–knees are discussed by W. McDade in his article, "Bowlegs and Knock-knees" in *Pediatric Clinics of North America*, November 1977, vol. 24, pp. 825–31.

The high incidence of flat feet in children is substantiated by A. J. Morley in "Knock-knee in Children" in *The British Medical Journal*, October 26, 1957, vol. 2, p. 977.

The relationship between intelligence and the onset of walking is explored in "On the Growth of Intelligence" by N. Bayley in *American Psychologist*, December 1955, vol. 10, p. 805.

A discussion of feet that turn in and out appears in "The Natural History of Torsion and Other Factors Influencing Gait in Childhood" by G. M. Engel and Lynn T. Staheli in *Clinical Orthopaedics and*

Related Research, March–April 1974, vol. 99, pp. 12–17. Also see "The Natural History of Hooked Forefoot" by G. F. Rushforth in *Journal of Bone and Joint Surgery*, November 1978, vol. 60-B, pp. 530–32.

A review of the usage of corrective shoes is made by Lynn T. Staheli and Laura Giffin in "Corrective Shoes for Children: A Survey of Current Practice" in *Pediatrics*, January 1980, vol. 65, pp. 13–17.

Information on growing pains appears in "Growing Pains: Fact or Fiction?" by J. J. Calabro in *Acta Paediatrica Scandinavica*, March 1965, vol. 64, pp. 264–66.

Knuckle cracking is discussed by R. L. Swezey and S. E. Swezey in "The Consequences of Habitual Knuckle-Cracking" in *The Western Journal of Medicine*, May 1975, vol. 122, pp. 377–79. Also see "Cracking Joints: A Bioengineering Study of Cavitation in the Metacarpophalangeal Joint" by A. Unsworth et al. in *Annals of the Rheumatic Diseases*, July 1971, vol. 30, p. 348.

For a discussion of the effects of wearing shoes, refer to "A Comparison of Foot Forms Among the Non-Shoe and Shoe-Wearing Chinese Population" by L. Sim-Fook and A. Hodgson in the *Journal of Bone and Joint Surgery*, October 1958, vol. 40, pp. 1058–62.

The wearing of tennis shoes by children is addressed by E. E. Bleck in "The Shoeing of Children: Sham or Science" in *Developmental Medicine and Child Neurology*, April 1971, vol. 13, pp. 188–95.

Exercise and Sports

Although the material in this section was derived from many sources, the best overall review is contained in *The Sportsmedicine Book* by Gabe Mirkin and Marshall Hoffman (Boston, Little, Brown, 1978). *Also see* "Injuries in High School Sports" by James G. Garrick and Ralph K. Requa in *Pediatrics*, March 1978, vol. 61, pp. 465–69.

Nutrition

Vegetarian diets are discussed in "Nutritional Aspects of Vegetarianism, Health Foods and Fad Diets" by L. A. Barness, et al. in *Pediatrics*, March 1977, vol. 59, pp. 460–64.

The relationship between yogurt and cholesterol is examined by G. Hepner et al. in "Hypocholesterolemic Effects of Yogurt and Milk" in the *American Journal of Clinical Nutrition*, January 1979, vol. 32, pp. 19–24.

A discussion of diarrhea and intestinal bacteria appears in "A Complete Review of G. I. Tract Microflora" in the *Dairy Council Digest*, July–August 1976, vol. 47, pp. 19–24.

For a discussion of the negative effects of chocolate consumption, see "Chocolate: A Review of Published Reports of Allergic and Other Deleterious Effects, Real or Presumed" by J. H. Fries in the *Annals of Allergy*, October 1978, vol. 41, pp. 195–207.

Information on the Feingold diet appears in "Diet and Hyperkinesis: Is There a Relationship?" by F. J. Stare et al. in *Nutrition and the M.D.*, January 1980, vol. 6, pp. 1–3.

Research on childhood obesity is discussed by W. B. Weil in "Current Controversies in Childhood Obesity" in the *Journal of Pediatrics*, August 1977, vol. 91, pp. 175–87.

Infectious Diseases

The confusion over mumps when playing wind instruments is explained by H. F. Saunders in "Wind Parotitis" in the *New England Journal of Medicine*, September 27, 1973, vol. 289, p. 698.

For an examination of the relationship between polio and swimming pools, refer to "The Spread of Polio Infection During an Epidemic of Unusual Severity" by P. F. Wehrle in the *American Journal of Hygiene*, May 1957, vol. 65, pp. 386–403. A personal communication from Dr. Wehrle also provided information on this subject.

Honey and botulism is addressed by S. S. Arnon et al. in "Honey and Other Environmental Risk Factors for Infant Botulism" in the *Journal of Pediatrics*, February 1979, vol. 94, pp. 331–36.

James H. Gilbaugh Jr. and Peter C. Fuchs discuss "The Gonococcus and the Toilet Seat" in *New England Journal of Medicine*, July 12, 1979, vol. 31, pp. 91–93.

Accidents and Environmental Hazards

A discussion of poisoning by E. L. Keller, titled "Poisoning in Children," appears in *Postgraduate Medicine*, May 1979, vol. 65, pp. 177–86.

Burns caused by hot water are addressed by K. W. Feldman et al. in "Tap Water Scald Burns in Children" in *Pediatrics*, July 1978, vol. 62, pp. 1–4.

Information on automobile safety appears in "Motor Vehicle Occupant Deaths in Young Children" by S. P. Baker in *Pediatrics*, December 1979, vol. 64, pp. 860–61.

For an explanation of the risks of playgrounds, refer to an article by T. E. Reichelderfer et al. titled "Unsafe Playgrounds" in *Pediatrics*, December 1979, vol. 64, pp. 962–63.

"Dog Bites" by W. P. Graham et al. appears in *American Family Physician*, January 1977, vol. 15, p. 132.

The relationship between the full moon and lunacy is discussed by T. Stair in "Lunar Cycles and Emergency Room Visits" in the *New England Journal of Medicine*, June 8, 1971, vol. 298, pp. 976–78. Also see "Lunar Madness: An Empirical Study" by C. E. Clement and R. Plutchik in *Comprehensive Psychiatry*, July–August 1977, vol. 18, p. 369.

INDEX